Revision Guide

Cambridge

International AS and A Level

Economics

Terry Cook

Hodder Education, an Hachette UK company, 338 Euston Road, London NW1 3BH

Orders
Bookpoint Ltd, 130 Milton Park, Abingdon, Oxfordshire OX14 4SB
tel: 01235 827827
fax: 01235 400401
e-mail: education@bookpoint.co.uk
Lines are open 9.00 a.m.–5.00 p.m., Monday to Saturday, with a 24-hour message answering service. You can also order through the Hodder Education website: www.hoddereducation.co.uk

ISBN 978-1-4441-9197-4

First printed 2013
Impression number 5 4 3 2 1
Year 2018 2017 2016 2015 2014 2013

Cover photo reproduced by permission of Jean-Pierre Pieuchot/Getty

Typeset by Datapage (India) Pvt Ltd
Printed in Spain

This text has not been through the Cambridge endorsement process.

Hachette UK's policy is to use papers that are natural, renewable and recyclable products and made from wood grown in sustainable forests. The logging and manufacturing processes are expected to conform to the environmental regulations of the country of origin.

P2267

Get the most from this book

Everyone has to decide his or her own revision strategy, but it is essential to review your work, learn it and test your understanding. This Revision Guide will help you to do that in a planned way, topic by topic. Use this book as the cornerstone of your revision and don't hesitate to write in it — personalise your notes and check your progress by ticking off each section as you revise.

My revision planner

AS topics

	Revised	Tested	Exam ready
1 Basic economic ideas			
8 Scarcity, choice and resource allocation	☐	☐	☐
9 Different allocative mechanisms	☐	☐	☐
10 Problems of transition	☐	☐	☐
11 Production possibility curves	☐	☐	☐

☑ Tick to track your progress

Use the revision planner on pages 4–6 to plan your revision, topic by topic. Tick each box when you have:

- revised and understood a topic
- tested yourself
- practised the exam-style questions

You can also keep track of your revision by ticking off each topic heading in the book. You may find it helpful to add your own notes as you work through each topic.

Individual and market demand curves

Individual demand curves Revised ☐

An individual demand curve shows the quantity of a product that a particular consumer is willing and able to buy at each and every price in a given period of time, ceteris paribus (i.e. all other things unchanged). The individual demand curve will slope downwards from left to right, indicating that a consumer will be more likely to buy a product at a lower price than a higher price.

demand: the quantity of a product that consumers are willing to buy at a given price in a given period of time

law of demand: a law (or theory) which states that there is an inverse relationship between the quantity demanded of a product and the price of the product, ceteris paribus

Features to help you succeed

Expert tips

Throughout the book there are tips from the experts on how to maximise your chances.

Definitions and key words

Clear and concise definitions of the essential key terms from the syllabus are given on the page where they appear. The key terms are highlighted in bold and a glossary is provided at the back of the book.

Revision activities

The activities will help you to understand each topic in an interactive way.

Now test yourself

These short, knowledge-based questions provide the first step in testing your learning. Answers are at the back of the book.

Tested ☐

Questions and answers

Use the exam-style questions and answers to consolidate your revision and practise your exam skills.

My revision planner

AS topics

A level topics

My revision planner

Countdown to my exams

6–8 weeks to go

- Start by looking at the syllabus — make sure you know exactly what material you need to revise and the style of the examination. Use the revision planner on pages 4–6 to familiarise yourself with the topics.
- Organise your notes, making sure you have covered everything on the syllabus. The revision planner will help you to group your notes into topics.
- Work out a realistic revision plan that will allow you time for relaxation. Set aside days and times for all the subjects that you need to study, and stick to your timetable.
- Set yourself sensible targets. Break your revision down into focused sessions of around 40 minutes, divided by breaks. This Revision Guide organises the basic facts into short, memorable sections to make revising easier.

Revised

4–6 weeks to go

- Read through the relevant sections of this book and refer to the expert tips and key terms. Tick off the topics as you feel confident about them. Highlight those topics you find difficult and look at them again in detail.
- Test your understanding of each topic by working through the 'Now test yourself' questions in the book. Look up the answers at the back of the book.
- Make a note of any problem areas as you revise, and ask your teacher to go over these in class.
- Look at past papers. They are one of the best ways to revise and practise your exam skills. Write or prepare planned answers to the exam-style questions provided in this book. Check your answers with your teacher.
- Use the revision activities to try different revision methods. For example, you can make notes using mind maps, spider diagrams or flash cards.
- Track your progress using the revision planner and give yourself a reward when you have achieved your target.

Revised

1 week to go

- Try to fit in at least one more timed practice of an entire past paper and seek feedback from your teacher, comparing your work closely with the mark scheme.
- Check the revision planner to make sure you haven't missed out any topics. Brush up on any areas of difficulty by talking them over with a friend or getting help from your teacher.
- Attend any revision classes put on by your teacher. Remember, he or she is an expert at preparing people for examinations.

Revised

The day before the examination

- Flick through this Revision Guide for useful reminders, for example the expert tips and key terms.
- Check the time and place of your examination.
- Make sure you have everything you need — extra pens and pencils, tissues, a watch, bottled water, sweets.
- Allow some time to relax and have an early night to ensure you are fresh and alert for the examination.

Revised

My exams

Paper 1

Date: ....

Time: ....

Location: ....

Paper 2

Date: ....

Time: ....

Location: ....

Paper 3

Date: ....

Time: ....

Location: ....

Paper 4

Date: ....

Time: ....

Location: ....

1 Basic economic ideas

Scarcity, choice and resource allocation

Scarcity refers to the fact that at any moment in time, the output that an economy is able to produce will be limited by the resources and technology available. People's **wants** and **needs**, however, will always exceed the **resources** available to satisfy them, i.e. these wants and needs are unlimited. This is known as the **economic problem**.

As a result of this condition of scarcity, choices must be made. In all economies, therefore, there is an inevitability of choice at all levels of decision making, i.e. at the level of the individual, the firm and the government.

This focus on choice stresses the need to recognise the implications of not only choosing one thing, but also of *not* choosing something else. This is known as **opportunity cost**. For example, using a piece of land for farming purposes or to build a factory on.

wants: things that are not essential, e.g. a new car or television

needs: things that are essential for human survival, e.g. food or shelter

resources: the inputs available to an economy for use in the production of goods and services

economic problem: a situation where there are not enough resources to satisfy all human needs and wants

opportunity cost: the benefit foregone from not choosing the next best alternative

Expert tip

It is important that candidates fully understand the difference between a *want* and a *need*, and can clearly demonstrate this understanding to the examiner.

Expert tip

Candidates sometimes define opportunity cost as the benefit that is foregone as a result of taking a decision. But it is not the result of any random choice; it is the cost of the next best alternative foregone.

The emphasis on choice focuses on three basic economic questions:

- what will be produced
- how it will be produced
- for whom it will be produced

Expert tip

Candidates should emphasise the importance of needing to make a choice as a result of the condition of scarcity, and although choice can apply to various areas of economic activity, these three basic economic questions are the three most fundamental ones.

Now test yourself

1 Define what is meant by the 'economic problem'.

2 Explain what is meant by the term 'opportunity cost'.

Answers on p.154

Tested

These three basic economic problems are solved in different ways in various economies, i.e. resource allocation can be approached through different systems or **mechanisms**, as the next section shows.

Different allocative mechanisms

There are three different types of allocative mechanism:

- market economies
- planned economies
- mixed economies

allocative mechanism: an allocative mechanism is a method of taking decisions about the different uses that can be made of factors of production. A mechanism is needed for economic goods that are scarce. Free goods in sufficient supply to satisfy demand, such as air or sunshine, do not need an allocative mechanism.

Expert tip

Candidates should understand that every country in the world (and there are over 200 countries) will allocate its scarce resources in different ways. This range of allocative mechanisms is so broad that economists have focused on three main types: market economies, planned economies and mixed economies.

Market economies

Revised

This is where the allocation of resources is left to the **market** forces of demand and supply through the operation of the price mechanism. The advantages and disadvantages are shown in Table 1.

Table 1 Advantages and disadvantages of the market economy

Advantages of the market economy	Disadvantages of the market economy
• Decisions are made by individual consumers, who act in their own self-interest, i.e. the maximisation of their utility or satisfaction when they consume a product. • Decisions are made by individual producers, who act in their own self-interest, i.e. the maximisation of their profits. • The use of the price mechanism to allocate resources (referred to as 'the invisible hand' by the Scottish economist **Adam Smith**) means that there is no need for any government intervention in the allocation of resources.	• Some products will be under-provided and under-consumed in a market economy; these are known as merit goods, e.g. education and healthcare. • Some products will be over-provided and over-consumed in a market economy; these are known as demerit goods, e.g. alcohol and tobacco. • Some products will not be provided or consumed at all in a market economy because it would be impossible to charge a market price for them; these are known as public goods, e.g. defence and lighthouses.

market economy (or market system): an economy where decisions about the allocation of resources are taken through the price mechanism

market: a way in which buyers and sellers come together to exchange products

Adam Smith: one of the founding fathers of Economics (1723–90) and author of *The Wealth of Nations*, published in 1776

Planned economies

Revised

Planned economies, also known as **command economies**, involve the allocation of scarce resources through government intervention with no (or very little) scope for market forces to operate. The advantages and disadvantages are shown in Table 2.

Table 2 Advantages and disadvantages of the planned economy

Advantages of the planned economy	Disadvantages of the planned economy
• Government intervention in the allocation of resources means it can take decisions in the national interest, e.g. it can prevent the production of socially undesirable products, such as drugs or pornography. • The government can intervene to bring about a more equitable distribution of income and wealth.	• A system with such a large amount of government influence and control will tend to be bureaucratic and, as a result, may be inefficient. • The lack of competition and the lack of the profit motive mean that products are often of a poor quality with consumers having little choice.

planned (or command) economy: an economy where decisions about the allocation of resources are taken by the state

Mixed economies

Revised

A **mixed economy** combines elements of both market economies and planned economies, i.e. there is some degree of state ownership and state intervention but in many areas of the economy market forces will be allowed to operate.

It could be argued that all economies today are, to some extent, mixed economies. However, there are large differences between, say, China, where the government still plays an important role in the allocation of resources, and the United States, where the government has only a limited role in the allocation of resources.

mixed economy: an economy where the allocation of resources is decided both by market forces and by the state

Now test yourself

3 Distinguish between a market economy, a planned economy and a mixed economy.

Answer on p.154

Tested

Expert tip

Candidates need to demonstrate they understand that the degree of mixture in any economy is not static. For example, since the credit crunch began in 2007, a number of banks in many countries have either been brought under complete state ownership or have been given financial assistance by government to remain in business. One bank in the UK, RBS (Royal Bank of Scotland), became 84% state owned.

Revision activity

Make a list of the key features of market economies, planned economies and mixed economies.

Problems of transition

A number of economies are going through a period of change where the extent of central planning is being reduced and market forces are being allowed to have a greater degree of influence. China is an example of such a **transitional economy**. There are, however, possible problems associated with transition, as Table 3 shows.

Table 3 Problems of transitional economies

Unemployment	A planned economy is generally better able to keep down the rate of unemployment in an economy; when there is a move towards greater reliance on market forces, the rate of unemployment in an economy is likely to increase because in a market economy, firms aim to maximise profits and this may lead them to reduce costs of production, possibly by laying off some workers.
Inflation	In a planned economy, the state controls prices so it is easier to keep down the rate of inflation; when prices are determined by the free-market forces of demand and supply, it is more difficult to control prices and so inflation is more likely.
Output	In a planned economy, it is possible for the state to support inefficient firms and industries; when state support is ended, such firms and industries may not be able to compete and so output could fall.
Welfare	A planned economy is able to provide housing and healthcare to everyone; with the introduction of market forces, there may be a fall in welfare provision and this may have a detrimental effect on levels of productivity in the economy.

transitional economy: an economy which was previously a command or planned economy and which is now allowing a greater degree of scope for market forces to operate

Expert tip

Candidates should recognise that transitional economies can vary a great deal depending on the degree of change or transition that has taken place. Some of these economies will still be similar to a planned economy, with only a small degree of private sector involvement in the economy. On the other hand, some of these economies will have moved away from a planned economy towards more of a market economy. It should also be understood that such economies are changing rapidly, and a great deal of change can have taken place in a short period of time.

Now test yourself

4 Analyse what is meant by a transitional economy.

Answer on p.154

Tested

Production possibility curves

A **production possibility curve** (or **production possibility frontier**, as it is sometimes called) shows the different combinations of products that can be produced if the economy is working at full capacity. It can also be referred to as a 'production transformation curve'.

production possibility curve (or frontier): a graphic representation showing the maximum combination of goods or services which can be produced from given resources

The shape of the curve shows that there are a number of different combinations that can be used to produce products. It is drawn as a curve rather than as a straight line because not all factors of production are equally efficient. This can be seen in Figure 1.

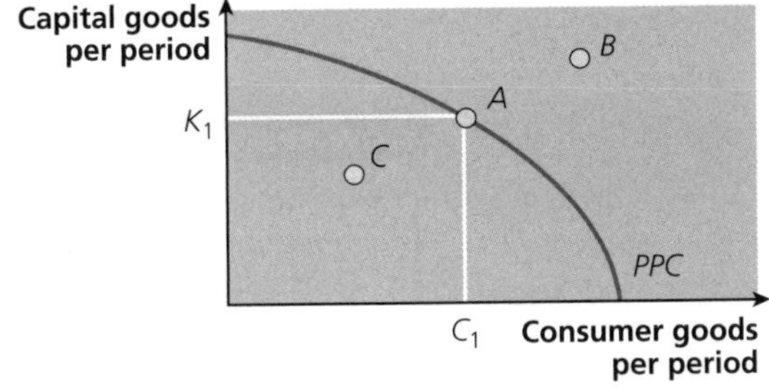

Figure 1 A production possibility curve

The production possibility curve (*PPC*) in Figure 1 shows the combination of capital goods (shown on the vertical axis) and consumer goods (shown on the horizontal axis) that an economy can produce at a particular period of time with the existing economic resources available. Point *A* shows one possible combination of outputs, i.e. where the economy produces K_1 capital goods and C_1 consumer goods. Any change along the curve from point *A* will show that the production of more of one type of goods will lead to production of less of the other (thus illustrating the concept of opportunity cost).

Point *C*, which is inside the *PPC*, shows that the economy is not using its resources efficiently and there is some degree of unemployment of resources. Output of both capital and consumer goods is lower than it could be.

Point *B*, which is outside the *PPC*, is unreachable at the present period of time given the resources that the economy currently has. However, over a period of time, it is possible for there to be **economic growth** resulting from the availability of more resources and/or the more productive use of resources, and this would enable point *B* to be reached. This can be seen in Figure 2.

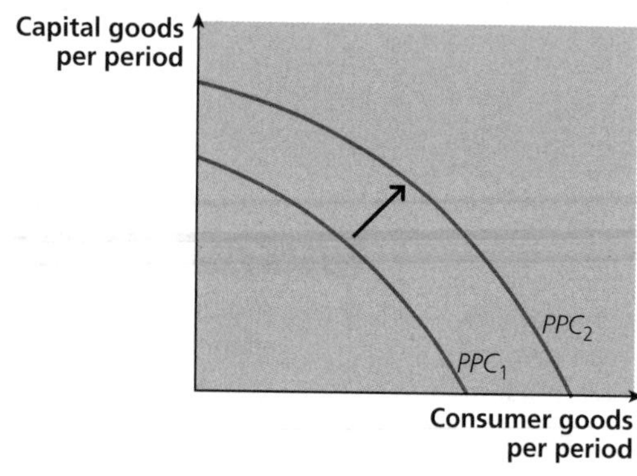

Figure 2 Economic growth

Economic growth enables an economy to produce more of both goods, i.e. more of both capital and consumer goods. It refers to a situation where there is an expansion in the productive capacity or potential output of an economy. This can be seen in Figure 2 by a rightward shift of the *PPC* from PPC_1 to PPC_2.

economic growth: an expansion in the productive capacity or potential of an economy

Expert tip

It is important that candidates understand the difference between *a movement along*, and *a shift of*, a production possibility curve. A movement along a curve indicates the different combinations of two goods that could be produced from the given resources in an economy. A shift of a curve to the right, however, would indicate an expansion in the productive potential or capacity of an economy, allowing more to be produced of both goods.

Now test yourself

5 Explain what is shown in a production possibility curve.

Answer on p.154

Tested

Production in an economy can take place in three sectors: the primary sector, the secondary sector and the tertiary sector.

- The **primary sector** is the extractive sector and is concerned with production in areas of an economy such as fishing, forestry and mining.
- The **secondary sector** is the manufacturing and construction sector and is concerned with production in areas of an economy such as car production and the construction of airport runways.
- The **tertiary sector** is the services sector and is concerned with areas of economic activity such as teaching, medicine and the law.

Now test yourself

6 Distinguish, with the aid of examples, between the primary, secondary and tertiary sectors of production.

Answer on p.154

Tested

primary sector: production that takes place in agriculture, fishing, forestry, mining, quarrying and oil extraction

secondary sector: production that takes place in manufacturing, construction and energy

tertiary sector: production that takes place through the provision of services

Revision activity

Research your own economy and make a list of the main primary, secondary and tertiary industries located in your country.

Decision making at the margin

Economists, in their analysis of decision making, are often concerned with decisions that are taken at the **margin**, i.e. the point at which the last unit of a product is produced or consumed.

There are many examples of 'marginal decision making' throughout this book. For example, marginal cost is the additional cost of producing one more unit of a product, and marginal utility is the extra or additional satisfaction that can be gained from the consumption of one more unit of a product. The marginal efficiency of capital is the additional output produced by the last unit of capital investment employed in the production process.

margin: the point at which the last unit of a product is produced or consumed

costs of production: these are the various costs involved in the production process and can be generally divided into fixed costs, which do not vary with changes in output, and variable costs, which do vary with changes in output

fixed capital formation: buildings, plant, machinery and vehicles for commercial use that are used in the production process

investment: spending on capital equipment, such as a machine or a piece of equipment that can be used in the production process

working capital: the part of the capital of a business that is available to pay for wages and materials and not tied up in fixed capital, such as land, buildings or equipment

Expert tip

The concept of the margin is of fundamental importance in economics and you will have opportunities to bring it in to many of your answers. For example, it is important, in the study of satisfaction, to distinguish between *marginal utility* and *total utility*.

Positive and normative statements

It is important in economics to be able to distinguish between two different types of statement. A **positive statement** is one which is factually correct. A **normative statement**, on the other hand, reflects the norms or values of the person expressing the statement, i.e. such a statement will involve a **value judgement** and will reflect someone's personal opinions. Normative statements often include the words 'should' or 'ought to'.

positive statement: a statement which is factual and objective

normative statement: a statement which is subjective and expresses a value judgement

value judgement: an opinion which reflects a particular point of view

Expert tip

Candidates should understand that economics is one of the social sciences so positive statements play an important role in the subject. Normative statements, on the other hand, are more subjective and are reflections of value judgements.

Revision activity

Write out three positive statements and three normative statements.

Ceteris paribus

Economics is one of the social sciences and there are many aspects of the subject that involve a scientific analysis. It is recognised, however, that the study of human behaviour is not really possible in laboratory conditions.

Economists do, nevertheless, put forward theories by assuming that certain other aspects of behaviour can be held constant. This enables economists to isolate a single change, assuming that all other possible influences are unchanged. The assumption of **ceteris paribus**, that other things are equal, means that economists can analyse one aspect of behaviour at a time. For example, in this way it has been possible to put forward **economic laws** of demand and supply.

These economic theories have been put forward in relation to both **microeconomics** and **macroeconomics**.

ceteris paribus: a Latin term that literally means 'other things being equal'

economic law: an economic theory put forward by economists, such as the laws of demand and supply

microeconomics: the study of the behaviour of relatively small economic units, such as particular individuals, households or firms

macroeconomics: the study of economics at the national and international levels

Expert tip

Candidates should appreciate that it is virtually impossible to keep all variables constant, and this is why economists use the concept of ceteris paribus to indicate the idea of 'everything else being held constant'. This idea can be brought into a number of answers, such as in relation to showing the relationship between changes in the price of a product and changes in the demand for that product. If ceteris paribus applies, all other possible influences, such as changes in income, can be assumed to be constant.

Revision activity

Note down why the concept of ceteris paribus is important in economics.

Factors of production

There are four factors of production:

- **Land** — this refers to all the natural resources that can be used in the process of production. It can include farmland, forests, lakes and rivers and all the mineral deposits of a country, such as coal or oil.
- **Labour** — this refers to all the human input into the process of production. It refers not just to the people themselves, but to their skills, training, education and qualifications. It can also be referred to as 'human capital' or 'intellectual capital'.
- **Capital** — this refers to the human-made aids to production that can be used in the process of production. It can refer to equipment, machinery and factories.
- **Enterprise** — this refers to the factor that brings the other factors of production together to produce products in order to make a profit (**profit maximisation**). The individual who combines the other factors of production, and takes a risk in doing so, is an **entrepreneur**.

land: the factor of production that includes all the gifts of nature, or natural resources, that can be used in the process of production, such as minerals, forests and the sea

labour: the factor of production that includes all the human effort that goes into the process of production, both mental and physical

capital: the factor of production that includes all the human-made aids to production, such as tools, equipment and machinery

enterprise: the factor of production that refers to the taking of a risk in organising the other three factors of production

profit maximisation: the idea that the main aim of a firm is profit maximisation

entrepreneur: the individual who takes a risk in combining the other factors of production

Now test yourself

7 Explain the meaning of the term 'capital' when used as a factor of production.

Answer on p.154

Tested

Expert tip

Candidates often confuse the meaning of the term 'capital' as a factor of production with another meaning when it is used to refer to money. It is important that these two meanings of the term are carefully distinguished.

Revision activity

Choose a particular form of production, such as car production or agriculture, and identify examples of the four factors of production involved.

Division of labour

A car assembly line is a good example of the way in which a manufacturing process can be broken down into a sequence of specific tasks. Workers will concentrate on, or **specialise** in, these particular tasks, giving rise to the existence of **division of labour**. One of the first studies of this process was by the Scottish economist, Adam Smith, who described in his book *The Wealth of Nations* (1776) how division of labour in a pin factory enabled a great deal more to be produced than if each worker tried to do everything him- or herself. The process of producing pins involved 18 specific operations. If one person did all of these, that person would be able to produce 20 pins a day. However, if division of labour was applied, it would be possible for each worker to produce 4,800 pins a day.

specialisation: the process whereby individuals, firms and economies concentrate on producing those products in which they have an advantage. Individuals working for a particular firm are an example, in the form of division of labour. Whole economies can also benefit from specialisation through the principle of comparative advantage

division of labour: the way in which production is divided into a sequence of specific tasks which enables workers to specialise in a particular type of job

Revision activity

Make a list of the main advantages and disadvantages of the division of labour.

Money: its functions and characteristics

Money is defined as anything which is generally acceptable as a means of payment in an economy. **Liquidity** is defined in relation to how easy it is to turn a financial asset into cash, with cash being 100% liquid.

money: anything which is generally acceptable in a society as a means of payment

cheques: cheques are a method of payment, i.e. they are a means of transferring money from one account to another. They are not, however, a form of money

liquidity: the extent to which a financial asset can be turned into cash. For example, if some shares in a company are sold, the paper asset becomes money

interest: the reward for parting with liquidity. This means that if a person deposits cash in a savings account, which they can no longer use for a period of time, their reward is an additional sum of money that they will get back with the amount of money originally deposited

The functions of money

Revised

Money is said to have four functions:

- a medium of exchange
- a unit of account or measure of value
- a store of value or wealth
- a standard of deferred payment

A medium of exchange

One function of money is that it operates as a **medium of exchange**. It works much more effectively than **barter**, in that money is generally acceptable as a means of payment for goods and services. This is the main reason that money is usually preferred to barter, i.e. there is not a need to establish a **double coincidence of wants** between two people.

medium of exchange: the use of money as an acceptable means of payment between buyers and sellers of a product

barter: the direct exchange of one good or service for another

double coincidence of wants: a situation in a system of barter where a seller needs to find a buyer who wants what is being sold and where the seller also wants something that the buyer has got and is willing to trade in exchange

Expert tip

Candidates should understand that the great advantage of money over barter is that it avoids the need for a 'double coincidence of wants'. This does not mean, however, that barter has completely disappeared. In many economies, barter still exists.

A unit of account

A second function of money is that it operates as a **unit of account** or as a **measure of value**. Money enables the value of different products to be compared. This is another distinct advantage of money over barter.

unit of account (or measure of value): the use of money to establish the value of a product

A store of value or wealth

A third function of money is that it operates as a **store of value or wealth**. Wealth can be stored as money and this is much more convenient than storing items that might have been used in a barter system, such as cattle. Of course, one problem with this particular function of money is that inflation will reduce its purchasing power and therefore its value.

store of value or wealth: the use of money to store wealth

A standard of deferred payment

As a **standard of deferred payment**, this fourth function of money enables people to borrow money and pay it back at a later date. This encourages **credit** and can act as an incentive to trade. Payment can be spread over a period of time, something that was not possible with barter.

standard of deferred payment: the use of money to purchase a product now and repay the debt in the future

credit: refers to a situation where a person can take possession of a product immediately, but not be required to pay for it until a later time

Now test yourself

8 Identify the four functions of money.

Answer on p.154

Tested

Revision activity

Make a list of the various reasons why money is to be preferred to barter.

The characteristics of money

Revised

Table 4 summarises the main characteristics of money.

Table 4 The main characteristics of money

Acceptability	Money needs to be generally acceptable in a society if it is going to be used as a means of buying and selling goods and services.
Portability	Money needs to be easily carried around if it is going to perform its functions effectively.
Scarcity	Unless money is relatively scarce, it will become worthless.
Recognisability	Money needs to be easily recognised; this will help to establish it and maintain people's confidence in it.
Stability of value	Money needs to be reasonably stable in value over a given period of time if people are going to have confidence in it, although inflation can negatively affect this characteristic.
Divisibility	It must be possible to divide money into smaller parts, or denominations, if it is going to be able to carry out its functions.
Durability	Money needs to be durable, i.e. relatively hard-wearing, over time.

Expert tip

Don't confuse the *functions* of money with the *characteristics* of money.

Revision activity

Consider the various characteristics of money and decide which is the most important.

2 The price system and the theory of the firm

Individual and market demand curves

Individual demand curves

Revised

An individual demand curve shows the quantity of a product that a particular consumer is willing and able to buy at each and every price in a given period of time, ceteris paribus (i.e. all other things unchanged). The individual demand curve will slope downwards from left to right, indicating that a consumer will be more likely to buy a product at a lower price than at a higher price.

demand: the quantity of a product that consumers are willing to buy at a given price in a given period of time

law of demand: a law (or theory) which states that there is an inverse relationship between the quantity demanded of a product and the price of the product, ceteris paribus

Aggregation of individual demand curves to give market demand

Revised

A **demand curve** can be drawn for every consumer in a society for every product, but in economics it is more usual to focus on market demand curves. Market demand for a product is derived from bringing together (or aggregating) all the potential buyers of a product. It is the total quantity of a product that all potential buyers would choose to buy at a given price in a given period of time.

demand curve: a curve that shows how much of a good or service will be demanded by consumers at a given price in a given period of time

effective demand: consumers must not only want to buy a particular product but be able to afford to pay for it. Effective demand refers to demand that is backed by the ability and the willingness to pay for a product

Expert tip

It is important that candidates demonstrate in their answers an understanding that demand needs to be *effective demand*, i.e. it is not enough that consumers want something; they have to be in a position to actually pay for it.

A **demand schedule** could be produced for a particular product, such as DVDs. This schedule can then be plotted to give a market demand curve. This can be seen in Figure 1.

The price of DVDs is shown on the vertical axis and the quantity of DVDs bought is shown on the horizontal axis.

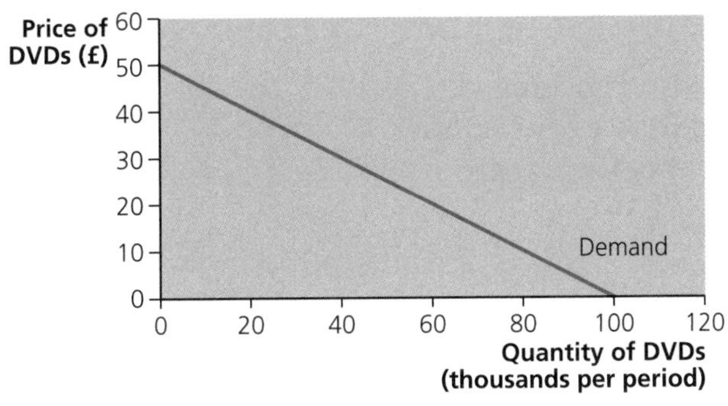

Figure 1 A demand curve for DVDs

The demand curve shows the relationship between price and the quantity demanded. It is downward sloping, indicating an inverse relationship between the price of a product and the quantity demanded of a product, i.e. as the price falls, the demand rises.

demand schedule: this gives the quantities sold of a product at different prices and enables a demand curve to be drawn from the information in the schedule

derived demand: this is where the demand for a component depends upon the final demand for a product that uses that component. For example, the demand for rubber is derived from the demand for car tyres. Derived demand can also be used in relation to the demand for workers, e.g. the demand for bus drivers derives from the demand for bus transport from people

Now test yourself

1 State the law or theory of demand.

Answer on p.154

Tested

Revision activity

Produce a demand schedule for a particular product and plot this in a demand curve.

Factors influencing demand

Revised

Price

A major influence on the demand for a product is its price. Figure 1 shows that there is an inverse relationship between a **change** in the price of a product and the quantity demanded of a product, all other things unchanged.

When it is only the price of a product that changes, this can be shown on a demand curve by a movement along the curve. This can be seen in Figure 2.

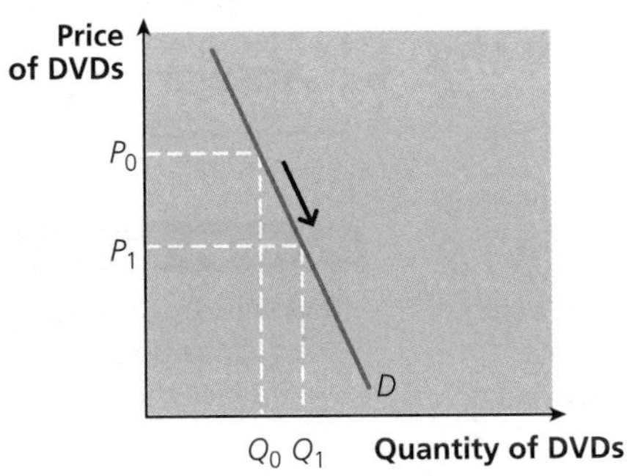

Figure 2 A movement along the demand curve

When the price of a product is reduced, e.g. from P_0 to P_1, the quantity demanded goes up from Q_0 to Q_1. This is shown as a downward movement along the demand curve, indicated in the diagram by the arrow in a downwards direction. If, on the other hand, the price of a product was increased, the quantity demanded would fall and this would be shown as an upward movement along the demand curve.

change in quantity demanded: this is where demand for a product changes as a result of a change in the price of the product; change in quantity demanded is shown by a movement along a demand curve

Other factors influencing demand

However, price is not the only factor that influences demand. If the ceteris paribus assumption is now removed, it is possible to consider all the other factors that were being held constant. These other factors could include the following:

- a change in the incomes of consumers
- a change in the price of a substitute product
- a change in the price of a complementary product
- an advertising campaign
- a change in population
- a change in the tastes and preferences of consumers
- a lowering of interest rates, making borrowing more affordable
- a change in the weather, possibly associated with different seasons

When it is one of these other influences on demand, this can be shown by a shift of a demand curve. This can be seen in Figure 3.

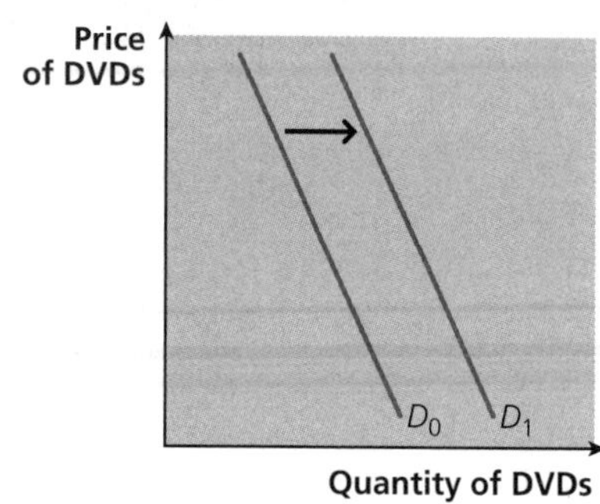

Figure 3 A shift in the demand curve

In this diagram, there could have been an increase in incomes and/or an effective advertising campaign and so the demand curve shifts to the right, from D_0 to D_1, shown by the rightward arrow.

change in demand: this is where there is a change in the conditions of demand, i.e. something other than a change in the price of a product; this is shown by a shift of a demand curve

composite demand: this refers to the demand for a product which can be used for more than one purpose. Stone, for example, could be used for building purposes and could also be used in the construction of roads; a particular piece of land could be demanded to build both shops and houses

Now test yourself

2 Explain the difference between a movement along, and a shift of, a demand curve.

Answer on p.154

Tested

Expert tip

Candidates sometimes confuse movements along a demand curve and a shift of a demand curve. It is important that you understand what will cause a movement along a demand curve and what will cause a shift of a demand curve.

Revision activity

Choose one particular product and list all the possible factors that could influence the demand for it.

Normal and inferior goods

Figure 3 shows what usually happens when there is an increase in the incomes of consumers, i.e. more of the product is bought at every price and there is a rightward shift of the demand curve. Such goods are called **normal goods**.

However, it is possible that the demand for some goods and services *decreases* when there is an increase in incomes. For example, while there might be an increase in the demand for cars as a result of an increase in incomes, there might be a decrease in the demand for public transport, such as bus journeys. This can be seen in Figure 4 where there is a leftward shift of the demand curve for bus journeys. Such goods are called **inferior goods**.

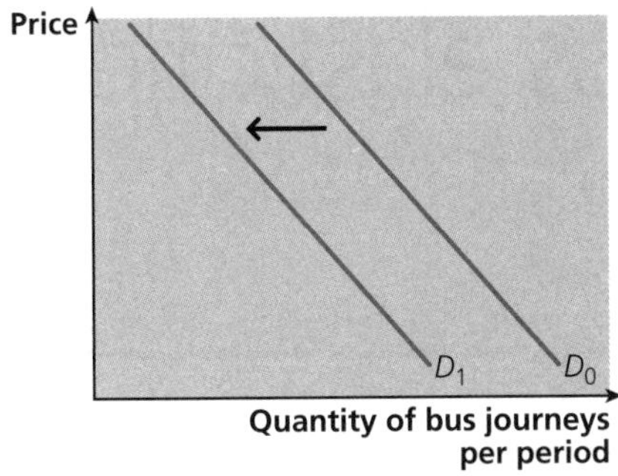

Figure 4 A shift in the demand curve following an increase in consumer incomes (an inferior good)

normal good: a good for which the demand rises with an increase in income

inferior good: a good for which the demand falls with an increase in income

Expert tip

Candidates need to ensure that they understand the difference between a *normal good* and an *inferior good* and can demonstrate this in their examination answers. A normal good is one where demand will increase as a result of a rise in income. An inferior good is the opposite: this is a good where demand will decrease as a result of a rise in income.

It is important to recognise that the demand for normal and inferior goods shows the relationship between a change in demand and a change in income, not price. Figure 5 shows this relationship for a normal good.

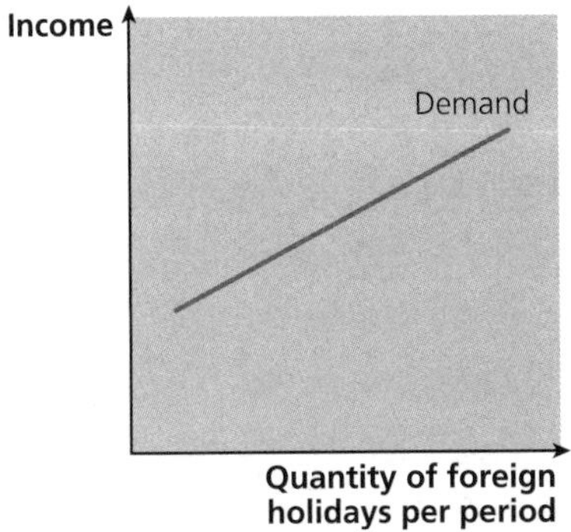

Figure 5 Demand and income for a normal good

Expert tip

Candidates can sometimes confuse the effect of a change in *price* and a change in *income* in examinations. These two effects need to be clearly distinguished. For example, the demand for normal and inferior goods is in response to a change in a person's income, not to changes in the prices of the goods.

Figure 6 shows this relationship for an inferior good.

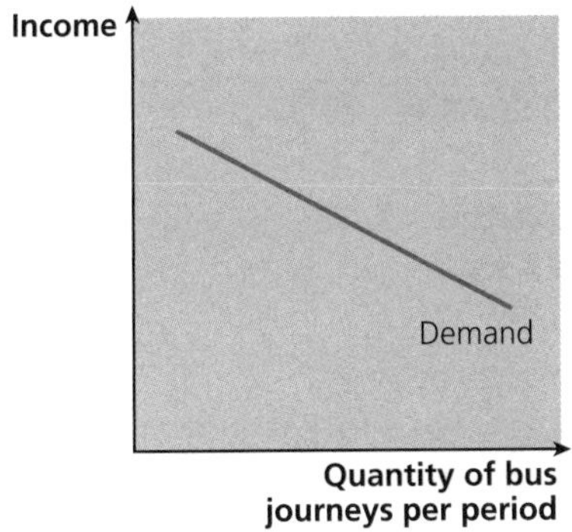

Figure 6 Demand and income for an inferior good

Now test yourself

3 Distinguish between a normal good and an inferior good.

Answer on p.154

Tested

Revision activity

Think of possible examples of inferior goods in your country.

Price, income and cross elasticities of demand

Price elasticity of demand

Revised

Price elasticity of demand measures the responsiveness of the demand for a product in relation to a change in its price. It is calculated by the following formula:

$$\frac{\text{percentage change in the quantity demanded of a product}}{\text{percentage change in the price of a product}}$$

For example, if the price of a good rises by 20%, and the quantity falls by 40%, then the price elasticity of demand is 40% divided by 20% = 2. There should really be a minus sign before 2 because it is a negative number, i.e. there is an inverse relationship between the change in price and the change in demand. However, the minus sign is usually left out.

price elasticity of demand: this measures the degree to which a change in the price of a product leads to a change in the quantity demanded of a product

Price elasticity of demand can vary from perfectly inelastic to perfectly elastic, as Table 1 shows.

Table 1 Elasticity

Elasticity	Figure
Perfectly inelastic	Zero
Inelastic	Greater than zero but less than one
Unitary elastic	One
Elastic	Greater than one but less than infinity
Perfectly elastic	Infinity

elastic: if the response of demand (or supply) is proportionately greater than the change in the independent variable, then the calculation is greater than one and is thus described as elastic

perfectly elastic: this refers to a situation where all that is produced is sold/bought at a given price; it is shown as a horizontal straight line

inelastic: if the response of demand (or supply) is proportionately less than the change in the independent variable, then the calculation is less than one and is thus described as inelastic

perfectly inelastic: this is where a change in price has no effect on the quantity demanded (or supplied); the calculation will be zero and it is shown as a vertical straight line

unitary elasticity: this is where the proportionate change in demand (or supply) is exactly equal to the change in the independent variable; the calculation will be equal to one

rectangular hyperbola: this is how unitary elasticity of demand is represented in a diagram; a movement up or down a demand curve will leave total revenue unchanged

total revenue: the total income that firms receive from sales; it is calculated by the price of a product multiplied by the number of products sold

A straight-line demand curve does not indicate constant elasticity of demand along the entire length. The price elasticity of demand will, in fact, vary along the line. This can be seen in Figure 7.

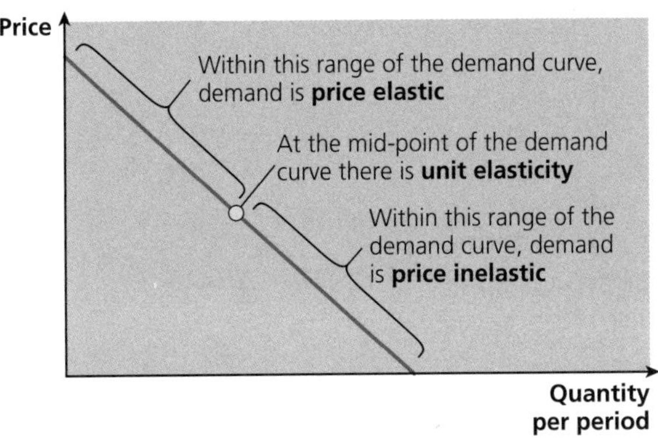

Figure 7 The price elasticity of demand varies along a straight line

There are a number of factors affecting price elasticity of demand, including the following:

- the availability of substitutes — the more substitutes that are available for a particular product, the more price elastic will be the demand, e.g. different brands of tea or coffee
- the definition of the product — the wider the definition of a product, the more price inelastic will be the demand, e.g. the demand for tea or coffee generally will be more inelastic than the demand for particular brands of tea or coffee
- the amount spent on the product — if the amount spent on a product is relatively small, the demand is likely to be inelastic, e.g. the amount spent on boxes of matches or on newspapers is likely to be a small proportion of weekly expenditure, so the demand for such products is likely to be relatively inelastic
- time — in the short run, demand for a product is likely to be more inelastic than in the long run when it might be possible to think about alternatives to the product

Price elasticity of demand is very important to an understanding of business decisions, especially because of the link with revenue. If the demand for a product is price elastic, a business should lower the price of the product because more products will be bought and this will be greater than the reduced amount received from each product sold. If the demand for a product is price inelastic, a business should increase the price of the product because even though fewer items will be bought, the increased revenue from each product sold will offset this.

Table 2 shows the link between price changes and revenue changes in relation to different price elasticities of demand.

Table 2 Elasticity and revenue

Price elasticity of demand	For a price increase, total revenue will...	For a price decrease, total revenue will...
Inelastic	...rise	...fall
Unitary elastic	...stay the same	...stay the same
Elastic	...fall	...rise

Expert tip

A common error in examinations is to describe a particular good as elastic or inelastic. It is important that you avoid this mistake. It is not that a good is elastic or inelastic, but that the *demand* for a particular good is elastic or inelastic.

Now test yourself

4 Explain what is meant when the price elasticity of demand for a product is said to be elastic.

Answer on p.154

Tested

Income elasticity of demand

Revised

Income elasticity of demand measures the responsiveness of the demand for a product in relation to a change in income. It is calculated by the following formula:

$$\frac{\text{percentage change in the quantity demanded of a product}}{\text{percentage change in income}}$$

The income elasticity of demand for most products will be positive, i.e. as incomes rise, the demand for products will rise. These are known as **normal goods**. However, the income elasticity of demand for some products will be negative, i.e. as incomes rise, the demand for products will fall. These are known as **inferior goods**.

income elasticity of demand: this measures the degree to which a change in incomes leads to a change in the quantity demanded of a product

There are a number of factors affecting income elasticity of demand, including the following:

- the proportion of income that is spent on a particular good — the demand for some products will not be very sensitive to a change in income because they are not very expensive, such as matches. Income elasticity of demand will be virtually zero
- the definition of the product — the income elasticity of demand for cars will be positive, but it may be negative for particular, cheaper, models of cars
- the economic development of a particular economy — in some economies, a motorcycle may be regarded as a normal good and so the income elasticity of demand will be positive, but as the economy develops and more people can afford cars, the demand for motorcycles may fall as incomes rise

Income elasticity of demand is important to an understanding of business decisions. Changes in an economy, and particularly changes in the level of incomes, can influence what a business is going to produce or stock; for example, if an economy is growing, and incomes are rising, a business might want to move from inferior goods towards producing normal goods. This will influence the planning of businesses in the future, such as in relation to employment requirements. On the other hand, if an economy is facing a recession, a business will want to be producing or stocking products with a relatively low income elasticity of demand; for example, people will still want to buy food in a recession, but they will be much less likely to want to buy expensive cars.

Now test yourself

5 Distinguish between price elasticity of demand and income elasticity of demand.

Answer on p.154

Tested

Cross elasticity of demand

Revised

Cross elasticity of demand or **cross price elasticity of demand** measures the responsiveness of demand for one product in relation to a change in price of another product. It is calculated by the following formula:

$$\frac{\text{percentage change in the quantity demanded of good A}}{\text{percentage change in the price of good B}}$$

If the two goods are **substitutes**, such as tea and coffee, the cross elasticity of demand will be positive. If good B increases in price, a number of people will switch to the substitute, good A, and so the demand for good A increases.

If the two goods are **complements**, such as DVDs and DVD players, the cross elasticity of demand will be negative. As the price of good B rises, fewer people will buy it and so fewer people will buy good A as well.

The existence of complements gives rise to the concept of **joint demand**. This occurs when two products are consumed together, such as the example of DVDs and DVD players. An increase in the sales of one product may lead to an increase in the sales of the other product.

Cross elasticity of demand is also important to an understanding of business decisions. In terms of a substitute, a firm would be able to estimate the effect on the demand of its product as a result of a change in the price charged by another firm in the market, such as in relation to a change in the price of tea and the demand for coffee. In terms of a complement, a firm would be able to estimate the effect on the demand for a product if there was a change in the price of a complement; for example, a fall in the price of DVD players would be likely to lead to an increase in the demand for DVD players and, therefore, an increase in the demand for DVDs.

cross elasticity of demand (or cross price elasticity of demand): this measures the degree to which a change in the price of one product leads to a change in the quantity demanded of another product

substitute goods: goods which are possible alternatives, e.g. gas or electricity as a source of energy in a home. These goods have a positive cross elasticity of demand, i.e. a rise in the price of one of them will lead to an increase in the demand for the other good

complementary goods: goods which are consumed together, e.g. DVDs and DVD players. These goods have a negative cross elasticity of demand, i.e. a rise in the price of one of them will lead to a decrease in the demand for the other

joint demand: this is a situation where two items are consumed together, i.e. they are complements. An example would be shoes and shoe laces

Now test yourself

6 What is the formula for cross elasticity of demand?

Answer on p.154

Tested

Expert tip

A number of candidates write the formula for the three elasticities of demand the wrong way round in examinations. To avoid making this mistake, remember that in all three calculations, i.e. price, income and cross elasticity of demand, the percentage change in the quantity demanded is always on the top.

Revision activity

A business person will be interested in price, income and cross elasticity of demand. Identify the different ways that these elasticities can affect business decisions.

Firms' supply curves

A firm's **supply curve** shows the quantity of a particular product that a firm is willing and able to sell at each and every price in a given time period, ceteris paribus (all other things unchanged). A firm's supply curve will slope upwards from left to right, indicating that a producer will be more likely to sell a product at a higher price than at a lower price.

supply: the quantity of a product that producers are willing to sell at a given price in a given period of time

law of supply: a law (or theory) which states that there is a direct relationship between the quantity supplied of a product and the price of the product, ceteris paribus

supply curve: a curve that shows how much of a good or service will be supplied by producers at a given price in a given period of time

Aggregation of individual firms' supply curves to give market supply

Revised

A supply curve can be drawn for every producer in an economy for every product, but in economics it is more usual to focus on market supply curves. Market supply of a product is derived from bringing together (or aggregating) all the potential suppliers of a product. It is the total quantity of a product that all potential sellers would choose to sell at a given price in a given period of time.

A supply schedule could be produced for a particular product, such as DVDs. This schedule can then be plotted to give a market supply curve. This can be seen in Figure 8.

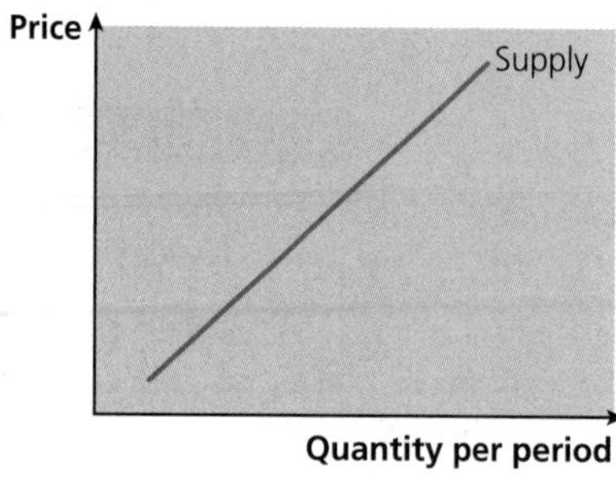

Figure 8 A supply curve

The price of DVDs is shown on the vertical axis and the quantity of DVDs sold is shown on the horizontal axis. The supply curve shows the relationship between price and the quantity supplied. It is upward sloping, indicating a direct relationship between the price of a product and the quantity supplied of a product, i.e. as the price rises, the supply rises.

Now test yourself

7 State the law or theory of supply.

Answer on p.154

Tested

Factors influencing market supply

Revised

Indirect taxes

A government may decide to impose an **indirect tax**, such as a sales tax, on a particular good or service. Examples could include VAT (value-added tax) or GST (goods and services tax). The effect of the imposition of such a tax can be seen in Figure 9. In this case, the tax is a **specific tax** with a fixed amount of tax per unit and so the supply curve shifts upwards parallel to the original supply curve.

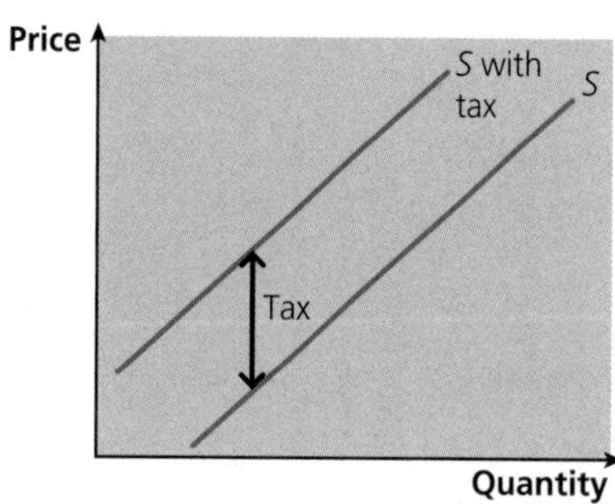

Figure 9 The effect of a sales tax on supply

Figure 9 shows how the imposition of an indirect tax will affect the price of a product. As there is an upward movement of the supply curve, this will lead to an increase in price. In order to determine the exact price charged, it would be necessary to include a demand curve in the diagram.

indirect tax: a tax that is imposed on expenditure; it is indirect in that the tax is only paid when the product on which the tax is levied is purchased

specific tax: an indirect tax that is a fixed amount per unit of output

ad valorem tax: an indirect tax with a percentage rate, e.g. a tax rate of 20% per product sold

incidence of tax: this refers to the burden of taxation. For example, with an indirect tax on expenditure, the burden of the tax is likely to be shared between the producer and the consumer. However, if the price elasticity of demand is perfectly inelastic, and there is a vertical demand curve, the incidence of the tax will be entirely on the consumer. On the other hand, if the price elasticity of demand is perfectly elastic, and there is a horizontal demand curve, the incidence of the tax will be entirely on the producer

impact of tax: this refers to the person, company or transaction on which a tax is levied, i.e. someone is responsible for handing the money to the tax authorities. The impact of a tax, therefore, is essentially concerned with the legal situation. As indicated above, the eventual incidence of a tax could be different if the burden of the tax is passed to someone else

direct taxation: whereas an indirect tax is imposed on expenditure, a direct tax is imposed on the incomes of individuals and firms. Examples of direct taxation include income tax (on the incomes of individuals), corporation tax (on the profits of companies) and inheritance tax (on the wealth of individuals)

income tax: a direct tax on the incomes of individuals. There is usually a personal allowance, which is tax free, and then different tax rates for different levels of income over the tax-free allowance. Income tax, therefore, is usually progressive as the tax rates change as incomes rise, i.e. it takes a higher proportion of a higher income and a lower proportion of a lower income

Expert tip

Candidates often seem confused about the progressive nature of income tax. It is not simply that a government takes more from a person who has a high income; it takes a higher percentage of that person's income.

Subsidies

The effect of a **subsidy** can be seen in Figure 10. Whereas the imposition of a tax shifted the supply curve upwards to the left, a subsidy has the opposite effect. If a government pays firms a subsidy to produce a particular product, this will have the effect of reducing their costs. This will encourage firms to supply more output at any given price. This can be seen in Figure 10 with the supply curve shifting downwards to the right.

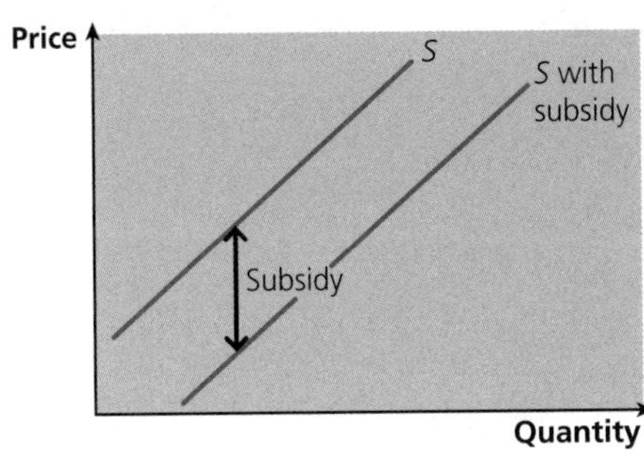

Figure 10 The effect of a subsidy on supply

The effect of the subsidy, in shifting the supply curve to the right, will be a lowering of price. The actual price will be determined where the S with subsidy line intersects with the demand curve. The effect of the subsidy is that both producers and consumers may benefit.

subsidy: an amount of money that is paid by a government to a producer. This is done so that the price charged to the customer will be lower than would otherwise have been the case without the subsidy

Expert tip

The distinction between the effect of a tax and the effect of a subsidy is another area that candidates often confuse in examinations. You need to remember that the effect of a tax is to shift the supply curve to the left, whereas the effect of a subsidy is to shift the supply curve to the right.

Now test yourself

8 Explain how a subsidy can affect the supply of a product.

Answer on p.154

Tested

Revision activity

Make a list of the arguments for and against the provision of a subsidy on a particular product.

Production costs

An important influence on supply is the costs of production. If the costs of the inputs in the production process, i.e. the costs of the factors of production, increase, then firms will be inclined to supply less output at any given price.

This can be seen in Figure 11. The increase in production costs causes the supply curve to shift to the left from S_0 to S_1. The increase in costs can be seen by the vertical distance between S_0 and S_1.

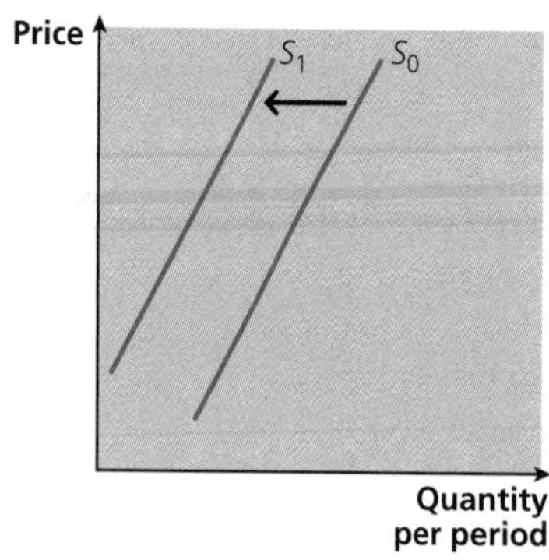

Figure 11 The supply curve shifts to the left if production costs increase

Technology of production

Another important influence on supply is the technology of production. If the technology of production is improved, this means that firms will be able to produce more effectively than before.

This can be seen in Figure 12 where improved technology leads to firms supplying a greater output at any given price. This can be seen in the diagram by the supply curve shifting to the right from S_0 to S_1.

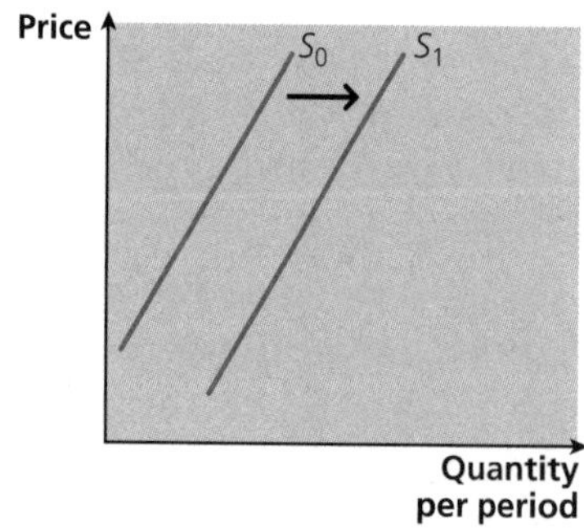

Figure 12 The supply curve shifts to the right if production costs fall

The prices of other goods

There may be a degree of substitution on the supply side if the prices of different products change. In many cases, the factors of production that a firm has can have alternative uses, and so a firm may be influenced by changes in prices of different products to produce more of one product and less of another.

A rise in the price of a product could increase profitability and so a firm may decide to switch production from one product to another.

The influence of price changes on the decisions of firms to supply particular products can also be seen in terms of a situation of **joint supply**.

In a situation of joint supply, one product may be a by-product of the production process of another product. An increase in the price of one of the products could mean that a firm will decide to produce more of both goods.

joint supply: a situation where the process of producing one product leads to the production of another product, such as meat and leather. It can sometimes happen in the chemical industry where one chemical can be produced as a by-product of the production of another

Expected prices

A final influence on market supply relates to the expectations of firms about possible future prices. This is especially the case in those situations where the production process takes quite a long time. Firms will thus need to take supply decisions on the basis of expected prices in the future. This is often the case in agriculture.

Movements along and shifts of a supply curve

Revised

It is important to distinguish between a movement along a supply curve and a shift of a supply curve. If there is a change in the market price of a product, and nothing else changes (i.e. assuming ceteris paribus), this will involve a movement along a supply curve. This will show how firms react to a change in the price of a product. This can be seen in Figure 8.

If the situation of ceteris paribus cannot be assumed, however, and there is a change in any of the other possible influences on supply, then the supply curve will shift because this will affect the willingness of firms to supply at any given price. As has already been indicated, this could involve a shift to the left, for example as a result of the imposition of an indirect tax on the consumption of a product (see Figure 9) or as a result of an increase in production costs (see Figure 11), or a shift to the right, for example as a result of the introduction of a subsidy (see Figure 10) or as a result of an improvement in technology (see Figure 12).

Expert tip

The possible confusion between a movement along a demand curve and a shift of a demand curve has already been pointed out. The possibility of confusion also applies to supply. You will need to be absolutely certain that you understand the difference between a movement along a supply curve and a shift of a supply curve before taking the examination.

Now test yourself

9 Distinguish between a movement along a supply curve and a shift of a supply curve.

Answer on p.154

Tested

Price elasticity of supply

Calculating price elasticity of supply

Revised

Price elasticity of supply measures the responsiveness of the supply of a product in relation to a change in its price. It is calculated by the following formula:

$$\frac{\text{percentage change in the quantity supplied of a product}}{\text{percentage change in the price of a product}}$$

If the percentage change in supply is greater than the percentage change in price, then supply is price elastic and the figure for the price elasticity of supply will be greater than one. If the percentage change in supply is less than the percentage change in price, then supply is inelastic and the figure for the price elasticity of supply is less than one.

price elasticity of supply: measures the degree to which a change in the price of a product leads to a change in the quantity supplied of a product

Expert tip

As with elasticity of demand, make sure you remember that the quantity goes on top of the formula.

Determinants affecting price elasticity of supply

Revised

There are a number of determinants affecting price elasticity of supply, including the following:

- the number of producers — the greater the number of suppliers, the more it is likely for the industry to increase output in response to a price increase and so supply is likely to be relatively elastic
- the amount of **stock** — some products will be easier to stock than others, and this will make the supply of them relatively more elastic, but some products will be **perishable** and so more difficult to stock for long periods, making supply less elastic
- the time period — supply is likely to be more elastic over a longer period of time (see Figure 13) as it gives firms more time to invest in more factors of production and also gives more time for new firms to join the industry
- the existence of spare capacity — the greater the degree of capacity in the industry, the easier it will be for firms to increase output if the price of products increases and this is likely to make supply more elastic
- the length of the production period — supply is usually more elastic in manufacturing than in agriculture because manufacturing usually involves a shorter production period than agriculture
- the degree of factor mobility — the easier it is for economic resources to be transferred into the industry, the more elastic the supply is likely to be

These various determinants give an indication of the speed and ease with which firms in an industry can respond to changed market conditions.

stocks: goods which have been produced, but which are unsold and stored for sale in the future. For example, a firm which sells car tyres will usually have considerable stocks of tyres to fit a wide range of different cars

perishability: the length of time in which a product is likely to decay or go bad; the shorter the time, the more perishable the product. For example, cheese will usually have a sell-by date and a date by which it should be consumed

Expert tip

Some candidates seem to believe that unitary elasticity, where the price elasticity of supply is equal to one, is a 45-degree line. In fact, any straight line which passes through the origin has a unitary price elasticity of supply.

Figure 13 shows the relationship between the price elasticity of supply and the time period. Supply curve S_S shows supply in the short run when it will usually be more difficult to alter supply at relatively short notice and so supply tends to be relatively inelastic. Supply curve S_l, however, shows supply in the long run when firms are usually more able to increase production and so supply tends to be relatively elastic.

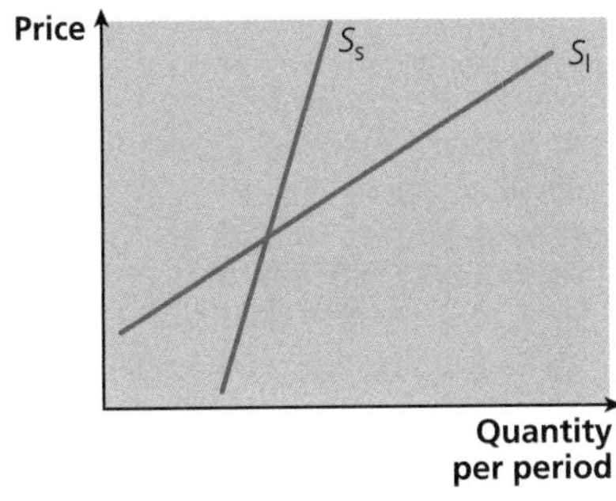

Figure 13 Short- and long-run supply

Of course, it is possible that there may be a situation of perfectly inelastic supply; in this situation, it is not possible to increase supply no matter how much price increases by. Agricultural products are a good example of perfectly inelastic supply as it can take a number of years to bring such products to the market. This is shown by the supply curve S_i in Figure 14.

At the other extreme, it is possible that there may be a situation of perfectly elastic supply; in this situation, the firms in the industry would be willing to supply any amount of the product at a given price. For example, if resources are available, the supply of batteries by firms in the industry may become perfectly elastic. This is shown by the supply curve S_e in Figure 14.

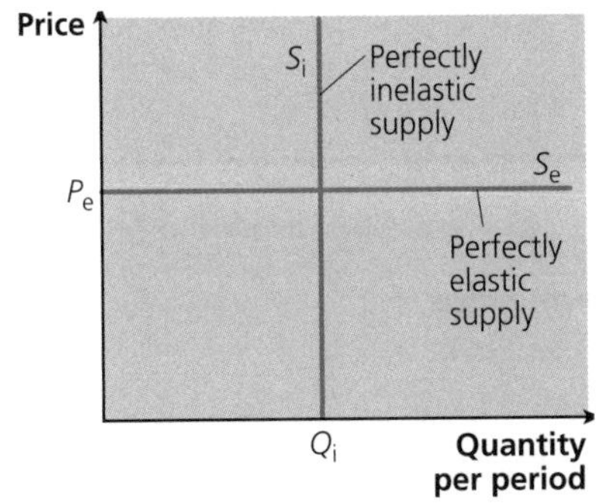

Figure 14 Perfectly elastic and inelastic supply

Now test yourself

10 What is the formula for price elasticity of supply?

Answer on p.154

Tested

Interaction of demand and supply

Equilibrium and disequilibrium

Revised

Having considered both demand and supply, it is now necessary to bring them together to establish what is meant by market **equilibrium**.

Market equilibrium is shown in Figure 15. The downward-sloping demand curve and the upward-sloping supply curve cross at the equilibrium position of price P^* and quantity Q^*. If the price were higher than this, there would be excess supply and this would cause the price to move downwards to the equilibrium position. If the price was lower than this, there would be excess demand and this would cause the price to move upwards to the equilibrium position.

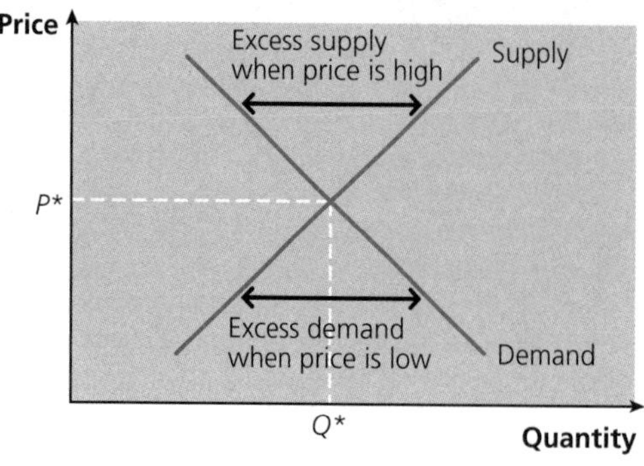

Figure 15 Bringing demand and supply together

If a situation of excess supply or excess demand were to exist for a period of time, this would be called **disequilibrium** until a position of equilibrium was eventually restored.

equilibrium: a situation where the quantity demanded in the marketplace is exactly equal to the quantity supplied. There is neither excess demand nor excess supply in the market. It is sometimes referred to as a state of rest or balance

disequilibrium: a situation where there is an imbalance between demand and supply in a market, i.e. there will be a situation of excess demand or excess supply

Now test yourself

11 Explain what is meant by 'market equilibrium'.

Answer on p.154

Tested

Expert tip

It is important that candidates can distinguish between a situation of *equilibrium* and one of *disequilibrium* in a market.

Equilibrium price and quantity

Revised

Now that demand and supply have been brought together, it is possible to consider the effects of changes in demand and supply on **equilibrium price** and **equilibrium quantity**.

equilibrium price: the price at which a market clears. The process of market clearing arises because the price is free to change and settle at the equilibrium level

equilibrium quantity: a situation where a market clears, with consumers getting all they want at the equilibrium price and producers not being left with unsold products, i.e. there is no excess demand or excess supply in the market

In Figure 16, there has been an increase in the demand for a product, for example as a result of an increase in incomes in an economy. The demand curve shifts to the right and there is a movement along the supply curve. Equilibrium price goes up from P_0 to P_1 and equilibrium quantity goes up from Q_0 to Q_1.

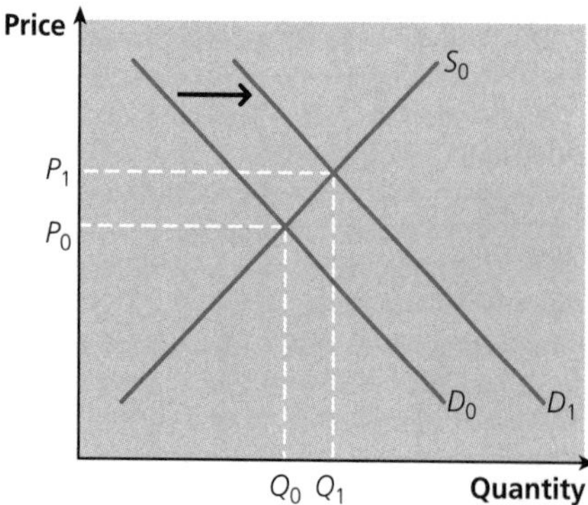

Figure 16 The effect of a shift of a demand curve to the right on equilibrium price and equilibrium quantity in a market

In Figure 17, there has been an increase in the supply of a product, for example as a result of a reduction in the costs of production. The supply curve shifts to the right and there is a movement along the demand curve. Equilibrium price comes down from P_0 to P_1 and equilibrium quantity goes up from Q_0 to Q_1.

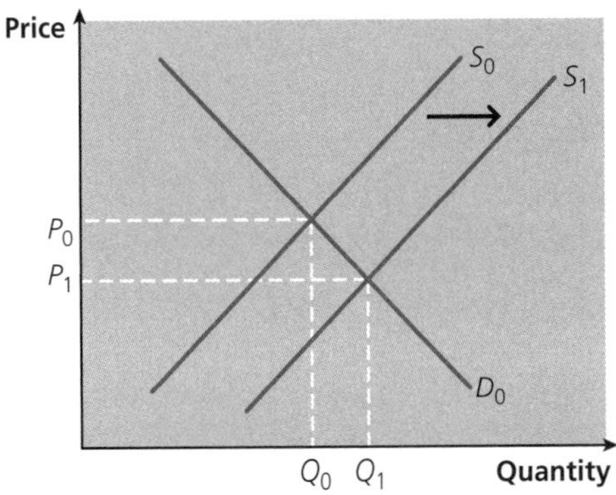

Figure 17 The effect of a shift of a supply curve to the right on equilibrium price and equilibrium quantity in a market

Now test yourself

12 Explain what is meant by an equilibrium in a market.

Answer on p.154

Tested

Applications of demand and supply analysis

Revised

Demand and supply analysis can be applied to a wide variety of different situations. For example, if an economy is experiencing an increase in incomes, there is likely to be an increase in the demand for cars, shifting the demand curve to the right. At the same time, an improvement in technology has reduced the cost of producing cars, shifting the supply curve to the right. The effect of these two changes can be seen in Figure 18. The demand curve shifts to the right; the effect of this is that equilibrium price goes up from P_0 to P_1 and equilibrium quantity goes up from Q_0 to Q_1. The supply curve also shifts to the right; the effect of this is that equilibrium price goes back down to P_0 and equilibrium quantity goes up from Q_1 to Q_2. Of course, whether equilibrium price actually returns to its original position will depend on the extent of the shifts of the demand and supply curves.

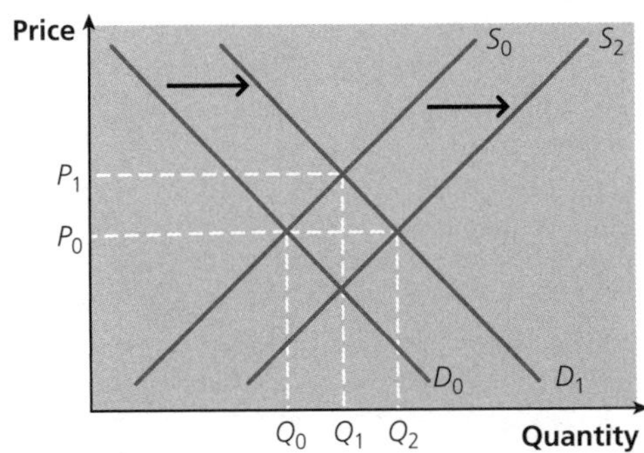

Figure 18 An application of demand and supply analysis to cars

Consumer and producer surplus

Consumer surplus

Revised

Consumer surplus is shown in Figure 19. Consumers are able to obtain a value from consuming a particular product that is above the price paid until at some point consumers pay a price that is exactly equal to the value gained. In the diagram, this is P^*. All the consumers up to Q^* have gained a value that is above the price and this is shown by the shaded area between the price line and the demand curve. When price is P^* and quantity is Q^*, the consumer surplus has disappeared. The demand curve is actually showing the marginal social benefit (*MSB*) of the consumption. This means that the demand curve combines all the points where consumers are gaining from the fact that one price is being charged to all consumers in the market, despite the fact that they would have been prepared to pay more. They are gaining a marginal social benefit by being able to buy a product at a lower price than they were originally prepared to pay, i.e. they gain from the additional benefit received.

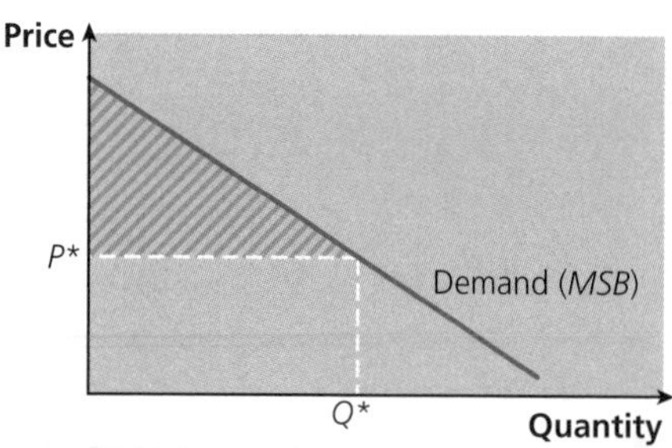

Figure 19 Consumer surplus

consumer surplus: a situation that comes about because some consumers will value a particular product more highly than other consumers and yet they will pay exactly the same price for it as the other consumers. Consumer surplus refers to the value of this extra satisfaction; it is shown on a demand and supply diagram by the triangle between the price line and the demand curve

Now test yourself

13 What is meant by the term 'consumer surplus'?

Answer on p.154

Tested

Producer surplus

Revised

Producer surplus is shown in Figure 20. Producers are able to gain because for all the units sold up to Q^*, they have received a price that is above the cost of producing those units. The supply curve is actually showing the marginal social cost of the production. This means that while the supply curve is made up of the points indicating the cost of producing that output, a firm will gain because the price charged is higher than the cost, i.e. it will gain from the additional benefit received where the price is greater than the cost. When the producer surplus disappears, that additional benefit disappears. The producer surplus is shown by the shaded area between the price line and the supply curve. When price is P^* and quantity is Q^*, the producer surplus has disappeared.

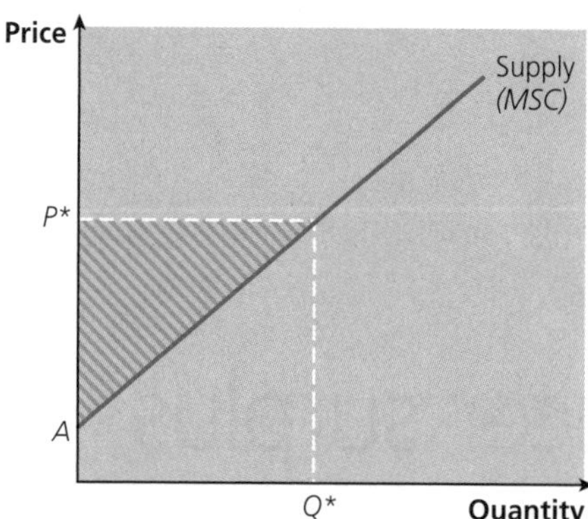

Figure 20 Producer surplus

producer surplus: the difference between the price that consumers are willing to pay for a particular product and the price that producers require in order to supply the product. Firms will stop increasing supply if the price is just equal to the marginal cost of production, but for all the output that firms have supplied up to that point they have received a price above the cost of production. This is the producer surplus; it is shown on a demand and supply diagram by the triangle between the price line and the supply curve

Revision activity

Using a diagram, distinguish between consumer surplus and producer surplus.

Prices as rationing and allocative mechanisms

The role of prices

Revised

Prices perform an important role in the allocation of resources in a market. The **price mechanism** allocates resources because price changes act as signals as the conditions of demand and supply in a market change. The Scottish economist Adam Smith (1723–90) argued that prices in a market therefore acted as an 'invisible hand' in allocating scarce resources.

Prices also perform an important function in a market as a rationing mechanism. For example, if a producer has a limited capacity to produce certain products, and if these products are expensive, this high price will have the effect of rationing demand. For example, in the case of exclusive brands of cars, which tend to be very expensive, the high price will limit demand to only those people who can afford to pay the high price of the cars.

Now test yourself

14 Analyse why price is so important in a market.

Answer on p.154

Tested

price mechanism: the operation of changes in prices in a market to act as signals to producers to allocate resources according to changes in consumer demand

Revision activity

Explain what Adam Smith meant when he referred to the price mechanism as an 'invisible hand'.

3 Government intervention in the price system

Externalities

An **externality** arises if a **third party** is affected by the actions and behaviour of others. A third party can be regarded as someone who is not directly involved. An externality can also be described as a situation where there is a **spillover effect**. An externality is external to a market transaction and so is not reflected in market prices. It can occur in relation to consumption or production. It is a form of **market failure** because if the cost or benefit is not reflected in market prices, it cannot be taken into account by all the parties involved in a transaction. That is why the costs or benefits that result from such a transaction affect a third party that is not directly involved in the transaction.

externalities: costs or benefits of either consumption or production which have spillover or third party effects that are not paid for by the consumer or by the producer

third party: individuals or groups that are not the main parties in a transaction, but are still affected by it

spillover effect: the effect of certain decisions which have an impact on third parties, i.e. those who are neither the producers nor the consumers of a particular product

market failure: a market imperfection which gives rise to an allocation of scarce resources which is not as efficient as it might have otherwise been

Expert tip

Candidates need to understand what is meant by a 'third party', i.e. someone who is not directly involved in the consumption and/or the production of a product. The third party, however, can still be affected in different ways by consumption and/or production decisions taken by others. For example, in the case of passive smoking, a person who is not actually smoking a cigarette can be badly affected by the actions of others around them. Similarly, in the case of drink driving, a motorist may be sober and driving very well, but may be involved in an accident as a result of the poor driving of another motorist.

Positive externality

Revised

A **positive externality** refers to the benefit that can be gained by a third party, i.e. someone who is not directly involved in a transaction. A positive externality can be seen in relation to either consumption or production.

positive externality: the external benefit that may occur as a result of an action, bringing some benefit to a third party

A positive consumption externality

A **positive consumption externality** is where there is a beneficial spillover effect on a third party arising from the consumption of a good or service. For example, the enjoyment provided by the views of private gardens. This can be seen in Figure 1. *MPB* shows the marginal private benefit, but *MSB* shows the marginal social benefit. The equilibrium which takes into account the marginal social benefit would be at quantity *Q**, a greater output than would be the case if there was only marginal private benefit at *Q*, because at this point it is only the marginal private benefit that is being taken into account, not the marginal social benefit. The welfare gain from the equilibrium being where *MSC* crosses *MSB*, rather than *MPB*, is shown by the shaded triangle.

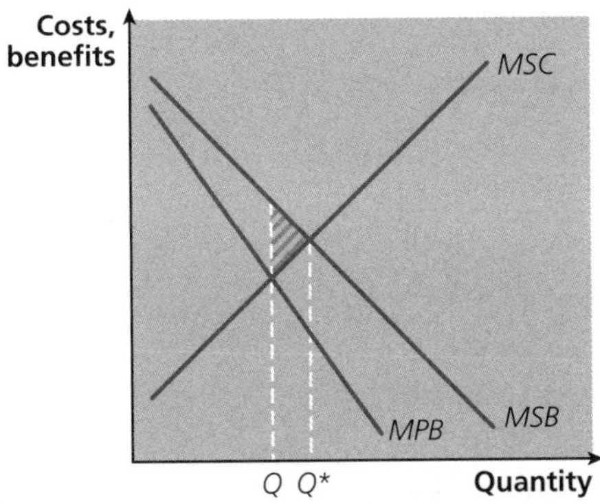

Figure 1 A positive consumption externality

positive consumption externality: an externality that affects the consumption side of a market in a positive or beneficial way

A positive production externality

A **positive production externality** is where there is a beneficial spillover effect on a third party arising from the production of a good or service. For example, if a firm purifies its waste water, this will be beneficial to a local fish farm in the area. This can be seen in Figure 2. *MPC* shows a firm's marginal private cost, but *MSC* shows the marginal social cost. This is lower than the *MPC*. The equilibrium should be at output *Q** which is where *MSC* = *MSB*. The output at *Q** is greater than at *Q*. The **welfare gain** resulting from the extra output is shown by the shaded triangle.

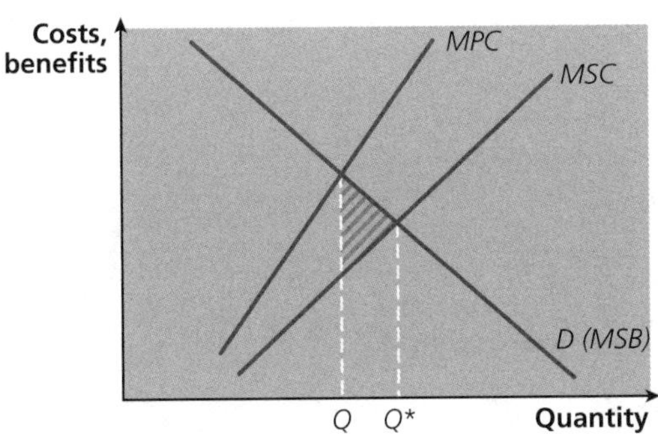

Figure 2 A positive production externality

positive production externality: an externality that affects the production side of a market in a positive or beneficial way

welfare gain: an additional benefit resulting from more being produced in a market

Negative externality

Revised

A **negative externality** refers to the disadvantage that can affect a third party, i.e. someone who is not directly involved in a transaction. A negative externality can also be seen in relation to either consumption or production. For example, a third party might be negatively affected by the consumption of a loud music system by a neighbour. In terms of production, a third party might be negatively affected by pollution caused by a factory in the neighbourhood.

negative externality: the external cost that may occur as a result of an action, bringing some disadvantage to a third party

A negative consumption externality

A **negative consumption externality** is where there is a negative spillover effect on a third party arising from the consumption. For example, a person playing loud music that irritates the neighbours living nearby. This can be seen in Figure 3. An individual's appreciation of the music can be seen by *MPB*, the marginal private benefit, but the negative effect on the neighbours means that *MSB*, the marginal social benefit, is lower than this. The equilibrium position for the person playing the music is at *Q*, where *MPB* and *MSC* cross, but the equilibrium position for the whole community, taking into account the negative effect of the loud music on the neighbours, is at *Q** where *MSC* and *MSB* intersect. The **welfare loss** is shown by the shaded triangle.

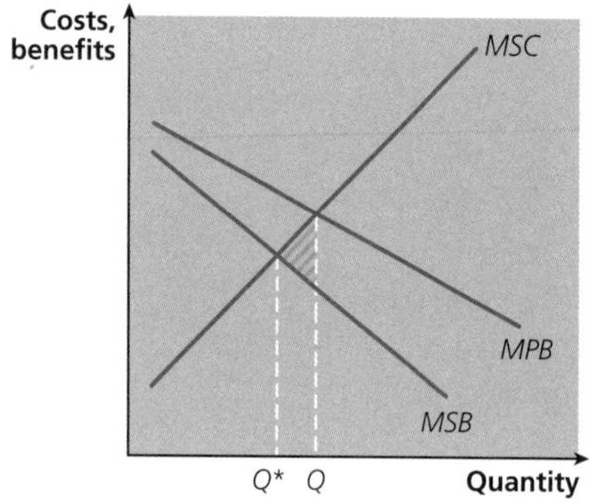

Figure 3 A negative consumption externality

negative consumption externality: an externality that affects the consumption side of a market in a negative or disadvantageous way

welfare loss: a situation which arises when *MSC* exceeds *MSB*, leading to a socially inefficient allocation of resources

A negative production externality

A **negative production externality** is where there is a negative spillover effect on a third party arising from the production of a good or service. For example, a factory producing noise and/or air pollution. This can be seen in Figure 4. The marginal private cost, *MPC*, only takes into account the cost of production to the firm. The marginal social cost, *MSC*, takes into account the full social costs of the production. For the firm, the equilibrium position would be at *Q*, but for the whole society the equilibrium position would be at *Q** where *MSC* and *MSB* intersect. If output was at Q rather than Q*, there would be a welfare loss shown by the shaded triangle.

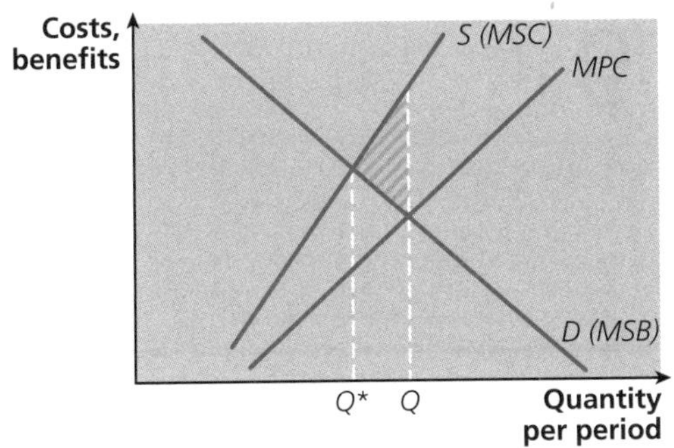

Figure 4 A negative production externality

negative production externality: an externality that affects the production side of a market in a negative or disadvantageous way

Now test yourself

1 Explain what is meant by an 'externality'.

Answer on p.154

Tested

Revision activity

Make a list of the main distinctions between the various types of externality that can exist in an economy.

Social costs and social benefits

Social costs

Revised

Social costs represent the true cost of something to society, i.e. they do not only include internal or private costs, but also the **external costs** imposed on the whole society as a result of an action.

social costs: the sum of private costs and external costs

external costs: the costs imposed on third parties

Expert tip

Candidates need to demonstrate that they understand that social costs include *both* private costs *and* external costs. A common mistake is to confuse social costs and external costs.

Now test yourself

2 Define the term 'social cost'.

Answer on p.155

Tested

Social benefits

Revised

Social benefits represent the true benefit of something to society, i.e. they do not only include internal or private benefits, but also the **external benefits** that are advantageous to the whole society as a result of an action. For example, the additional income that is created in an area when a new business locates there. This will lead to an increase in spending in the community.

social benefits: the sum of private benefits and external benefits

external benefits: the advantages gained by third parties, not just the consumer or the producer

Expert tip

Candidates need to demonstrate that they understand that social benefits include *both* private benefits *and* external benefits. A common mistake is to confuse social benefits and external benefits.

Revision activity

Make a list of some of the main social costs and social benefits that exist in your country.

Decision making using cost–benefit analysis

Cost–benefit analysis

Revised

Cost–benefit analysis provides a framework where all the costs and benefits of an investment project can be analysed, not only private ones. It is a particular feature of major transportation projects, such as the building of a road, a runway or a railway line. Its key feature is that the full social costs and the full social benefits need to be taken into account before a decision can be taken as to whether a particular investment project should go ahead or not. In this way, the true cost and benefit to society can be taken into account before a final decision is taken. The advantage of cost–benefit analysis is that a wide view can be taken of a project by taking into account its full impact on an economy over a period of time.

cost–benefit analysis: an analysis of a project which includes a valuation of the total costs and total benefits involved, i.e. including private and external costs and private and external benefits

Expert tip

In an answer to a question on cost-benefit analysis, candidates should emphasise that the advantage of this approach is that it can take into account the full social costs and social benefits involved in an investment project.

Despite these advantages, however, the process of cost–benefit analysis does face a number of problems, as can be seen in Table 1.

Table 1 Problems of cost–benefit analysis

Problem	Explanation
Absence of market prices	Cost–benefit analysis takes into account all costs and benefits, but not all of these will have a market price. For example, it is difficult, if not impossible, to establish the price of pollution.
Need to use shadow prices, i.e. prices that are estimated rather than accurately calculated	In the absence of market prices, values will need to be estimated through the use of shadow prices, but this will not always be accurate, e.g. the valuation of time or an accident.
The future	The costs and benefits of any project, such as the building of a road or a runway, will be spread over a long period of time, so it will be difficult to compare the interests of present and future generations.
Discounted values	Future costs and benefits will need to be converted into present values through discounting future values, but this is quite a complex process.
Spillover effects	It is recognised that a project will have spillover effects, but it may be difficult to establish what these are and how far they extend.
Political versus economic decisions	Cost–benefit analysis may produce a decision in favour of a particular project, but it may still be rejected because of political decisions.

Now test yourself

3 Explain what is meant by 'cost–benefit analysis'.

Answer on p.155

Tested

Revision activity

Contrast the main advantages and disadvantages of using cost-benefit analysis to decide on whether an investment project should go ahead.

Private and public goods

Private goods

Revised

A **private good** is one which is consumed by an individual for their own private benefit. This would apply to most products in an economy. The key feature of a private good is that there is **rivalry** in consumption, i.e. once a product has been consumed by one person, it cannot be consumed by another because other people are **excluded** from consumption. There is rivalry in such a situation because different consumers are in competition with other consumers to consume a particular product. Examples could include food and clothing.

private goods: goods that are bought and consumed by individuals for their own benefit

excludable: a situation that occurs with private goods in that when a product is consumed by one person, all others are excluded from it

rivalry: rivalry in consumption means that when a product is consumed by one person, it cannot be consumed by another

Expert tip

It is important that candidates can clearly distinguish between *private goods* and *public goods* in their examination answers on this topic. The key characteristic of a private good is that it involves rivalry, i.e. it is possible to exclude people from the consumption of such a good.

Public goods

Revised

In contrast to private goods, **public goods** are provided by society as a whole so that everyone can benefit from them. No one is excluded from benefiting from such products and consumption by one person does not prevent others consuming them. Examples could include street lighting, defence and the police.

These products need to be provided by the state or the public sector because it would be impossible to exclude someone who had not paid if the products were provided in the private sector. This gives rise to the **free rider** problem; it would not be possible to provide street lighting through the private sector because it would be impossible to exclude someone who had not paid. When such products are provided by the public sector, they are part of **government expenditure** and are financed out of taxation.

In addition to being non-rival and non-excludable, public goods are also **non-rejectable**. This means that even if a person did not want to be protected by their country's defence and police system, they would not actually be able to reject it.

public goods: goods and services that are provided by the public sector, otherwise they would not be provided

non-rivalness (or non-rivalry): where the consumption of one product does not prevent its consumption by someone else

non-excludability (or non-excludable): where the consumption of a product by one person does not exclude others from consuming the same product

free rider: the idea that it would be impossible to charge people for the use of something because it would be virtually impossible to charge each person for the use of a product; this is why street lighting, for example, is provided as a public good rather than as a private good

government expenditure: the total of all spending by a government

non-rejectability: a situation where individuals cannot actually abstain from the consumption of a public good, even if they wanted to, e.g. an individual cannot reject being defended by the armed forces of a country

Expert tip

Whereas a key feature of a private good is that it involves rivalry, candidates need to emphasise in their answers that a key feature of a public good is that it is non-rival, i.e. it is not possible to exclude people from the consumption of such a good. It is, therefore, non-excludable as well as being non-rival.

Now test yourself

4 Distinguish between a private good and a public good.

Answer on p.155

Tested

Revision activity

Find out which public goods exist in your country.

Merit and demerit goods

Merit goods

Revised

A **merit good** is a particular type of private good. Like other private goods, they are both rival and excludable, but what distinguishes a merit good is the fact that it would be likely to be under-produced and under-consumed if provided through the private sector as they generate positive externalities, with the social benefit from consumption exceeding the private benefit. This could be regarded as a **market imperfection**.

A merit good has intrinsic benefits for an individual, but it also has external benefits to the wider society. Examples include education and healthcare. The problem is that there is **information failure**, i.e. the allocation of resources is sub-optimal because people lack full information. For example, people don't fully appreciate the value of a good education. Without government intervention, it is likely that there would be market failure because merit goods would be under-produced and under-consumed in the private sector. They are provided through the public sector, alongside private sector provision, so that those who could not afford to consume them in the private sector would be able to do so in the public sector.

merit goods: products which are rivalrous and excludable but, if left to a free market, would be likely to be under-produced and under-consumed

market imperfections: these occur in an imperfect market, such as a need for government intervention in a market

information failure: a situation where people lack the full information that would allow them to make the best decisions about consumption

Expert tip

Candidates sometimes get confused and describe merit goods as examples of public goods. They are not examples of public goods, but of private goods. Like all private goods, they are rivalrous and excludable.

Expert tip

Candidates can also sometimes confuse a merit good with a **free good**, especially given that some merit goods are free at the point of consumption, e.g. entry to a particular lesson. A free good, however, is something completely different; this is where there is so much of a product that demand can be satisfied without a need for an allocative mechanism and supply will equal demand at zero price, e.g. air.

Demerit goods

Revised

Demerit goods are the opposite of merit goods. Whereas merit goods would be under-produced and under-consumed in a free market, demerit goods would be over-produced and over-consumed in a free market. A demerit good is socially undesirable in some way. Examples include alcohol and tobacco. Without government intervention, it is likely that there would be market failure because demerit goods would be over-produced and over-consumed in the private sector.

demerit goods: products which are rivalrous and excludable which, if left to a free market, would be likely to be over-produced and over-consumed. The social costs of production/consumption outweigh the private costs

Expert tip

It is important that candidates clearly indicate how a demerit good is fundamentally different from a merit good. Whereas a merit good is likely to be under-produced and under-consumed, a demerit good is likely to be over-produced and over-consumed in a free market. This is a concern to society because of the harmful side-effects of demerit goods.

Now test yourself

5 Distinguish between a merit good and a demerit good.

Answer on p.155

Tested

Revision activity

Find out what actions the government of your country is taking to encourage the consumption of merit goods and to discourage the consumption of demerit goods.

Examples of government intervention

Maximum price controls

Revised

One form of government intervention in an economy is to establish a **maximum price** in a market for a product which prevents the price rising above a specific level. The maximum price will need to be established below the equilibrium price which would otherwise have established a price resulting from the intersection of demand and supply. Examples could include bread and rice, because without maximum price controls, the price of these could rise so high that poorer sections of a community would not be able to afford them and this could have detrimental effects on their health and standard of living.

maximum price controls: controls which establish a maximum price for a product; price is not allowed to rise above this specific level

Now test yourself

6 Explain why a maximum price might be introduced in an economy.

Answer on p.155

Tested

Price stabilisation

Revised

If left to free-market forces, there is always a chance that prices will fluctuate widely in those markets where there can be great variations in supply over a period of time. This is especially the case with agricultural markets. In such a situation, a government could intervene through what is called a **buffer stock** scheme. When supply is very high, the government purchases some of the stock and stops it from entering the market; the effect of this is to stop the price going too low. When supply is very low, the government releases some of this stock; the effect of this is to stop the price going too high.

price stabilisation: a situation where a government intervenes to purchase stocks of a product when supply is high and to sell stocks of a product when supply is low

buffer stock: a stock of a commodity which is held back from the market in times of high production and released onto the market in times of low production

Revision activity

Outline the main advantages and disadvantages of a government intervening in an economy to influence prices of particular products.

Taxes

Revised

In the case of a demerit good, a government could intervene in a market through taxation in an attempt to discourage consumption of the demerit good. For example, if expenditure taxes, such as **excise duties**, were placed on demerit goods to such an extent that the price was substantially increased, this would be likely to discourage the level of consumption of the demerit good.

excise duties: an indirect tax on expenditure

This can be seen in Figure 5. *MPB* shows the marginal private benefit of the consumption of a demerit good, tobacco, but given the potential health dangers of smoking tobacco, the social benefit can actually be shown by *MSB*, the marginal social benefit. The equilibrium in a market without government intervention would be at Q where *MPC* (marginal private cost) is equal to *MPB*, giving a quantity Q. A government, however, decides to intervene by imposing an indirect tax so that the supply curve shifts upwards by the extent of the tax to Supply + tax. This gives an equilibrium output of *Q**.

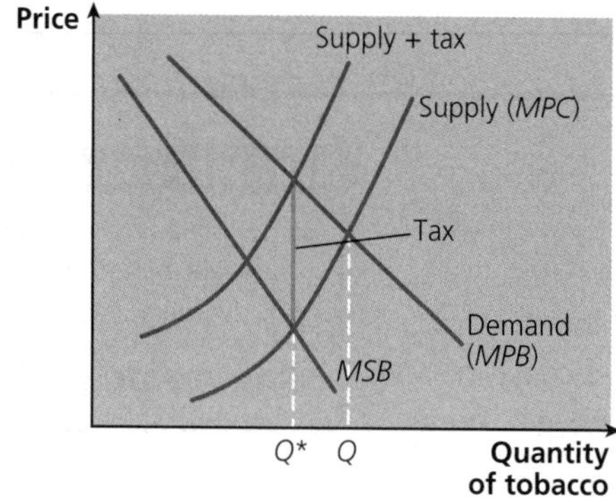

Figure 5 Taxing tobacco

Subsidies

Revised

Whereas in the case of a demerit good, a government will aim to intervene in a market to discourage consumption, it is the opposite with merit goods where a government will seek to encourage consumption. This could be achieved through a subsidy.

This can be seen in Figure 6 in relation to a subsidy on museums. The original equilibrium, without government intervention, would have been at a quantity of Q and a price of *P* where *MPC* is equal to *MPB*. A museum, however, can be regarded as an example of a merit good and so if a government decides to encourage the number of people visiting museums, it could provide a subsidy shown by the vertical distance between Supply (*MPC*) and Supply with subsidy. The new equilibrium will produce a quantity of *Q** and a price of *P**.

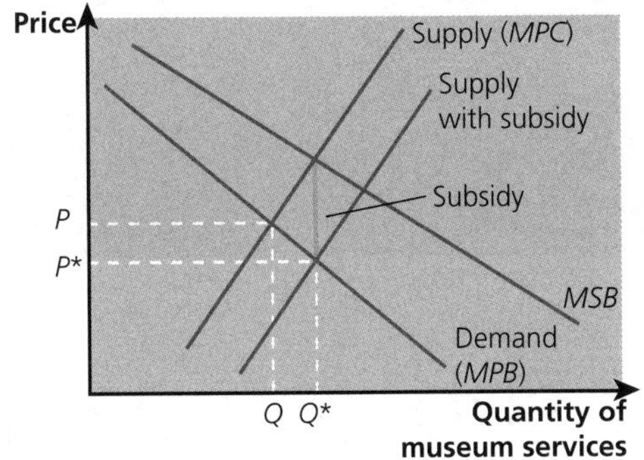

Figure 6 Subsidising museums

Direct provision of goods and services

Revised

Although a government can intervene in a market, such as through indirect taxes and subsidies, it is also possible for a government to directly provide goods and services. For example, a government may provide a service through the public sector by nationalising an industry, i.e. taking it under state control.

Revision activity

Find out which sectors of your country's economy are directly controlled by the state.

4 International trade

Principles of absolute and comparative advantage

International trade between countries is based on specialisation whereby one country is more efficient than another at producing a particular product. This gives rise to two types of advantage: **absolute advantage** and **comparative advantage**.

absolute advantage: a situation where a country can produce a particular good using fewer resources than another country

comparative advantage: a situation where a country might be more efficient at producing everything compared to another country, but where there would still be an advantage if it produced something that it was least bad at producing

Absolute advantage

Revised

Absolute advantage refers to a situation where one country is able to produce a particular good with fewer resources than another country. As a result of this, the country will enjoy a cost advantage and this is why absolute advantage is often referred to as 'absolute cost advantage'.

The reason for this advantage is that each country is endowed with a particular mix of factors of production and so one country may be more efficient than another country at producing a particular good. For example, a country in the Caribbean, such as Jamaica, would have an absolute advantage over the UK in the production of bananas because of the fact that the weather conditions would be much more favourable.

Comparative advantage

Revised

The principle of comparative or relative advantage is different to that of absolute advantage because it takes into account not just the absolute efficiency of one country compared to another, but its relative efficiency. This then allows a country to produce something in which it does not have an absolute advantage, but in which it is relatively good compared to other goods that it might produce. To put it another way, a country will specialise in the production of something in which its comparative disadvantage is less than for another country.

This can be seen in Figure 1. Two countries, country 1 and country 2, have different comparative advantages which can be seen by the slope of their respective production possibility curves. Country 1 has a comparative advantage in the production of manufactured goods whereas country 2 has a comparative advantage in the production of agricultural goods. At point *A*, if each country produced 20 units of manufactured goods and 20 units of agricultural goods, total world output with no trade would be at point *B*, i.e. there would be 40 units of manufactured goods and 40 units of agricultural goods.

If, however, country 1 specialised on the production of manufactured goods and country 2 specialised on the production of agricultural goods, the total world output with trade would be at point *C* with 60 units of manufactured goods and 60 units of agricultural goods. As a result of applying the principle of comparative advantage, total world output with trade would be greater than the situation without any trade taking place.

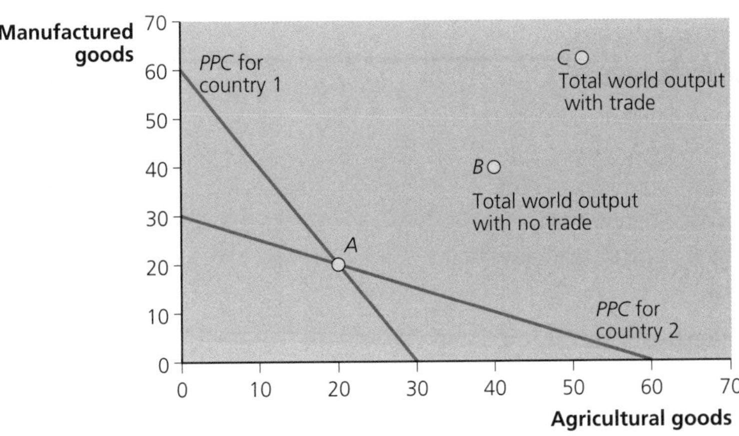

Figure 1 PPCs for two countries

Figure 1 shows the situation where just two countries are trading with each other. This is known as **bilateral trade**. Of course, in the real world, the situation is more complex than this, given the existence of **multilateral trade**.

bilateral trade: where trade takes place between two countries

multilateral trade: a more realistic situation where trade takes place between a number of countries

globalisation: the process whereby there is an increasing world market in goods and services, making an increase in multilateral trade more likely. It has been made possible by a number of factors, including progress in trade liberalisation

exports: goods and/or services that are produced domestically in one country and sold to other countries

imports: goods and/or services that are produced in foreign countries and consumed by people in the domestic economy

Now test yourself

1 Distinguish between absolute advantage and comparative advantage.
2 Distinguish between bilateral trade and multilateral trade.

Answers on p.155

Tested

Expert tip

It is important that candidates can demonstrate their understanding of the distinction between *bilateral trade* and *multilateral trade*. Economists use two countries on production possibility curve diagrams, but in reality trade will involve the participation of many more countries in the world.

Revision activity

Find out as much as you can about the trading patterns of your country, both in terms of the countries involved and the various products imported and exported.

Real-world limitations

Revised

The principle of comparative advantage is helpful in explaining how total world output can be increased as a result of specialisation, but there are a number of real-world limitations. These include the following:

- It is assumed that there are no transport costs involved in international trade, but this is unrealistic and transport costs may actually offset any cost advantages arising from the application of the principle of comparative advantage.
- It is assumed that there are constant returns to scale and constant costs of production, but it is always possible that an increase in output leads to diseconomies of scale and a situation of rising costs of production.
- It is assumed that there is free trade between countries, but in reality there are many import restrictions which exist in different parts of the world.
- It is assumed that the benefits of international trade will not be affected by exchange rates, but movements in exchange rates can help to make trade more or less advantageous to a country in the real world.

Opportunity cost concept allied to trade

Revised

The principle of comparative advantage is reflected in differences in opportunity cost. World trade will substantially increase if each country concentrates on producing the product(s) in which it has the lowest opportunity cost. International trade will always be beneficial if there is a difference in the opportunity cost ratios between countries and if each country specialises in the product in which it has the lowest opportunity cost.

It is possible to appreciate the importance of opportunity cost in international trade through a **trading possibility curve**. This will show the extent to which output can be increased without the need for any additional resources. By specialising according to the principle of comparative advantage, countries will minimise the opportunity cost of production. When countries trade their surplus output, there will be more for everyone to consume in the world.

trading possibility curve: a means of showing the advantages of two countries trading with each other as long as the opportunity costs of production are different

Other explanations and determinants of trade flows

Revised

Traditionally, economists have always focused on the principle of comparative advantage as the main explanation of trade flows. However, given the existence of the real-world limitations to the principle already discussed, economists have begun to look at other possible explanations and determinants of trade flows. These include the following:

- competitive advantage — this is the idea that it is not so much opportunity cost that is important, but the actual cost of production in different countries, e.g. the decision of multinational companies to locate production in particular countries to take advantage of differences in labour costs
- factor endowment — differences in endowments of factors of production in various countries are already an element in the principle of comparative advantage, but some economists have greatly stressed the significance of differences in the quality and quantity of factors of production between countries
- government policy — a government may be concerned about the possible disadvantages of over-specialisation on particular products and so might decide to encourage a greater degree of diversification of production than might otherwise have been the case

Arguments for free trade and motives for protection

Arguments for free trade

Revised

For many years, economists have stressed the potential advantages of **free trade** for a country. These include the following:

- world output can be increased
- resources are allocated more efficiently
- consumers can have a wider range of products to choose from
- this can contribute to a substantial increase in economic growth
- it will lead to an improved standard of living and quality of life

A reduction in trade barriers will bring about a greater degree of free trade and this process of trade liberalisation will lead to **trade creation**.

free trade: trade which is not restricted or limited by different types of import controls

trade creation: the creation of new trade as a result of the reduction or elimination of trade barriers

The World Trade Organisation

Revised

The **World Trade Organisation** was set up in 1995 to encourage free trade. It replaced another organisation which had previously existed since 1948 with the same purpose, the General Agreement on Tariffs and Trade (GATT). Its head office is in Geneva, Switzerland, and it currently has 157 member countries. It has sought to regulate trade between countries through a series of discussions. The latest round of discussions has been the Doha Round and these have been taking place since 2001.

World Trade Organisation: an organisation set up in 1995 to promote free trade in the world through the reduction of trade barriers

Now test yourself

3 Explain the purpose of the World Trade Organisation.

Answer on p.155

Tested

Motives for protection

Revised

Despite the undoubted potential advantages of free trade, economists emphasise that there can be a number of motives in favour of protection. These include the following:

- **Infant** or **sunrise industries** need protection, at least as a temporary measure, to allow firms to be strong enough to compete with other already established firms.
- **Sunset** or **declining industries** need to be protected, at least temporarily, to give sufficient time for the factors of production to be transferred to alternative productive use.
- A strategic industry may need to be protected, such as weapon production, because if not a country may be vulnerable to attack by an enemy.

- Firms which sell products that have been imported into a country may sell them not only cheaply to establish a market foothold, but at a price that is actually below the cost of production; this is known as **dumping** and a country may decide to use protectionist methods to protect themselves from such 'dumping'.
- A country may be experiencing a balance of payments deficit on current account, e.g. the value of the imports may exceed the value of the exports, and so protectionism may be employed to try to overcome this deficit by restricting the imports coming into the country (such a policy will not overcome the underlying reason for the deficit).
- Some protectionist methods, such as tariffs, raise revenue and so a government may use tariffs as a way of increasing its revenue.

When trade barriers are established, it can lead to a process of **trade diversion**, i.e. a certain amount of trade will be lost as a result of the establishment of the barriers.

infant industry argument: the idea that a newly established industry should be given time to establish itself; it will, therefore, need to be protected, at least temporarily

sunrise industries: industries that are new, or relatively new, and which are growing fast. It is also expected that they will become very important in the future

sunset industries: industries that have passed their peak and are now in decline, with no realistic hope of recovery

dumping: the practice of selling a product at a price that is less than the cost of production

trade diversion: where a certain amount of trade is lost as a result of the imposition of trade barriers

Expert tip

Candidates often state that dumping is where a product is sold cheaply to gain access in to a market. It may well be sold at a price that is cheaper than that charged by domestic producers, but that does not mean that it is an example of dumping. For dumping to take place, the product has to be sold at a price that fails to cover the cost of production.

Now test yourself

4 Distinguish between a sunrise industry and a sunset industry.

Answer on p.155

Tested

Revision activity

Summarise the main arguments for and against free trade.

Types of protection and their effects

Methods to protect domestic industries

Revised

There are a number of different methods that can be used to protect domestic industries. These include the following:

- **tariffs** — these are taxes or duties that are imposed on imported products; the effect is to make the imported products more expensive than they would otherwise be and this should lead to a reduction in the demand for them, although the actual effect will depend on the price elasticity of demand for the imported product
- **quotas** — these are restrictions on imports into a country in terms of the number of goods imported, the value of goods imported or the proportion of market share that they represent; the effect is that as there are fewer of them, less will be purchased by domestic consumers

- **subsidies** — these are payments by a government to a domestic firm to help it keep down the costs of production; the effect is that if the lower cost is passed on to consumers in the form of lower prices, the demand for them is likely to increase and make them a more competitively priced product to compete with the imports
- **exchange controls** — these are restrictions on the buying and selling of foreign currency; the effect is to make it more difficult to actually finance the purchase of imported products
- **embargoes** — these are complete bans on certain imported products, a decision that is usually taken for political, rather than economic, reasons; the effect is to make it impossible to purchase imported products from particular countries
- **administrative procedures** — this is where the paperwork, or 'red tape', is made more difficult than it would otherwise be; the effect is to make it much more difficult to get the imported products actually into the country

tariff: a tax or duty that is imposed on an imported product to make it more expensive in the hope that this will reduce demand for the product

quota: a limit on the imported products that are allowed to enter a country; a quota can be in the form of a limited quantity, a limited value or a limited market share

embargoes: bans on imports from particular countries. They can either apply to particular products or to all products from particular countries. They are usually imposed for political, diplomatic or military, rather than economic, reasons

Now test yourself

5 Explain the difference between a tariff and a quota.

Answer on p.155

Tested

Expert tip

It is important that candidates can distinguish between a *tariff* and a *quota* as these two forms of trade protection are often confused in examination answers. A tariff refers to a tax or duty that is placed on an imported good. A quota is a restriction on the import of certain products, and this can be by quantity, value or market share.

Revision activity

Outline the main advantages and disadvantages of the various import controls.

Voluntary export restraints

Revised

In some situations, one country might be fearful that another country to which it is exporting may decide to impose protectionist barriers on that trade, which could have dramatic consequences on the exporting country's economy. To reduce the likelihood of such import controls being established, the exporting country could establish a **voluntary export restraint** or restriction, limiting the amount that the country could export. The idea is that the other importing country would now decide against imposing import controls on the exporting country.

voluntary export restraints: a decision, taken by an exporting country, to voluntarily restrict its exports in the hope that a country that it exports to will decide against imposing import controls

Economic integration

Revised

There are different forms of economic integration in various parts of the world and it is important that these different types of integration are clearly distinguished.

Free trade area

A **free trade area** refers to a situation where a number of countries come together to trade freely between each other, but where each of these countries maintains their own trade barriers with other countries outside the free trade area, i.e. there is no **common external tariff** barrier between the member countries and other countries.

> **free trade area:** a group of countries which promote free trade between themselves, but which retain a separate set of trade barriers against other countries
>
> **common external tariff:** where all of the countries in an economic organisation impose the same tariff with other countries outside of the organisation

Customs union

A **customs union** refers to a situation where a number of countries come together to trade freely between each other, and in addition to this, the countries establish a common external tariff against all other countries that are not members of the customs union.

> **customs union:** a group of countries which promote free trade between themselves, and which impose a common external tariff on imports from countries outside the area

Now test yourself

6 Distinguish between a free trade area and a customs union.

Answer on p.155

Tested

Expert tip

Candidates often confuse a free trade area with a customs union. Both types of integration encourage free trade between the member countries, but the key difference between them is that in a free trade area the member countries retain their own trade barriers with countries outside the area, whereas in a customs union the member countries adopt a common external tariff with countries outside the union.

Economic union

An **economic union** refers to a situation which goes further than a customs union and which establishes a number of economic policies, rules and regulations which affect all the member countries. An economic union may have a single currency, but it is not necessary that all member countries agree to use that currency. For example, in the European Union, there are 27 countries, but only 17 of them use the single currency.

> **economic union:** a group of countries which agree to integrate their economies as much as possible through various rules, laws, policies and regulations

Expert tip

Latvia will become the 28th member country of the European Union in 2014 and Lithuania is due to become the 29th member country in 2015.

Monetary union

A **monetary union** refers to a situation where a group of countries come together and adopt a single currency. They may also adopt a number of common monetary policies to support the operation of that currency.

> **monetary union:** a group of countries who decide to bring their economies closer together through the adoption of a single currency

Revision activity

Find out if your country is a member of a form of economic integration. If it is, try to discover the impact that this has had on your country's economy.

Expert tip

A number of candidates seem to believe that all countries in the European Union use the single currency, the euro. This is not the case. In 2013, 17 of the 27 member countries did use the euro. The UK is one of the 10 countries that does not use it, although it is possible that it may decide to use it at some point in the future.

Terms of trade

Calculating terms of trade

Revised

The **terms of trade** refer to the relative changes of export prices and import prices. It is calculated by:

$$\frac{\text{index number showing the average price of exports}}{\text{index number showing the average price of imports}}$$

If, in one year, the terms of trade are equal to 100 and the import prices rise by more than the export prices, the terms of trade will fall below 100. This is an unfavourable change because more exports will need to be sold to buy the same number of imports.

However, if in another year, the terms of trade are equal to 100 and the import prices rise by less than the export prices, the terms of trade will be above 100. This is a favourable change because fewer exports will need to be sold to buy the same number of imports, assuming a situation of ceteris paribus.

terms of trade: the price of exports in relation to the price of imports

Expert tip

Another confusion that candidates sometimes make is to regard a fall in the terms of trade as something that is unhelpful to a country's trading position. In actual fact, a fall in the terms of trade means that export prices have become relatively cheaper than import prices; if the price elasticity of demand for both exports and imports is elastic, this will help to improve a country's balance of trade situation.

Expert tip

Candidates often confuse the terms of trade with the balance of trade. The terms of trade simply indicate the relationship between changes in the prices of exports and imports; they give no indication of the changes in the quantity or value of exports and imports that are traded between countries.

Now test yourself

7 State the formula to calculate the terms of trade.

Answer on p.155

Tested

Components of the balance of payments

The **balance of payments** is a record of the transactions that a country has with the rest of the world. It shows the payments and receipts arising from this international trade. It consists of three accounts: the current account, the capital account and the financial account.

balance of payments: a record of all transactions linked with exports and imports, together with international capital movements. It consists of the current account, the capital account and the financial account

The current account of the balance of payments

Revised

The **current account** is made up of the following four parts:

- trade in goods — this is the balance of trade in terms of visible exports and visible imports (**visible balance**)
- trade in services — this is the balance of trade in terms of invisible exports and invisible imports (**invisible balance**)
- income — this is the net income from investments (**net investment income**)
- **current transfers** — this refers to transfers of money by governments and individuals; in the case of individuals, this could relate to gifts, charitable donations and money sent to, and received from, relatives who live abroad

current account of balance of payments: this is made up of four elements — the trade in goods, the trade in services, income and current transfers

visible balance: this refers to the trade in visible goods, such as cars, between countries

invisible balance: this refers to the trade in invisible services, such as banking, between countries

net investment income: this refers to the net income that relates to investments, such as dividends on shares or interest payments

current transfers: this refers to the net payments by governments and private individuals, such as grants for overseas aid or cash remittances sent home to their own countries by migrant workers

Now test yourself

8 Explain the difference between a visible and an invisible in relation to the current account of the balance of payments.

Answer on p.155

Tested

Expert tip

It is important that candidates demonstrate an awareness of the four elements of the current account of the balance of payments in their examination answers.

The capital account of the balance of payments

Revised

The **capital account** is that part of the balance of payments which records capital movements, in terms of assets and liabilities, into and out of a country. These could include physical assets such as the purchase of land.

capital account of the balance of payments: this is made up of transactions where there is a transfer of financial assets between one country and another. For example, such a financial asset could include the purchase of a physical asset such as land

The financial account of the balance of payments

Revised

The **financial account** is that part of the balance of payments which records the capital inflows into a country and the capital outflows out of a country resulting from investments, such as the building of factories.

There is a final part of the balance of payments that needs to be mentioned. This is known as **net errors and omissions**. It is not always possible to identify all payments accurately and so there may well be some transactions that go unrecorded: these are shown in the balance of payments as net errors and omissions.

financial account of the balance of payments: this is made up of the capital inflows and capital outflows resulting from investment in different countries

net errors and omissions: those transactions in the balance of payments that go unrecorded

Deficits and surpluses

Revised

The balance of payments as a whole, or one particular part of it, can have a **deficit** or a **surplus**. A deficit in the balance of payments means that the money going out of a country is greater than the money coming into the country. On the other hand, a surplus in the balance of payments means that the money coming into a country is greater than the money going out of the country. The term 'deficit' or 'surplus' is therefore said to refer to the **external balance** of a country.

deficit: a negative balance when expenditure exceeds income

surplus: a positive balance when income exceeds expenditure

external balance: the balance between receipts and payments in relation to international transactions between one country and other countries in the world

Revision activity

Try to find out as much as you can about the composition of the balance of payments of your country.

5 Theory and measurement in the macroeconomy

Employment statistics

The size and components of the labour force

Revised

The **labour force** refers to all the people in a country who are employed or who are looking for work. It is therefore both the employed people and the people who are unemployed. The best way of defining it is the number of people in a country who are available for work.

The size of a country's labour force depends on a number of factors, including the following:

- the total size of the population
- the birth rate
- the death rate
- the school leaving age
- the number of people who stay in full-time education after leaving school
- the retirement age
- the availability and value of welfare benefits to those who do not have a job
- the availability and cost of childcare
- the attitudes in the society to women working
- the state of the economy

labour force: the number of people that are available for work in a country

Expert tip

Candidates often seem to believe that the term 'labour force' only applies to those people who are employed, i.e. to those people who actually have a job. It does, however, refer not only to those people who have a job, but also to those who are unemployed.

Now test yourself

1 Define the term 'labour force'.

Answer on p.155

Tested

The working population

Another way of expressing the number of people in a country who are available to work is to refer to the **working population**.

There will always be some people who are too young to work, or who stay on in education beyond the school leaving age, or who are too old, or who are too disabled. All these people determine the **dependency ratio** of a country.

working population: the people in a country who are working or who are actively seeking work

dependency ratio: the ratio of those people in a country who are unable to work divided by those who are able to work

Revision activity

Find out as much as you can about the labour force and the dependency ratio in your country.

The participation rate

The labour **participation rate** is an indication of the people in a country who are either in work or who are officially registered as unemployed. It gives an indication of the extent to which the population of a country is economically active.

participation rate: the proportion of the population which is either in employment or officially registered as unemployed

Labour productivity

Revised

Labour productivity is the measurement of the efficiency of labour in terms of the output per worker per period of time, such as 1 hour, 1 day or 1 week.

The productivity of workers can vary for a number of reasons, including differences in:

- education
- training
- skills
- experience
- technical knowledge
- level of capital available
- working methods and practices
- motivation

labour productivity: productivity measures the level of efficiency in the use of resources. Labour productivity, therefore, measures the efficiency of labour in terms of the output per person per period of time

Expert tip

It is important to distinguish between productivity and production. Candidates often confuse these two terms. 'Production' refers to total output from resources, whereas 'productivity' refers to the efficiency of an input into the production process, such as labour.

Now test yourself

2 Explain what is meant by 'labour productivity'.

Answer on p.155

Tested

Revision activity

Choose one type of production in your country. Outline the different ways in which the productivity of the workers in this industry could be improved.

Definition of unemployment

Revised

Unemployment refers to the situation which occurs when people are able and willing to work, but are unable to find employment.

unemployment: a situation where people who are able and willing to work are unable to find work

Difficulties involved in measuring unemployment

Revised

There is no one agreed method of measuring unemployment. This is significant because different ways of measuring unemployment can give different results. Most countries use one of the two following methods.

The claimant count

The **claimant count** is one method of measuring unemployment in a country. This is where the number of people who officially register as unemployed is counted; they register so that they are eligible to claim any benefits (known as transfer payments) that the state may provide for those people who are unemployed.

claimant count: the number of people who officially register as unemployed

The labour force survey

An alternative way of measuring the number of people who are unemployed in a country is to take the claimant count and then add to it those people who are able and willing to work, but who have not officially registered themselves as unemployed. This is known as a **labour force survey**.

labour force survey: this will include not only those who are officially registered as unemployed but also those who are available for work but who have not officially registered themselves as unemployed

Expert tip

It is important that candidates can demonstrate that they understand there are two different ways to measure the number of unemployed people in an economy. One is the claimant count and one is the labour force survey. Countries usually use one or the other, although some countries use both methods.

Now test yourself

3 Distinguish between the two different methods of measuring the number of people unemployed in a country.

Answer on p.155

Tested

The unemployment rate: patterns and trends in (un)employment

Revised

It is important to distinguish between the number of people who are unemployed in a country and the **unemployment rate**. The of unemployment rate refers to the total number of people who are unemployed in a country divided by the labour force.

Economists are interested in discovering patterns and trends in the rate of unemployment in a country over a period of time. It is useful to establish whether the trend is upward or downward; if it is upward, the government will need to devise appropriate policies to try to reduce the rate.

unemployment rate: the number of unemployed people divided by the labour force

Expert tip

Candidates need to distinguish between the *number of people who are unemployed* in an economy and the *rate of unemployment* in the economy. In the first case, it will be a number; in the second case, it will be a percentage.

Revision activity

Find out about the pattern of unemployment in your country. Is the trend in recent years going up or down?

General price level: price indices

The general price level

Revised

The **general price level** of an economy gives an indication of the average price level of the various consumer goods and services in an economy at a given period of time. It is a way of measuring the **cost of living** in an economy.

The general price level in an economy is measured through the use of an index.

general price level: the average level of prices of all consumer goods and services in an economy at a given period of time

cost of living: the cost of a selection of goods and services that are consumed by an average household in an economy at a given period of time

Price indices

Revised

There are a number of different price indices that can be used to measure changes in the cost of living in an economy over a period of time, but the two most common ones are the **consumer prices index (CPI)** and the **retail prices index (RPI)**.

consumer prices index: a way of measuring changes in the prices of a number of consumer goods and services in an economy over a period of time

retail prices index: an index, just like the consumer prices index, which measures changes in the prices of a number of goods and services in an economy over a period of time, but it includes a number of items that are not included in the CPI, such as the costs of housing

There are a number of stages involved in the construction of a price index, as Table 1 indicates.

Table 1 The construction of a price index

Stage	Explanation
Basket of goods and services	A selection of a number of goods and services is included in a representative basket; the number of items is often around 600.
Household expenditure	A survey is carried out, usually every month, which monitors changes in the prices of these goods and services.
Weights	An index is constructed to show the changes in these prices, but it is recognised that some items are more important than others; these differences in importance are reflected in **weights** that are given to the different items in the basket.
Base year	To show the changes in the general level of prices over a period of time, a starting point is chosen; this is called a **base year** and is given a value of 100.
Calculation of the index figure	The percentage change in price for each item is then multiplied by its weight and this will give the average change in the index; this is usually calculated each month and shows the change in the general price level, over the previous 12 months.

weights: the items in a representative sample of goods and services bought by people in an economy will not all be of the same importance; weights are given to each of the items to reflect the relative importance of the different components in the basket, and so a price index involves a weighted average

base year: a year chosen so that comparisons can be made over a period of time; the base year for an index is given a value of 100

household expenditure: a survey is taken on a regular basis (usually every month) to record changes in the prices of a selection of goods and services that constitutes a representative basket

sampling: the use of a representative sample of goods and services consumed in an economy to give an indication of changes in the cost of living

Now test yourself

4 What is meant by 'weighting' in the construction of a prices index?

Answer on p.155

Tested

Money and real data

It is important to distinguish between **nominal value** and **real value**.

The nominal value of a given sum of money does not take into account the effects of inflation. No allowance at all is made for inflation.

The real value of a given sum of money, however, shows the value after the effects of inflation have been removed. This can be achieved with a price index by expressing the data at constant prices using a base year. This means that the value of money is calculated by assuming that the prices of goods and services in an economy have not changed and have remained constant.

An example of nominal value is if a person receives a wage rise of 8%. An example of real value is if, at that time, inflation is 7%; this 7% has to be subtracted from the 8% so that the real value of the wage increase is 8% – 7% = 1%.

nominal value: the value of a sum of money without taking into account the effect of inflation

real value: the value of a sum of money after taking into account the effect of inflation, i.e. the effects of inflation have been removed

Expert tip

It is important that candidates can demonstrate they understand what is meant by a *real value* in terms of the value of something after the effects of inflation have been taken into account.

Now test yourself

5 Distinguish between 'nominal' and 'real' data.

Answer on p.155

Tested

Revision activity

Consider why it is important to distinguish between nominal and real data.

Aggregate demand (*AD*) and aggregate supply (*AS*)

Aggregate demand

Revised

Aggregate demand refers to the total demand for all the goods and services in an economy. There are four sources of this demand:

- consumer spending
- investment by firms in machinery, equipment and plant
- government spending
- the net effect of international trade, i.e. exports minus imports

aggregate demand: the total amount that is spent on an economy's goods and services over a given period of time; it is made up of four elements — consumption, investment, government spending and net exports

The aggregate demand curve slopes downwards from left to right. This can be seen in Figure 1. If there is a change in the price level, this will cause a movement along the *AD* curve.

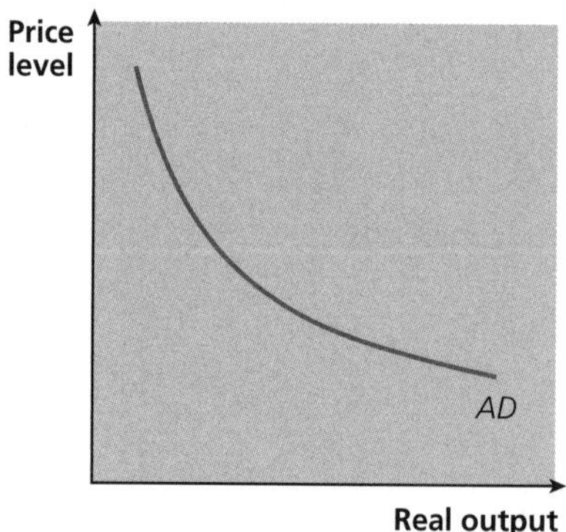

Figure 1 An aggregate demand curve

If there is a change for any reason other than price, however, the *AD* curve will shift. If there is an increase in aggregate demand, the curve will shift to the right. This can be seen in Figure 2 (from AD_0 to AD_1). If there is a decrease in aggregate demand, the curve will shift to the left.

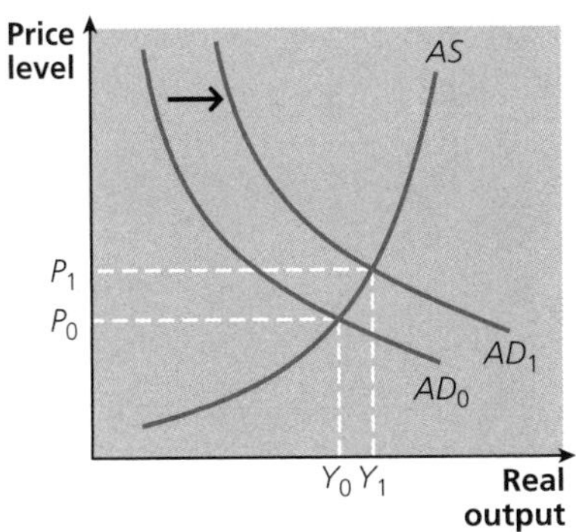

Figure 2 A shift in aggregate demand

Now test yourself

6 Name the four elements that make up aggregate demand.

Answer on p.155

Tested

Aggregate supply

Revised

The short-run **aggregate supply** curve slopes upwards from left to right. This can be seen in Figure 3. If there is a change in the price level, this will cause a movement along the *AS* curve.

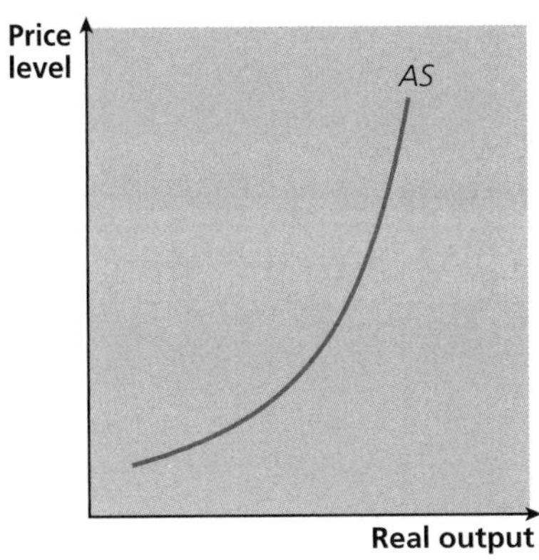

Figure 3 Aggregate supply in the short run

aggregate supply: the total output that the various firms in an economy are able and willing to supply at different price levels in a given period of time; it includes both consumer and capital products

If there is a change for any reason other than price, however, the *AS* curve will shift. If there is an increase in aggregate supply, the curve will shift to the right, as can be seen in Figure 4 (from AS_0 to AS_1). If there is a decrease in aggregate supply, the curve will shift to the left.

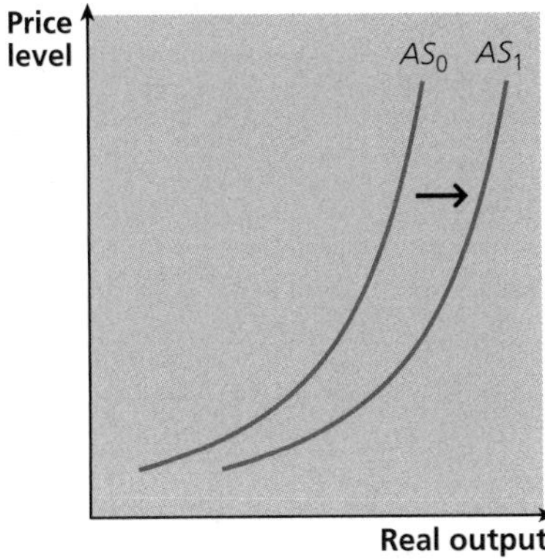

Figure 4 A shift in aggregate supply

In the long run, however, the shape of the *AS* curve will change. At low levels of output, the *AS* curve can be horizontal, indicating that it is perfectly elastic. At high levels of output, the *AS* curve can be vertical, indicating that it is perfectly inelastic. Indeed, some economists argue that the long-run *AS* curve is perfectly inelastic to indicate that an economy will operate at full capacity.

Interaction of *AD* and *AS*

Equilibrium is determined when *AD* and *AS* intersect. This can be seen in Figure 5, where the equilibrium price level is *P* and the equilibrium real output level is *Y*.

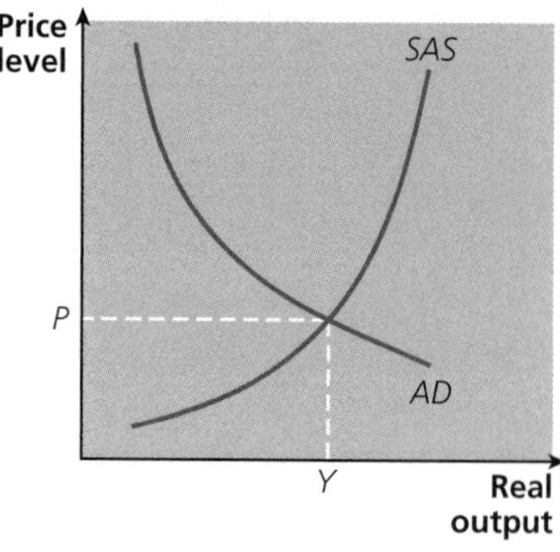

Figure 5 Macroeconomic equilibrium

This equilibrium position will not necessarily be at the full employment level for an economy. This can be seen in Figure 6. The equilibrium where AD^* crosses *SAS* (short-run aggregate supply) is at price P^* and real output Y^*; at this point, the macroeconomic equilibrium is at full employment. However, the equilibrium where AD_1 crosses *SAS* is at price P_1 and real output Y_1; at this point, the equilibrium is below the full employment level in the economy, so there is surplus capacity.

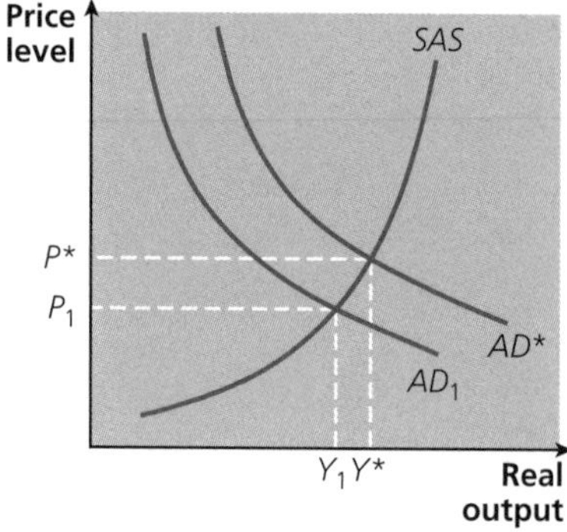

Figure 6 Will macroeconomic equilibrium be at full employment?

Figure 7 shows the equilibrium position in relation to long-run aggregate supply. As indicated above, aggregate supply is initially elastic, but as it gets nearer to the full employment level, shown by Y^*, it becomes increasingly inelastic until it eventually becomes perfectly inelastic when the full employment (Y^*) level of output is eventually reached.

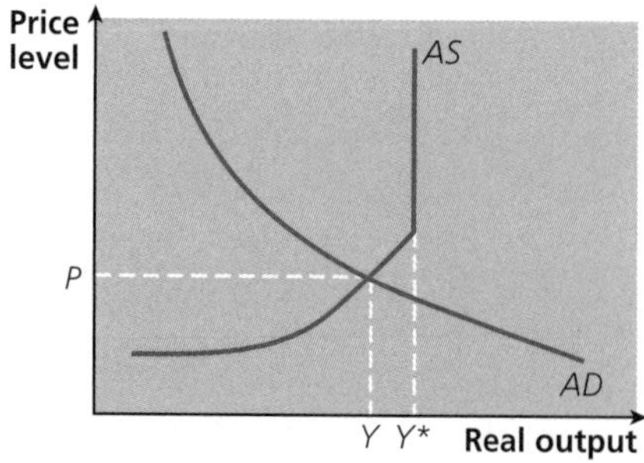

Figure 7 Macroeconomic equilibrium revisited

Expert tip

It is important to recognise that the equilibrium of *AD* and *AS* will not necessarily be at the full employment level of an economy.

6 Macroeconomic problems

Inflation

Definition of inflation

Revised

Inflation refers to a situation of a rise in the general level of prices in an economy over a period of time.

inflation: a general increase in the average level of prices in an economy over a period of time

Expert tip

Candidates need to realise that it is not necessary for all prices in an economy to be rising to constitute a situation of inflation. It is often the case that, at any one time, the prices of some products will be falling while the prices of other products are rising. What is important in an inflationary situation is that the general level of prices on the whole is rising.

Now test yourself

1 Define the term 'inflation'.

Answer on p.155

Tested

Degrees of inflation

Inflation, as has been stated, is a situation of rising prices in an economy, but there are varying degrees of inflation. In many economies, the government aims to keep the rate of inflation down to, say, about 2%, but in some economies a rate of inflation of, say, 4% or 5% would not be regarded as a major problem.

In some economies, however, the rate of inflation has been significantly higher than this. In some cases, countries have experienced a rate of inflation of over 1,000%. Germany in the early 1920s, Hungary in the mid-1940s and Zimbabwe in the mid-2000s are three examples of countries which have experienced excessive rates of inflation in the last 100 years.

It is not inevitable that a country must always be faced with inflation. It is possible that a country could experience a situation of **deflation**, or falling prices. This has happened in Japan in recent years.

deflation: a general decrease in the average level of prices in an economy over a period of time. Deflation can also mean a reduction in the level of aggregate demand in an economy, in contrast to **reflation** which means an increase in the level of aggregate demand in an economy

Expert tip

Candidates can sometimes confuse *inflation* and *deflation* in their examination answers. It is important to clearly distinguish between a situation of inflation, which refers to rising prices, and a situation of deflation, which refers to falling prices.

Revision activity

Distinguish between inflation and deflation.

Types of inflation

Revised

Economists have distinguished between different types of inflation.

Creeping inflation

When the rate of inflation in an economy is relatively low, say about 2%, and is reasonably stable over a period of time, the situation is one of **creeping inflation**.

creeping inflation: a situation where the rate of inflation is reasonably low, say about 2%

Accelerating inflation

Accelerating inflation is a situation where the rate of inflation in an economy is getting significantly higher and is becoming a major problem in the economy.

accelerating inflation: a situation where the rate of inflation is rising, say from 5% to 25%, and is beginning to become a serious problem in an economy

Hyperinflation

It is difficult to be precise as to exactly when an economy has reached a situation of **hyperinflation**, but it is generally where the rate of inflation has reached such a high level that it affects confidence in the economy. It may lead to the collapse of a country's currency. For example, the rate of inflation in Germany reached over 20,000% in 1923, leading to the replacement of the currency. In Zimbabwe, the rate of inflation reached over 230 million % in 2008, and this caused many people to move away from the Zimbabwe dollar to the US dollar.

hyperinflation: a situation where the rate of inflation is becoming very high, say over 100%, and is damaging confidence in the country's economy

Expert tip

Candidates should understand that it is not possible to give a precise percentage figure to indicate when a situation of hyperinflation exists in an economy.

One particular feature of a high rate of inflation is what are called **shoe leather costs**. This term is used to refer to those people who prefer to hold only a small amount of money at any one time and so need to make more visits to a financial institution to obtain cash. Such costs can be regarded as 'search costs' that come about as a result of the state of inflation in an economy.

Another feature of a high rate of inflation is what are called **menu costs**. If a country is experiencing a high rate of inflation, it means that prices are continuously changing. Having to alter the prices again and again involves time and expense.

shoe leather costs: in a situation of very high inflation, people need to ensure that their money is gaining interest and so will be less inclined to have large cash deposits. These costs are, in fact, search costs that are caused by the high rate of inflation in an economy

menu costs: the costs of continually having to change the prices of goods and services as a result of an inflationary situation

Now test yourself

2 Explain why hyperinflation is such a serious problem.
3 Explain the difference between menu costs and shoe leather costs.

Answers on p.155–6

Tested

Causes of inflation

Revised

There are broadly four possible causes of inflation: demand-pull, cost-push, monetary and imported.

Demand-pull inflation

One cause of inflation is a situation where there is too much demand in an economy, i.e. aggregate demand is greater than aggregate supply. Where an economy is at a situation of full employment, and an increase in demand cannot be met by an increase in output, the general price level will rise.

demand-pull inflation: a rise in the general level of prices in an economy, caused primarily by too much demand for products

Cost-push inflation

Whereas demand-pull inflation is essentially brought about from the demand side, **cost-push inflation** is due to the increase in the costs of production that are passed on to consumers in the form of higher prices. Labour costs, for example, could rise significantly, forcing firms to raise the prices of products.

There is also an element of **anticipated inflation** in relation to labour costs. If inflation is anticipated or expected, workers will build this into their wage demands. It is therefore possible that the anticipated inflation actually contributes to the inflation. In such a situation, inflation becomes self-perpetuating and a self-fulfilling prophecy.

Inflation can also be **unanticipated**; this is the difference between the actual rate of inflation in an economy and the anticipated or expected rate of inflation.

cost-push inflation: a rise in the general level of prices in an economy, caused primarily by a significant rise in the costs of production

anticipated inflation: the expected future rate of inflation in an economy

unanticipated inflation: the actual rate of inflation in an economy minus the anticipated or expected rate of inflation

Now test yourself

4 Distinguish between 'demand-pull' and 'cost-push' inflation.

Answer on p.156

Tested

Monetary inflation

This explanation of the cause of inflation is also from the demand side, but it stresses the importance of an excessive increase in the money supply making such an increase in demand possible.

Monetary inflation is closely associated with the Monetarist perspective on economics, which stresses the importance of the **quantity theory of money**.

monetary inflation: a rise in the general level of prices in an economy, caused primarily by too much money in an economy

quantity theory of money: the idea that $MV = PT$ where M is the money stock, V is the velocity of circulation, P is the general price level and T is the volume of transactions. This theory is actually an identity because MV, which represents total spending in an economy, must necessarily equal PT, which represents the total amount of money received for products. It is assumed that V and T are constant, and so the theory puts forward the idea that changes in the price level in an economy are directly proportional to changes in the money supply in the economy

velocity of circulation: the average number of times one particular unit of money is used over a given period of time

Revision activity

Outline what is meant by 'the quantity theory of money'.

Imported inflation

This explanation of the cause of inflation is from the supply side, but it emphasises the increase in the costs of imports in particular. This can either be in the form of imported raw materials and component parts that are used in domestic production or the higher prices of imported finished goods.

imported inflation: a rise in the general level of prices in an economy, caused primarily by a significant increase in the price of imports

The consequences of inflation

Revised

It is certainly the case that inflation has a number of negative consequences for an economy, but it should also be recognised that it is possible that inflation can have some positive consequences. Table 1 indicates the main consequences of inflation for an economy, both positive and negative.

Table 1 The consequences of inflation for an economy

Negative consequences	Positive consequences
• The purchasing power of a given sum of money will fall, i.e. it will be able to buy less in real terms. • A country's exports will become uncompetitive, although the effect of this will depend on the rate of inflation in one country compared to that in another. • There will be a redistribution of income, with some people adversely affected, e.g. those on fixed incomes, and creditors (people who lend money) unless the loans are index linked to the rate of inflation. Savers will also be negatively affected, unless they can find a savings account with a rate of interest that is greater than the rate of inflation. • Menu costs, i.e. the need to keep changing the prices that are being advertised for various products, can be expensive and time consuming. • Shoe leather costs, i.e. the need to continually search for the best possible returns to try to keep ahead of inflation, also involve extra time and effort. • Uncertainty in investment, i.e. some firms may be reluctant to plan investment as inflation creates a great deal of uncertainty in an economy. • A situation of **fiscal drag** can occur if tax allowances are left unchanged in an inflationary situation; more people will be caught in the 'tax net'.	• A relatively low rate of inflation, caused by an increase in aggregate demand, could lead to people feeling more optimistic about future economic prospects. • If prices rise by more than costs, this will help to increase the profits of firms, assuming that demand is price elastic. • Redistribution of income may work in favour of some people in an economy, such as borrowers; inflation will make the debt less in real terms. This may encourage people to spend more, improving their standard of living. • If the real cost of debt is reduced, but the price of property rises in line with inflation, property owners will benefit significantly. • If firms experience an increase in their profits, they may be encouraged to expand and this could lead to a reduction in unemployment (although high inflation can also be associated with high unemployment, a situation known as **stagflation**).

fiscal drag: the idea that more people will be dragged into the 'tax net' in a situation of inflation if the tax allowances are not increased in line with the rate of inflation

stagflation: a situation where an economy is experiencing high inflation and high unemployment at the same time

Now test yourself

5 Explain what is meant by 'fiscal drag'.

Answer on p.156

Tested

It should be clear, therefore, that the overall effect of inflation will depend on a number of factors. These include:

- whether the inflation is anticipated or not
- the extent of the increase in prices
- whether the inflation rate is accelerating or stable
- the extent to which other countries are experiencing inflation

Expert tip

Candidates often make broad generalisations in examinations in relation to the possible effects of inflation. You will need to make sure that you demonstrate an understanding of the fact that the effects of inflation in any particular country will depend on a number of possible factors.

Revision activity

Consider whether the positive consequences of inflation outweigh the negative ones.

Expert tip

Candidates often assume that inflation can only have negative consequences, but it is important to realise that there can be winners, as well as losers, as a result of inflation. If an examination question requires candidates to discuss or evaluate the consequences of inflation, an answer should include reference to *both* the possible positive *and* negative consequences.

Balance of payments problems

Balance of payments equilibrium and disequilibrium

Revised

'Balance of payments equilibrium' refers to a situation where the deficits and surpluses of a country are cancelled out, both in a given year and over a period of time. For example, a current account deficit could be cancelled out by a financial account surplus.

'Balance of payments disequilibrium' refers to a situation where a country is experiencing a persistent deficit or surplus over a period of time.

The **International Monetary Fund (IMF)** exists to help countries with a persistent deficit. It can provide a loan to a country which will help it to finance the deficit in the short term. This will hopefully allow time for economic policies to improve the situation in the long term.

International Monetary Fund: set up in 1944 to promote international trade through such measures as providing financial support in the form of a loan which will help a country to overcome, or at least reduce, a deficit in the balance of payments. It now has 188 member countries

Now test yourself

6 Explain the role of the International Monetary Fund.

Answer on p.156

Tested

The causes of balance of payments disequilibrium

Revised

There are a number of possible reasons why a country might be experiencing a persistent balance of payments disequilibrium. In relation to a persistent deficit, reasons could include the following:

- The foreign exchange rate could be too high, causing exports to be more expensive than they should otherwise be; if demand for these exports is price elastic, this could have a significant effect on the balance of payments.
- Consumers in a country could have begun to increase their demand for imported products, i.e. as incomes have risen, there has been an increase in the **marginal propensity to import.**
- A country could have borrowed funds from other countries to finance development projects, but these projects have not been as successful as had been anticipated and yet the debt still has to be paid off.

marginal propensity to import: the proportion of an increase in income that is spent on imported products

Expert tip

In examination questions on balance of payments disequilibrium, candidates tend to assume that it can only apply to a deficit. However, it should be remembered that it is possible that a country could experience a persistent surplus, such as has been the case with China.

The consequences of balance of payments disequilibrium

Revised

Balance of payments disequilibrium will affect a domestic economy in various ways. These include the following:

- There will be an increase in unemployment if there has been a decrease in the demand for exports and an increase in the demand for imports.
- There will be a reduction in business confidence, leading to a fall in the level of investment in the domestic economy.
- If corrective action is taken in an attempt to reduce, and hopefully eliminate, the disequilibrium, consumers will either have a restricted range of imported products to choose from (if quotas have been introduced) or will have to pay much more for the imported products (if tariffs have been introduced).
- This increase in prices could have an inflationary effect on the economy.

The disequilibrium in the balance of payments will also have an effect on the external economy:

- There is likely to be a move towards greater protectionism in the international economy, reducing the extent of the benefits that would otherwise have been obtained.

Now test yourself

7 Analyse how a balance of payments of disequilibrium can affect an economy.

Answer on p.156

Tested

Fluctuations in foreign exchange rates

Definitions and measurement of exchange rates

Revised

A **foreign exchange rate** refers to the value of one currency in relation to another. It is the price of one particular currency expressed in terms of another.

The usual way to express the value of one currency in terms of another is through a nominal exchange rate. However, this will not take into account the purchasing power of a nominal sum of one currency in relation to the purchasing power of another currency. It is for this reason that exchange rates are often expressed in terms of **purchasing power parity**, i.e. by taking into account price levels in different countries, exchange rates can be adjusted so as to give a more accurate comparison of the purchasing power of currencies.

foreign exchange: the foreign currency that is used in other countries as a medium of exchange

Forex (or Foreign Exchange) Market: the coming together of buyers and sellers of currencies to establish a price

purchasing power parity: the value of a currency in terms of what it would be able to buy in other countries

Expert tip

Candidates need to demonstrate a clear understanding of the concept of purchasing power parity. This concept is important because it enables the purchasing power of a currency to be established by taking into account different price levels in various countries.

Now test yourself

8 What is meant by the term 'purchasing power parity'?

Answer on p.156

Tested

Another way of expressing changes in an exchange rate is to relate it to changes not in one other currency, but in a number of other currencies. These different currencies are weighted to take into account their importance in international trade. As with other indices, a base year is selected and given a value of 100. The **trade-weighted exchange rate** can also be called the 'effective exchange rate'.

trade-weighted exchange rate: a way of measuring changes in an exchange rate in terms of a weighted average of changes in other currencies

The determination of exchange rates

Revised

Exchange rates can be determined in a number of different ways, but the three most common ways are floating, fixed and managed float.

Floating exchange rate

A **floating exchange rate** is one that allows the value of a currency to be determined by the forces of demand and supply in an economy, just like the price of anything else in a free market.

This can be seen in Figure 1. The demand for a currency is determined by the demand for a country's exports that leave the country and the supply of a currency is determined by the demand for the imports which come into the country. The vertical axis shows the price of UK£ in US$ and the horizontal axis shows the quantity of UK£. The equilibrium is established where demand and supply intersect, i.e. at a price of *P* and a quantity of *Q*.

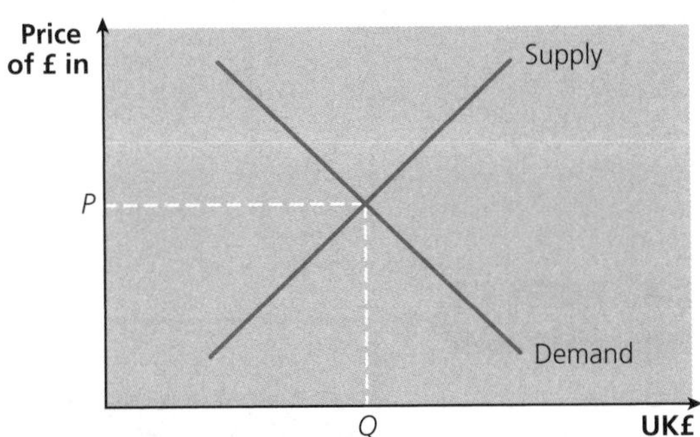

Figure 1 The price of sterling

When the value of a floating exchange rate goes up, it is known as an **appreciation**.

When the value of a floating exchange rate goes down, it is known as a **depreciation**.

floating exchange rate: an exchange rate that is determined, like any other price, by the market forces of demand and supply

appreciation: the rise in value of a currency that is floating

depreciation: the fall in value of a currency that is floating

Fixed exchange rate

Whereas a floating system allows exchange rates to be determined by the forces of demand and supply in a free market, a **fixed** system is where exchange rates are set at a particular level by a government. They are not determined by the forces of demand and supply. The central bank of a country will continually buy and sell the currency in order to maintain its value.

When the value of a fixed exchange rate goes up, it is known as a **revaluation**.

When the value of a fixed exchange rate goes down, it is known as a **devaluation**.

fixed exchange rate: an exchange rate that is determined at a particular level by a government

revaluation: the rise in value of a currency that is fixed

devaluation: the fall in value of a currency that is fixed

Now test yourself

9 Distinguish between a 'depreciation' and a 'devaluation' of a currency.

Answer on p.156

Tested

Expert tip

In the examination, candidates need to clearly distinguish between a revaluation/devaluation that will occur in a fixed exchange rate system and an appreciation/depreciation that will occur in a floating exchange rate system.

Managed exchange rate

Sometimes a government may allow the rate of a currency to be determined by market forces to some extent, but will intervene to restrict the degree of floating between a minimum and maximum price. This is often referred to as a '**dirty float**'.

managed (dirty) float: an exchange rate that is determined, to some extent, by the forces of demand and supply, but where the rate is managed by a government, i.e. it will only be allowed to float between certain parameters

Expert tip

Candidates need to demonstrate they understand that a managed exchange rate system is a mixture of a floating and a fixed exchange rate system.

Factors underlying fluctuations in exchange rates

Revised

Fluctuations in a country's exchange rate can be caused by a number of factors, including the following:

- the demand for the country's exports from other countries
- the demand for imports into the country
- inflation rates in different countries affecting international competitiveness
- perceptions of quality/reliability in relation to both exports and imports
- interest rates in different countries, affecting movements of '**hot money**'
- changes in unit costs in various countries
- differences in the state of technology in various countries
- trends in tourism

hot money: flows of money that move from one country to another to take advantage of different rates of interest in various countries

Now test yourself

10 Identify what is meant by 'hot money'.

Answer on p.156

Tested

Revision activity

Consider whether a managed float is the best form of exchange rate system.

The effects of changing exchange rates on the economy

Revised

A country's exchange rate could be lowered in value in order to encourage an increase in exports and a decrease in imports. This effect, however, may not happen immediately and there may be a period of time when the situation becomes worse before it gets better. This is known as the **J-curve effect**.

The reason for this J-curve effect is that buyers take time to adjust to price changes. A lower price for exports and a higher price for imports may eventually have an effect on demand, but the expected changes will not happen immediately.

J-curve effect: the period of time, after a depreciation, when the current account of the balance of payments gets worse before it gets better

Expert tip

Candidates need to demonstrate in their examination answers that they understand what is meant by a J-curve effect. This is the idea that there will be a period of time, after a depreciation, when the current account of the balance of payments is likely to get worse before it gets better. You need to make it clear that you understand that the J-curve effect will depend on the price elasticity of demand for both exports and imports. It is impossible to be precise about how long this period of time is likely to be because it will vary from one country to another.

Another factor to take into account when assessing the effect of a change in the exchange rate on an economy is in relation to the price elasticity of demand. A depreciation will make exports cheaper and imports dearer, but the ultimate effect of these price changes will depend on the price elasticity of demand for both the exports and the imports.

A depreciation is generally expected to bring about an increase in the demand for exports, because they are now relatively cheaper than they were, and a reduction in the demand for imports, because they are now relatively dearer than they were. This may not, however, necessarily happen, as it will depend on the price elasticity of demand for both exports and imports. If a depreciation, or a devaluation, is to be successful in terms of improving the balance of payments situation, the sum of the price elasticity of demand for exports and the price elasticity of demand for imports will need to be greater than one. This is known as the **Marshall-Lerner condition**.

Marshall-Lerner condition: the requirement that for a depreciation to be successful, the sum of the price elasticity of demand for exports and the price elasticity of demand for imports must be greater than one

Now test yourself

11 Explain what is meant by a 'J-curve effect'.

12 What is meant by 'the Marshall-Lerner' condition'?

Answers on p.156

Tested

7 Macroeconomic policies

Policies designed to correct balance of payments disequilibrium

There are two approaches that can be used in an economy to correct a balance of payments deficit: expenditure switching policies and expenditure dampening policies.

Expenditure switching policies

Revised

Expenditure switching is concerned with policies that will actually switch demand away from some products and towards others. In particular, it will lead to an increase in the demand for exports and a decrease in the demand for imports.

expenditure switching: a policy which attempts to bring about a change in the pattern of demand in an economy by reducing the demand for imports and increasing the demand for exports

Different methods can be used to reduce the demand for imports and encourage the demand for exports. These have been covered above on pages 50–51. They can include the following:

- tariffs
- quotas
- subsidies
- exchange controls
- embargoes
- administrative restrictions

The main problem associated with such policies is that they involve restraints on free trade and are therefore generally opposed by the World Trade Organisation. This is why many economies decide to use expenditure dampening policies rather than expenditure switching policies.

Now test yourself

1 Explain what is meant by 'expenditure switching'.

Answer on p.156

Tested

Expenditure dampening policies

Revised

Whereas an expenditure switching policy is concerned with the change in the patterns of demand for different products, an **expenditure dampening** or reducing policy is concerned with a more general reduction in the demand for all products in an economy. This will have two effects. First, the demand for imported goods will fall. Second, the demand from within an economy for all goods will fall, and so domestic producers will need to compensate for this by increasing the level of exports.

expenditure dampening (or expenditure reducing): a policy which attempts to bring about a reduction in the level of aggregate demand in an economy

This process of expenditure dampening will be carried out by various strategies, including the following:

- deflationary fiscal policy, e.g. through an increase in taxation and/or a reduction in government expenditure; the effect will be to create a downward multiplier effect (see page 125) in the economy, bringing down the level of aggregate demand
- deflationary monetary policy, e.g. through an increase in interest rates and/or a reduction in the money supply

Economists are agreed that the main way to reduce or eliminate a balance of payments deficit is to improve the quality of the goods produced in an economy so that more people will buy them, both within the domestic market and abroad. Many economies have adopted a variety of supply-side policies to improve the competitiveness of products.

Now test yourself

2 Explain what is meant by 'expenditure dampening'.

3 What is meant by a 'balance of payments disequilibrium'?

Answers on p.156

Tested

Expert tip

Balance of payments disequilibrium has been discussed in terms of a persistent deficit, but don't forget that disequilibrium can also refer to persistent surpluses in the balance of payments.

Revision activity

Contrast expenditure switching policies and expenditure dampening policies.

Policies to influence the exchange rate

Another way of changing the aggregate demand in an economy is through the exchange rate. If the exchange rate of a country's currency falls, either through depreciation or through devaluation, the demand for exports will rise, as they are now relatively cheaper, while the demand for imports will fall, as they are now relatively dearer. However, the extent to which this actually happens will depend on the price elasticity of demand for both exports and imports.

In a floating exchange rate system, the external value of a currency will be determined by the forces of demand and supply, but policies can be used to influence this. For example, **interest rate policy** could be used to bring about a depreciation in the external value of a currency if a country's interest rates are lower than in other countries. In such a situation, more money is likely to leave a country than be attracted to it because money will be attracted by higher rates of interest in other countries.

interest rate policy: the use of changes in interest rates in an economy to bring about particular objectives, such as a change in the exchange rate

Possible conflicts between macroeconomic policy objectives

It is not always easy for a government to achieve success in all its policy objectives and so there may often be a conflict between the objectives. For example, a depreciation or devaluation of an exchange rate could be used to increase the demand for exports and decrease the demand for imports, thus reducing the size of a balance of payments deficit. If, however, the price elasticity of demand for imports is relatively inelastic, as it often is in many countries, the demand for the more expensive imports will not be affected very much. The consequence of this is that it will contribute to inflation in an economy, both in terms of the import of raw materials and component parts and in relation to the import of finished goods.

Revision activity

Consider whether it is inevitable that there will be a conflict between the macroeconomic objectives of a government.

AS questions and answers

This section contains AS exam-style questions. The key to the multiple-choice answers is given on p.72. The data-response and essay questions are followed by expert comments (shown by the icon ⓔ) that indicate where credit is due and where there are areas for improvement.

Multiple-choice questions

Question 1

In a command economy, how are resources allocated? According to:

A the needs of the country
B the needs of the consumers
C the needs of the workers
D the needs of the young [1]

Question 2

Which of the following is a positive statement?

A Trade unions should be more powerful.
B Income ought to be distributed more evenly.
C Economic growth is measured through gross domestic product.
D The retirement age should not be increased. [1]

Question 3

Which of the following would cause a shift of the demand curve for a product to the right?

A An increase in price
B An increase in income tax
C An increase in the price of a complement
D An increase in the price of a substitute [1]

Question 4

Which of the following is a positive externality?

A An increase in noise pollution
B An increase in air quality
C An increase in traffic congestion
D An increase in the number of shops in an area closing [1]

Question 5

Which of the following is an example of a public good?

A Education
B Healthcare
C Transport
D Defence [1]

Question 6

Which of the following is a definite advantage of international trade?

A A wider choice of products for consumers
B A guaranteed increase in the quality of life
C An end to balance of payments deficits
D An increase in the costs of production [1]

Question 7

Which of the following will happen if a customs union becomes an economic union?

A The exchange rate of all the currencies will rise.
B Standards of living will definitely increase.
C Member countries will attempt to integrate their economies more closely.
D A common external quota will be imposed on imports from non-members. [1]

Question 8

Which of the following states the quantity theory of money?

A $MP = VT$
B $M + T = V + P$
C $MT = VP$
D $MV = PT$ [1]

Question 9

Which of the following will not be likely to help correct a deficit in the current account of a country's balance of payments?

A A devaluation of the currency
B The elimination of tariffs
C The introduction of a quota on certain imports
D An increase in subsidies given to domestic firms [1]

Question 10

Which of the following is a reason why cost–benefit analysis is not always precise in its measurement of costs and benefits?

A None of the costs or benefits has a market price.

B External costs are difficult to estimate accurately.

C It is impossible to put a value on time.

D Prices will always go up. [1]

Key to the answers

1 A
2 C
3 D
4 B
5 D
6 A
7 C
8 D
9 B
10 B

Data-response question

Question 11

SACU SHOWS RESILIENCE

The Southern African Customs Union has seen an average economic growth rate of 3.4% over the past few years. There has been considerable expenditure on the development of infrastructure in the region and yet the rate of unemployment has remained stubbornly high in the member countries.

The member countries have taken measures to encourage trade between them, especially in terms of reducing tariffs and quotas, but it is recognised that the existence of the customs union will lead to both trade creation and trade diversion.

(a) Describe how economic growth is usually measured. [2]

(b) Explain the difficulties involved in measuring unemployment. [4]

(c) What are the gains from international trade? [4]

(d) Explain the difference between a tariff and a quota. [4]

(e) Discuss whether the creation of a customs union should always be encouraged. [6]

Candidate answer

(a) Economic growth is usually measured through changes in the gross domestic product of a country over a period of time, usually one year. It is usually measured in real terms to discount the effects of inflation.

This is a clear and accurate description of how economic growth is usually measured. Mark: 2/2.

(b) Many people who are unemployed do register, usually because this entitles them to some form of income. This method of measuring unemployment is based on the claimant count. However, not everybody who is unemployed will qualify for unemployment benefit and so there is another method called the labour force survey. The problems arise because people may not be actively seeking work, even though they are unemployed, and do not want to go through the embarrassment of officially registering as unemployed. It may also be the case that they do not actually need the income.

The candidate has explained some of the difficulties involved in measuring unemployment, but the explanation needs to be developed more fully, especially in terms of comparing the claimant count and the labour force survey approaches. Mark: 3/4.

(c) The gains from international trade include the increase in output resulting from specialisation in those areas of production where a country has a comparative advantage. This increase in output will provide a greater variety of choice for consumers in different countries, leading to an increase in standards of living.

The candidate makes an attempt to consider the gains from international trade, especially in terms of greater output, a wider choice for consumers and an increase in standards of living. The two key concepts of specialisation and comparative advantage, however, are only referred to in passing — the candidate needs to say much more on these two concepts. Mark: 2/4.

(d) A tariff is an indirect tax that is placed on the imports into a country. The idea is that the higher price, brought about by the imposition of the tariff, will lead to a reduction in consumption of the product. A quota is a limit imposed on goods entering a country. It can be in the form of either a physical amount of imports, a certain value of imports or a restriction on the degree of penetration in terms of a market share.

The candidate explains the difference between a tariff and a quota, but while the coverage of a quota is quite thorough, the treatment of the tariff needs to be developed more fully. In particular, the candidate needs to point out that the potential effectiveness of a tariff would depend on the price elasticity of demand for the imported goods on which the tariff is placed. Mark: 3/4.

(e) A customs union refers to a trading agreement between a number of countries. The member countries are able to trade freely among themselves, but a common external tariff is imposed on imports from outside the union. It brings about trade creation so that trade between the member countries is encouraged. Without trade barriers affecting trade between the member countries, it is possible for the member countries to benefit from greater specialisation, increasing production, reducing unemployment and encouraging growth and higher living standards. However, the establishment of a common external tariff could mean that there is a degree of trade diversion, i.e. trade with other countries that are not members of the customs union will be discouraged as a result of the common external tariff.

In conclusion, the creation of a customs union can sometimes be encouraged, especially when there is a large degree of trade creation within the union leading to higher living standards. However, this needs to be balanced by consideration of the possible trade diversion, losing traditional trading partners and trading links that may have been built up over many years, and so it may be the case that it is not always encouraged.

e *The candidate clearly explains what is meant by a customs union and goes on to contrast the possible advantages and disadvantages, recognising the distinction between trade creation and trade diversion. There is a useful conclusion which is always important in a 'discuss' question. The candidate recognises that there needs to be a balance in taking account of the advantages and disadvantages of such a decision. Mark: 6/6.*

e *On the whole, the answers to the five questions are of a reasonable standard, although the answer to (c) is rather limited when compared with the others. The overall mark is 16/20, equivalent to a Grade B.*

Essay questions

Question 12

Discuss whether all planned economies should become market economies. [12]

Candidate answer

Many planned or command economies, where the state or government plays a key role in the allocation of scarce resources, are in the process of moving towards more of a market economy, such as China or Cuba. This means that the government will play a less important role in the allocation of scarce resources and that free-market forces, through the operation of the price mechanism and the interaction of the influences of demand and supply, will play a more important role.

e *This is a good introductory paragraph. The candidate is focusing clearly on the actual question being asked. The candidate clearly demonstrates an understanding of what is meant by a planned or command economy and there is then a consideration of what is meant by a market economy, especially in terms of the importance of the price mechanism and the influence of demand and supply. The answer also includes some examples of countries where this has been happening, such as China and Cuba. The answer could be improved, however, by mentioning the term that is used to describe these economies that are moving from a planned economy towards more of a market economy, i.e. transitional economies. It would also be useful to include a diagram to show how the forces of demand and supply operate in a market economy through the price mechanism. Examiners are always keen to have diagrams included in answers, as long as they are relevant, clear and accurately drawn.*

There are clear advantages in this process. Many planned economies tend to be rather inefficient and so if the government played less of a role, and market forces played more of a role, the economy would be more likely to operate efficiently. If firms were part of the private sector, there would be more incentive for them to produce products of a good quality. They would be encouraged by the existence of the profit motive. Consumers would also benefit from the greater competition between private sector firms. Consumers would have more choice and would be able to exercise consumer sovereignty; this should lead to an increase in living standards.

e *The answer is clearly structured and this paragraph focuses on the potential advantages of this process of moving from a planned or command economy towards a more market economy. There is a useful reference to the importance of efficiency, although this term could be discussed more fully. There is a rather sweeping statement that 'many planned economies tend to be rather inefficient', but the candidate really needs to support this with some specific examples. Examiners are impressed when candidates use appropriate examples to support the points being made in a discussion. The candidate does provide some examples of possible advantages of a greater degree of market forces, such as in relation to the quality of goods, the importance of the profit motive and the greater scope for competition and consumer sovereignty, leading ultimately to an increase in living standards.*

There are also, however, possible disadvantages. There is likely to be greater instability in market economies than in planned economies and the level of unemployment is likely to be higher in the former than in the latter. There is also likely to be greater inequality in the distribution of income and wealth in a market economy than in a planned economy. There is also a greater likelihood of market failure in a market economy. For example, there is likely to be a higher level of consumption of demerit goods, such as tobacco or alcohol, and a lower level of consumption of merit goods, such as education or healthcare.

This paragraph also shows the clear structure of the candidate's answer. Here, the candidate focuses on the potential disadvantages of the move from a planned or command economy to more of a market economy. This is very important in a 'discuss' question, as examiners will want to see that a candidate has addressed both points of view in an answer. The candidate refers to the possibility of greater instability, a higher level of unemployment and a greater inequality in the distribution of income and wealth. There is a reference to the possible existence of market failure, but the candidate does not actually explain clearly what is meant by this term. There is a good use of examples of both merit goods and demerit goods, but the candidate does not clearly explain what is meant by these two terms. The last sentence would be better if further developed.

In conclusion, the reality is that both planned economies and market economies have their advantages and disadvantages, and so the solution is that the mixed economy is likely to be preferable. A mixed economy allows market forces to operate in many aspects of the economy, without any government intervention, but it also enables governments to intervene to avoid the worst examples of market failure. For example, taxes could be placed on demerit goods to encourage consumption. The answer to the question, therefore, is that all planned economies should become mixed, rather than market, economies.

A 'discuss' question should always end with a conclusion, and in this case the candidate does provide a useful conclusion. The candidate confidently points out that both of these systems have their advantages and disadvantages and that the solution, therefore, might be an economic system which combines both types of structure, i.e. a mixed economy. The candidate clearly understands what is meant by a mixed economy, but should develop the discussion of this a little more fully. Finally, the candidate does indicate that the conclusion is an answer to the precise question being asked.

This is clearly a good answer to this question. It is well structured and the logic of the argument is easy to follow. There are areas where it could be improved, as indicated in the comments, but it would gain a Grade A with a mark of 9/12.

Question 13

Explain why the division of labour in an economy depends on the ability of money to perform effectively. **[8]**

Candidate answer

The division of labour in an economy is based on the idea of dividing up the process of production into a number of different stages. This enables workers to specialise in particular parts of the production process and this will lead to a greater degree of efficiency. This was first studied by Adam Smith in the eighteenth century in relation to how a pin factory operated. By dividing the process of production into a sequence of particular tasks, a great deal more could be produced than would otherwise be the case.

The candidate is clear about the meaning of the term 'division of labour', stressing that it is concerned with the separation of the production process into a series of different stages. The candidate refers to the important concept of 'specialisation' and indicates the link here with efficiency, although the comment that 'this will lead to a greater degree of efficiency' is rather vague and could be developed more fully. There is a reference at the end of the paragraph to how this could have resulted in greater production, but the link with the division of labour needs to be made more explicit. The candidate also needed to elaborate more fully on the concept of specialisation.

In the past, the exchange of goods took place through the system of barter, but this depended upon the trade of one product for another. This worked well whenever there was a double coincidence of wants, i.e. you wanted something that somebody else had and they wanted what you had. The success of barter, however, still depended on an agreement being reached on the relative value of the products that were to be traded.

In this section, the candidate moves on to consider how the process of exchange used to take place before the modern development of money, i.e. when there was a situation of 'barter'. There is a brief explanation of what is meant by this term, but this really needs to be developed more fully. The candidate does, however, recognise the major limitation of barter, i.e. that it depended on the existence of a double coincidence of wants.

Barter limited the extent of specialisation in an economy and this is why it eventually gave way to a much better system of exchange, i.e. the use of money to enable transactions to be made. Money can be defined as anything that is generally acceptable as a means of payment and so it is a much more convenient and useful form of exchange.

The candidate now considers the link between the limitations of barter and the importance of specialisation to the development of the modern economy. The answer stresses the advantage of money over barter, defining it as 'anything that is generally acceptable as a means of payment', but would benefit from a more developed explanation of how money has enabled economies to progress in ways that would have been unimaginable in a situation of barter.

Money has four main functions — a medium of exchange, a unit of account, a store of value and a standard of deferred payments. The most important of these in relation to the division of labour is the first one. Workers can specialise in the process of production in the knowledge that the money that they receive in wages or salaries can then be used to purchase the products that they need.

The question refers to the need for money to 'perform effectively', and the candidate approaches this part of the question by clearly outlining the four functions of money, although each of these needs to be developed more fully. The candidate clearly recognises that the most important of these functions, in terms of the link with division of labour, is the function of a means of exchange. The last paragraph demonstrates a good understanding of this link between the division of labour and the function of money as a means of exchange, although it could perhaps be developed more fully.

e *This is an example of a good answer to a question which requires candidates to show how two parts of the syllabus can be integrated. There are areas where the answer could be developed more fully, but it is well structured and would gain a Grade B with a mark of 5/8.*

Question 14

Explain what is meant by (i) an inferior good and (ii) a complementary good. [8]

Candidate answer

An inferior good is one where the demand for the product is linked to changes in the incomes of consumers. As people have more money, they may decide to buy less of one good and more of another good. The good which has a reduction in demand is known as an inferior good.

e *The candidate clearly understands that the demand for an inferior good is related to income, and particularly to changes in incomes, but there needs to be more of a contrast with 'another good' which could be regarded as a normal good, i.e. where demand increases with a rise in income, as people are now better able to afford such goods.*

Examples of inferior goods could include bicycles, if they are replaced by motor cycles, or motor cycles, if they are replaced by cars.

e *The candidate could develop this section further by stating that examples of inferior goods can vary from one country to another. For example, in some countries a bicycle might not be regarded as an inferior good, but as a normal good. The answer could also point out that examples of inferior goods can change over time within a particular country. For example, if a country is experiencing a high level of economic growth, people will generally have higher levels of income, but if a country is experiencing a recession, people may turn towards products which were previously seen as inferior goods. In such a situation, producers of inferior goods may experience an increase in demand during a recession.*

The demand for an inferior good is linked to the income elasticity of demand, with demand falling as incomes rise.

e *The candidate is correct in stressing the link between the demand for an inferior good and the income elasticity of demand, but it would be useful to explain this concept more fully, such as in relation to the formula of percentage change in the quantity demanded of a good divided by the percentage change in incomes. In the case of an inferior good, the income elasticity of demand is negative, stressing that a rise in incomes will lead to a reduction in the quantity demanded.*

A complementary good is one that is demanded along with another good, i.e. if one good is demanded, so is the other.

e *The candidate clearly demonstrates an understanding of the link between the demand for the two goods, but it would be better if reference were made to the concept of joint demand. This would make it clearer that the two goods are consumed together.*

Examples of complementary goods could include coffee and cream, shoes and shoe laces, cars and petrol or diesel and DVDs and DVD players.

e *Linking this to the idea of joint demand, the examples could be used more effectively to explain that an increase in the demand for one good is likely to lead to an increase in the demand for the other good. It could also be pointed out that the complementarity of two goods, resulting from the nature of consumer tastes and preferences and/or the technical relationship between them, can change over a period of time as consumer tastes and preferences and/or the state of technology change.*

The demand for a complementary good is linked to the concept of cross price elasticity of demand. This measures how close the relationship is between the two complementary goods.

e *The candidate does well to link complementary goods to the idea of cross price elasticity of demand, but the answer could be significantly improved by pointing out that the cross price elasticity of demand is negative, indicating that as the price of one good rises, the quantity demanded of a complement reduces. It would also be useful to define the concept of cross price elasticity of demand in terms of the percentage change in the quantity demanded of good X divided by the percentage change in the price of good Y.*

e *It is a shame that the candidate has not finished the answer with a conclusion, stating that although the two types of products were linked to the concept of elasticity, these were different examples of elasticity, i.e. income elasticity of demand in the case of inferior goods and cross price elasticity of demand in the case of complementary goods, contrasting the link first with changes in incomes and second with changes in prices.*

e *Overall, this is an example of a reasonable answer which does make an attempt to explain the different types of good, but there are a number of areas where the answer could be improved, especially by going into more detail on the elasticity concepts involved with each good. It would gain a Grade C with a mark of 4/8.*

8 Basic economic ideas

Efficient resource allocation

The term 'efficiency' generally means using resources in the most economical way that is possible, i.e. it refers to a situation of making maximum use of the resources that are available. It can also refer to the idea of obtaining the maximum output for given inputs.

efficient resource allocation: the optimal use of scarce inputs to produce the largest possible output

Concept of economic efficiency

The concept of economic efficiency can be divided into two types of efficiency: productive efficiency and allocative efficiency.

Expert tip

Examination questions will sometimes simply refer to efficiency, but in such a situation it is important that both productive and allocative efficiency are addressed in an answer.

Productive efficiency

Revised

One way of measuring **productive efficiency** is in terms of the **average cost** (or **average total cost**) of production. Productive efficiency can be defined as the minimum average cost at which output can be produced.

Productive efficiency actually involves two elements. **Technical efficiency** is where the best possible use is made of the inputs, or factors of production, used in the production process. This means that as much output as possible is produced from given inputs. **Cost efficiency** relates to whether the best set of inputs has been used in the production process; this will be influenced by the relative costs of different inputs, such as labour and capital.

productive efficiency: a situation where a firm operates at the minimum of the average cost curve. It is made up of two elements: technical efficiency and cost efficiency. It can also be seen in terms of a whole economy when that economy is operating on its production possibility curve or frontier

average cost: the total cost of producing something divided by the quantity that is produced. This shows the cost of producing each unit of whatever it is that is being produced by a firm

technical efficiency: a situation where a firm produces the maximum output possible from given inputs

cost efficiency: a situation where a firm uses the most appropriate combination of inputs of factors of production, given the relative costs of those factors

As well as being seen in the micro context of a particular firm, the concept of productive efficiency can also be seen in the macro context of the whole economy. This can be seen in Figure 1.

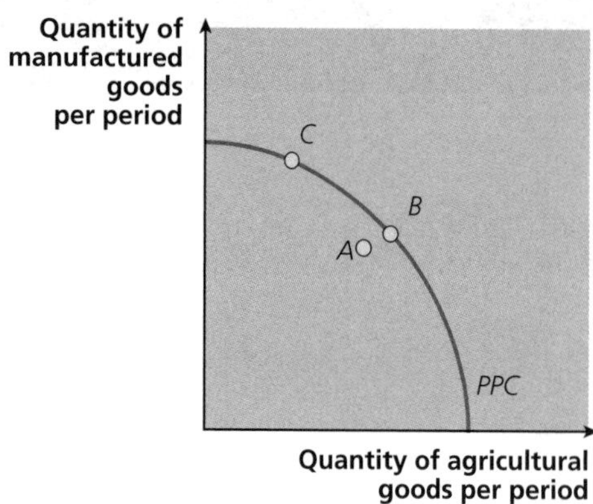

Figure 1 Productive efficiency

An economy can decide between the production of manufactured goods (shown on the vertical axis) and the production of agricultural goods (shown on the horizontal axis). The *PPC* shows the combination of these two types of goods that is possible in an economy. Productive efficiency is not taking place at point A, inside the *PPC*, because by moving to a point on the *PPC* it would be possible for the economy to produce more of both goods. Any point on the *PPC* will indicate productive efficiency, i.e. points *B* and *C* are both productively efficient.

There is a trade-off between the production of manufactured goods and the production of agricultural goods. For example, at point *C*, more manufactured goods will be produced in the economy than at point *B*, but fewer agricultural goods will be produced in the economy. Both points *B* and *C* are productively efficient, but it is not possible to make a judgement as to whether the society is better off at point *B* or *C* without knowing the preferences of the consumers in the society. There is therefore a need to consider another type of efficiency, allocative efficiency.

Revision activity

Outline the main features of productive efficiency.

Allocative efficiency

Revised

The most efficient allocation of resources in an economy will be the one which fits the needs and wants of the consumers most closely. The more that firms in an economy can respond effectively to changes in the demand of consumers, the closer the economy can get to a situation of **allocative efficiency**.

This can be clearly seen in the relationship between price and marginal cost. The marginal cost of production is the cost of producing one more product. When this cost is equal to the price charged for the product, there is a situation of allocative efficiency. This is because the value that is put on the resources used to produce the product by the producer is equal to the value put on the product by the consumer. If a greater or lesser amount of the product was produced, price and marginal cost would no longer be equal.

allocative efficiency: a situation that describes the extent to which the allocation of resources in an economy matches consumer preferences

Expert tip

In a question on economic efficiency, it is important that both productive efficiency and allocative efficiency are considered.

Now test yourself

1 Distinguish between productive efficiency and allocative efficiency.

Answer on p.156

Tested

Optimum resource allocation

Revised

The word 'optimum' means the best possible outcome in a given situation. **Optimum resource allocation** refers to a situation where the best possible allocation of scarce resources exists. It exists when both productive efficiency and allocative efficiency occur. The idea of an optimum, or optimality, is an important concept in economics, given that resources are scarce; when resources are allocated in an optimum way, it means that they are used in the most efficient way possible.

optimum resource allocation: the best allocation of resources possible in given circumstances

Expert tip

In examination questions on the concept of efficiency, candidates should ensure the idea of optimality is included in their answer, emphasising that this means the best possible allocation of scarce resources in a given situation.

Now test yourself

2 Explain what is meant by an 'optimum resource allocation'.

Answer on p.156

Tested

Pareto optimality

Revised

Vilfredo Pareto (1848–1923), an Italian economist, was interested in the concept of economic efficiency. He argued that the best possible allocation of scarce resources existed when it was impossible to make one person better off without making another person worse off. In such a situation, there must be an optimal allocation of resources, i.e. the inputs or resources are used in the most efficient possible way (productive efficiency) and the output produced by the resources provides the maximum possible utility or satisfaction to consumers (allocative efficiency). An improvement in optimality can only occur when one person is made better off without making anyone else worse off.

Pareto optimality: a particular use of the term 'optimality' associated with the Italian economist Vilfredo Pareto, who stated that this situation existed when it was not possible to reallocate resources to make someone better off without making someone else worse off

Expert tip

It is important that candidates can demonstrate they understand what is meant by Pareto optimality, i.e. the idea that an improvement can only take place when one person is made better off without making another person worse off. If somebody else would be made worse off as a result of a reallocation of scarce resources, the reallocation should not take place.

Now test yourself

3 Explain what is meant by 'Pareto optimality'.

Answer on p.156

Tested

9 The price system and the theory of the firm

Law of diminishing marginal utility

Its relationship to the derivation of an individual demand schedule and curve

Revised

'Utility' refers to the satisfaction that is derived from the consumption of a particular product. **Marginal utility** is the additional satisfaction that is gained from consuming an additional unit of a product, whereas total utility is the total satisfaction obtained from the consumption of a given number of units of a particular product.

The **law of diminishing marginal utility** states that the consumption of successive units of a product will eventually lead to a fall in marginal utility, i.e. as a person consumes more units of a product, the satisfaction provided by each unit will be progressively less and less.

There is a relationship between the law of diminishing marginal utility and the derivation of an individual demand schedule and curve. If the marginal utility of consuming an extra item of a product continually falls, a consumer will be unwilling to pay as much for each successive unit consumed. This explains why a demand curve is downward sloping from left to right.

marginal utility: the additional utility or satisfaction obtained from the consumption of an extra unit of a product

law of diminishing marginal utility: the principle (or law) that the marginal utility of consuming successive units of the same product will fall

Now test yourself

1 What is meant by 'the principle or law of diminishing marginal utility'?

Answer on p.156

Tested

The equi-marginal principle

Revised

The **equi-marginal principle** shows the relationship between the marginal utility obtained from the consumption of different products and the prices paid for these products. It can be represented in the following way:

$$\frac{MUa}{Pa} = \frac{MUb}{Pb} = \frac{MUc}{Pc}$$

To maximise their utility or satisfaction, it is assumed that consumers will consume up to the point shown above, i.e. the extra satisfaction, in relation to the money spent, on the last unit of product A will equal the extra satisfaction, in relation to the money spent, on the last unit of product B and so on.

equi-marginal principle: this states that a consumer will maximise total satisfaction by equating the utility or satisfaction per unit of money spent on the marginal unit of each product consumed

Now test yourself

2 State the equi-marginal principle.

Answer on p.156

Tested

The limitations of marginal utility theory

Revised

The law of diminishing marginal utility is based on a number of assumptions and if these assumptions do not apply, there are clear limitations to the theory. The assumptions include the following:

- the idea of utility or satisfaction that a consumer gains from the consumption of particular items of a product, but this assumes that satisfaction can be easily measured
- the idea that consumers behave in a rational way, but is this always the case?
- the idea that consumers have limited incomes, but it is possible that incomes may significantly rise over a period of time
- the idea that consumers aim to maximise their **total utility**, but is this always going to be the case?
- the idea that prices are constant, but it may be the case that the prices of products are continually changing
- the idea that consumer tastes and preferences remain constant, but this may not always be the case

total utility: the total amount of satisfaction obtained from the purchase of a number of units of a product

Revision activity

Outline the main uses and limitations of marginal utility theory.

Paradox of value

Revised

Certain products that are vital to our survival, such as water, will not be as expensive as products that are less crucial, such as diamonds. This is known as the **paradox of value**. The explanation of this paradox can be seen in terms of marginal utility and total utility. People will consume water up to the point where marginal utility is zero and total utility is high, whereas people will demand diamonds where marginal utility is high, but total utility is low.

paradox of value: the fact that certain products that are essential to survival, such as water, are cheaper than less important products to survival, such as diamonds

Expert tip

Candidates need to show they understand why diamonds are more expensive than water, illustrating the concept of 'paradox of value'.

Revision activity

Outline what is meant by 'the paradox of value'.

Budget lines

Budget lines show the possible combinations of two products that a consumer is able to purchase with a given income and fixed prices. Each of the combinations would cost the same total amount. Any point along the line will show the maximisation of consumption at the given income level.

Figure 1 shows the combination of Products A and B that can be purchased by a consumer, assuming that the income of the consumer and the prices of the products remain fixed.

budget line: a line that shows all the possible combinations of two products that a consumer would be able to purchase with fixed prices and a given income. It is also sometimes known as a consumption possibility line

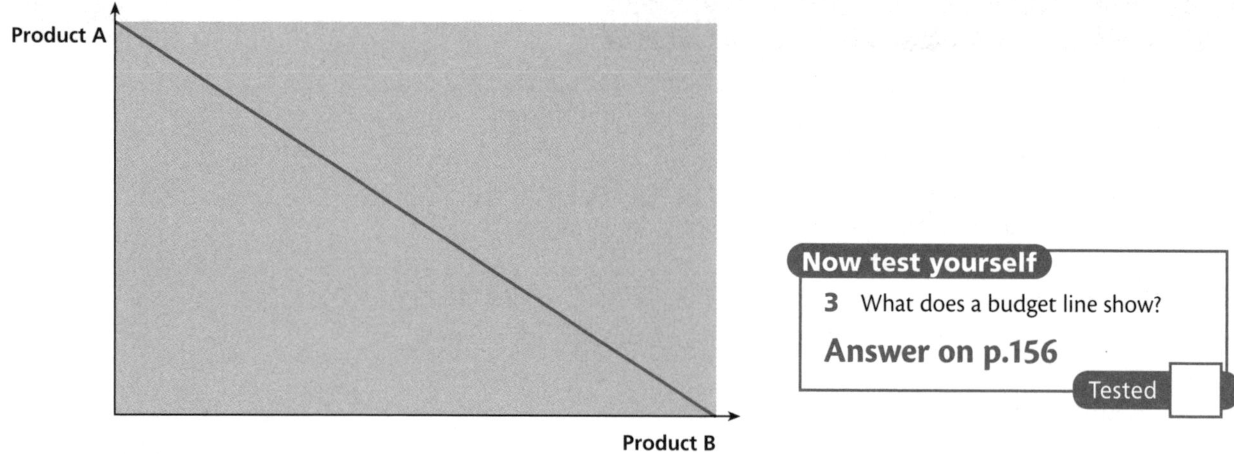

Figure 1 A budget line

Now test yourself

3 What does a budget line show?

Answer on p.156

Tested

Income and substitution effects

Revised

Income effect

A change in the price of a product can bring about two effects. One of these is known as the **income effect**; a change in the price of a product will bring about a change in real income. Although there is no change in nominal income, a rise or fall in the price of a product will have a real income effect, i.e. a person will be able to buy more or less of a product, and other products, as a result of the change in price of the product.

income effect: the effect on consumption of a change in real income which occurs as a result of a price change

Substitution effect

The second effect of a change in the price of a product relates to the utility or satisfaction obtained from the consumption of a product. A **substitution effect** means that a rational consumer will substitute in favour of a product which has now become relatively cheaper; this means that the substitution effect is always negative.

substitution effect: this shows the effect of a rise or fall in the price of a product on the utility or satisfaction obtained from each unit of money spent on that product. As a result of the price changes, expenditure can be rearranged to maximise the utility or satisfaction gained

Expert tip

It is important to remember that whereas the substitution effect is always negative for all goods, the income effect can be positive or negative and this is what determines whether a good is a normal good or an inferior good.

Revision activity

Distinguish between the income effect and substitution effect of a change in the price of a product.

Short-run and long-run production and cost functions

The short-run production function

Revised

Fixed and variable factors of production

In the short-run period of the production process, at least one **factor of production** or resource input will remain fixed. For example, it will be difficult to change the number of machines in a factory in the short run.

It will be possible, however, to change the quantity of other factors of production in the short run. For example, it will be relatively easy to buy in more component parts and raw materials in the short run.

The **production function** shows the relationship between inputs and output over a given time period, i.e. it indicates how a given level of output is produced as a result of the use of the various factors of production involved in the production process.

fixed factors of production: resource inputs that exist in the short run when the quantity of the factors used cannot be changed, e.g. capital equipment

variable factors of production: factors or resource inputs that can be varied in the short run, when at least one factor of production is fixed, e.g. raw materials

production function: refers to the ratio of inputs to output over a given time period. It shows the resources that will be needed to produce a maximum level of output, assuming that the inputs are used efficiently

Revision activity

Consider why it is important to distinguish between the short run and the long run in production.

Expert tip

It is difficult to be precise about just how long a period of time the short run is; it is simply defined as a period of time when at least one factor of production is fixed.

Total product, average product and marginal product

It is important to distinguish between these three different types of product. **Total product** is the total output resulting from the use of the factors in the production process. **Average product** is the output per unit of the variable factor, such as the output per worker per period of time. This is also known as productivity. **Marginal product** refers to the additional or extra output that is produced as a result of employing one more variable factor, e.g. one more worker.

total product: the total output produced by the factors of production

average product: the output per unit of the variable factor, e.g. output per worker per period of time. This is also referred to as productivity

marginal product: the additional output that is produced from employing another unit of a variable factor, e.g. the extra output from employing an additional worker

Now test yourself

4 Explain what is meant by 'average product'.

Answer on p.156

Tested

Expert tip

Questions on the different types of product can often feature in multiple-choice questions in Papers 1 and 3, so it is important that you are able to clearly distinguish between them.

The law of diminishing returns or law of variable proportions

In the short run, the production process involves the combination of fixed and variable factors. Additional units of a variable factor, such as labour, could be employed and combined with a fixed factor of production, such as capital equipment. The **law of diminishing returns** states that although the total output (or total product) is still increasing, it will increase at a diminishing rate. This is because the extra output, resulting from the employment of the additional worker, will eventually diminish. The law of diminishing returns is also known as the **law of variable proportions**.

law of diminishing returns: as additional units of a variable factor, such as labour, are added to a fixed factor, such as capital, the additional output (or marginal product) of the variable factor will eventually diminish.

Expert tip

It is important to remember that the law of diminishing returns is a short-run concept when one factor production, such as capital, remains fixed.

The short-run cost function

Revised

Fixed and variable costs of production

It has been pointed out that it is important to be able to clearly distinguish between fixed and variable factors of production. It is also important to distinguish between **fixed** and **variable costs** of production. If output is zero, there will be no need to pay for raw materials or component parts, so these are examples of variable costs. On the other hand, even if output is zero, there will be some costs of production, such as the cost of renting a factory or the cost of interest payments on a loan.

fixed costs: the costs of production that remain constant at all levels of output, including zero production; examples include rent and interest payments

variable costs: the costs of production that vary with changes in output, i.e. the cost is zero if nothing is produced; examples include the cost of raw materials and component parts

Explanation of the shape of short-run average cost (*SRAC*)

Figure 2 shows a number of short-run **average cost** curves. Each of these is U-shaped and each shows the relationship between output and cost on the basis that capital is fixed in the short run. If a firm wishes to change output, it will have to change the amount of the variable factor being used, such as labour. The position of the average cost curves in the short run will therefore depend on the quantity of capital being used in the production process, i.e. there is a short-run average cost curve for each level of output, e.g. $SRAC_1$ and $SRAC_4$.

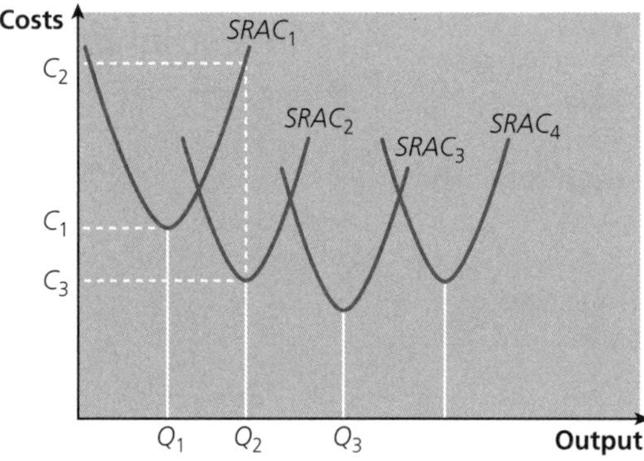

Figure 2 Short-run cost curves with different levels of capital input

average cost: the total cost of employing all the factor inputs divided by the number of units produced; also known as average total cost (ATC)

average fixed cost: the total fixed cost of production divided by the number of units produced

average variable cost: the total variable cost of production divided by the number of units produced

The long-run production function

Revised

The long-run production function takes into account the fact that, in the long run, all factors of production are variable.

The long-run cost function

Revised

Explanation of the shape of long-run average cost (*LRAC*)

Just as the short-run average cost curve is U-shaped, it is the same with the long-run average cost curve. This can be seen in Figure 3. As output increases, there is initially a decrease in the average cost of production and this is shown by the falling part of the *LRAC* curve. The curve reaches its minimum point at *Q** and then starts to rise again, indicating an increase in the average costs of production.

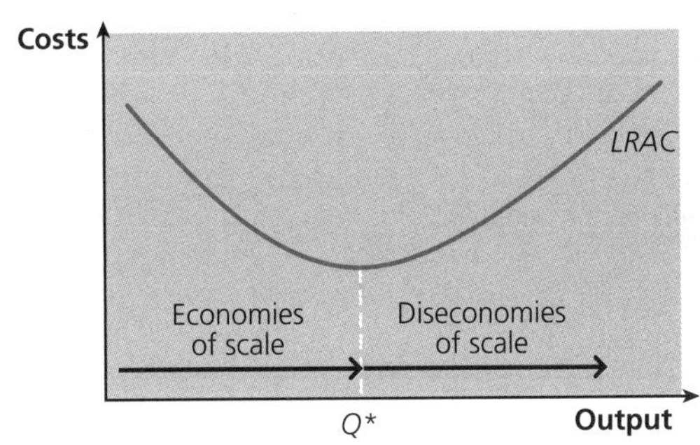

Figure 3 Long-run average cost curve, showing economies and diseconomies of scale

The level of output where the *LRAC* is first at its lowest point is known as the **minimum efficient scale**.

> **minimum efficient scale:** the lowest level of output where average cost is at the minimum

Returns to scale

Revised

In Figure 3, the *LRAC* curve is falling up to a point when it is at its minimum. These decreasing average costs of production resulting from an increase in output are known as **economies of scale**. It is possible to distinguish between internal and external economies of scale.

> **returns to scale:** the relationship between the level of output produced by a firm and the quantity of inputs required to produce that output
>
> **increasing returns to scale:** where output can be increased using proportionately fewer inputs; this gives rise to economies of scale

Internal economies of scale

Decreasing average costs of production can come about as a result of a firm becoming larger. There are various examples of these **internal economies of scale**, as can be seen in Table 1.

> **internal economies of scale:** these are the advantages of a firm growing in size in the form of a reduction in the average cost of production

Table 1 Internal economies of scale

Type of internal economy	Explanation
Financial	Larger firms may be able to benefit from negotiating a loan at a lower rate of interest than a smaller firm, largely because financial institutions regard them as less of a risk.
Purchasing	Larger firms are often able to take advantage of their size by negotiating favourable terms with suppliers as a result of bulk buying.
Managerial	As a firm increases in size, this does not usually mean that its employment of managers needs to grow at the same rate, and so the cost of management per unit of output is likely to fall. It is also the case that larger firms can employ specialist managers and this is likely to increase the efficiency of a firm.
Technical	Economies of increased or large dimensions can come about more easily in a large firm, reducing costs of production; for example, if a firm doubles the size of containers that it uses, it is not likely to lead to a doubling of the cost.
Marketing	A larger firm may be better able to negotiate a lower rate, such as in relation to buying advertising time on television.
Risk bearing	A larger firm is likely to be more diversified, spreading risks across a wider range of markets. This enables average costs to be reduced. For example, diversification will lead to more stable and predictable demand and this will mean that a firm will not need to keep as much stock as before, reducing the costs of stockholding.

Revision activity

Distinguish between the various types of internal economics of scale.

economies of large dimensions: the reduction in average cost as a result of using larger factors of production, such as larger containers in the transportation process

financial economies of scale: the reduction in average cost as a result of a firm being larger, such as the ability of a larger firm to negotiate more favourable borrowing terms on a loan

technical economies: the reduction in average cost as a result of the application of advanced technology in a firm which brings about a greater degree of efficiency

risk-bearing economies of scale: a situation where there is diversification so that a firm is not reliant on what happens in just one market. By diversifying into different markets, the overall pattern of demand is more predictable and so a firm can save costs, such as by reducing the amount of stocks held in reserve

diversification: a situation where a firm decides to operate in a number of markets to spread risk

External economies of scale

The fall in the average costs of production of a firm can also be the result of **external**, rather than purely internal, factors. Examples of these are included in Table 2.

external economies of scale: these are when costs of production fall because of developments outside a particular firm

Table 2 External economies of scale

Type of external economy	Explanation
Concentration	If a number of firms are located in a particular area, this may encourage the development of specialist ancillary or support firms in the area that supply component parts to the firms, reducing the average costs of production.
Specialised labour	A pool of specialised skilled labour may be available in a particular area, which all firms in that industry in the area can benefit from.
Knowledge	Firms in an industry may benefit from specialist research or marketing agencies, and so be able to reduce the costs of acquiring and using this information.

Expert tip

Whereas internal economies of scale involve a movement down a long-run average cost curve, external economies of scale will involve a downward shift of the whole long-run average cost curve.

Expert tip

Candidates need to demonstrate they clearly understand the distinction between *internal economies of scale*, which relate to a particular firm, and *external economies of scale*, which relate to a much wider aspect, such as a whole industry.

Revision activity

Consider whether the area in which you live, or an area with which you are familiar, has any particular external economies of scale to a firm located in that area.

Constant returns to scale

Revised

Constant returns to scale indicate a situation where average costs remain the same even as the output produced increases. In this situation, a firm will add factors of production in the same proportion so that there are constant additions to total output.

constant returns to scale: whereas economies of scale give rise to decreasing costs, it may be that there is a level of output where costs remain the same. This is known as constant returns to scale

Diseconomies of scale

Revised

In Figure 3, the long-run average cost curve, after initially falling, begins to rise as output is increased beyond Q^*. This indicates that there are **diseconomies of scale**. As with economies of scale, it is possible to distinguish between internal and external diseconomies of scale.

diseconomies of scale: a situation where the average cost of production rises with an increase in the level of output

decreasing returns to scale: where the same proportional increase in productive factors gives rise to decreasing additions to total output; this gives rise to diseconomies of scale

Internal diseconomies of scale

Increasing average costs of production can come about as a firm grows too large. There are various examples of these **internal diseconomies of scale**, as shown in Table 3.

internal diseconomies of scale: these are the disadvantages of a firm growing in size in the form of an increase in the average cost of production

Table 3 Internal diseconomies of scale

Type of external economy	Explanation
Communication	There may be poorer communication in a large firm, which adversely affects efficiency.
Motivation	There may be lower levels of motivation in a large firm, with some employees feeling alienated. This may lead to a greater likelihood of industrial disputes.
Management	Problems of poor communication and low levels of motivation can lead to difficulties in managing a firm effectively.
Flexibility	Larger firms may become less flexible, making it more difficult to respond to changing market conditions.

Revision activity

Consider possible reasons why a firm should not grow too large.

External diseconomies of scale

The rise in the average costs of production of a firm can also be the result of external, rather than purely internal, factors. Examples of these are included in Table 4.

external diseconomies of scale: these are when costs of production rise because of developments outside a particular firm

Table 4 External diseconomies of scale

Type of external economy	Explanation
Competition for inputs	The increase in the size of firms, and indeed the whole industry, can lead to greater competition for a limited number of productive inputs and, as a result, the cost of these inputs increases. For example, there could be an increase in the cost of labour or land.
Congestion	If a number of firms tend to be located in a particular area, this can lead to greater congestion, reducing the efficiency and effectiveness of the transport system and leading to an increase in costs.

Now test yourself

5 Explain the difference between an internal economy of scale and an external diseconomy of scale.

Answer on p.156

Tested

Types of cost, revenue and profit

Marginal cost and average cost

Revised

It is important to clearly distinguish between average cost and **marginal cost**. Average cost is the total cost of producing something divided by the number of units that are being produced. Marginal cost is the addition to the total cost of producing one additional unit and can be calculated by dividing the change in total cost by the change in output.

In diagrams, the marginal cost curve will always cross the average cost curve at its lowest point. When marginal cost is less than average cost, average cost will be falling; when marginal cost is more than average cost, average cost will be rising.

marginal cost: the additional cost of producing an extra unit of a product

Now test yourself

6 Distinguish between marginal cost and average cost.

Answer on p.157

Tested

Marginal, average and total revenue

Revised

It is important to distinguish between the different forms of revenue. **Marginal revenue** refers to the additional revenue received when one more unit of a product is sold. **Average revenue** indicates the **total revenue** obtained from selling a product divided by the number of units sold. Total revenue refers to the money received from the sales of a product.

> **marginal revenue:** the extra revenue obtained from the sale of an additional unit of a product
>
> **average revenue:** the total revenue obtained from sales divided by the number of units sold
>
> **total revenue:** the total revenue obtained from sales of a product, i.e. it is the total amount of income received and can be calculated by the number of units sold multiplied by the price of each unit

The relationship between elasticity and marginal, average and total revenue

Figure 4 shows the relationship between price elasticity of demand and marginal revenue, average revenue and total revenue for a downward-sloping demand curve. If the demand curve is perfectly elastic, then marginal revenue is equal to price. If, however, there is a downward-sloping demand curve, it means that marginal revenue is less than price. This is because price has to be reduced for all products to sell just one more product. Average revenue is in fact the downward-sloping demand curve. Total revenue is rising when demand is elastic, at its maximum when there is unitary elastic demand, and falling when demand is inelastic.

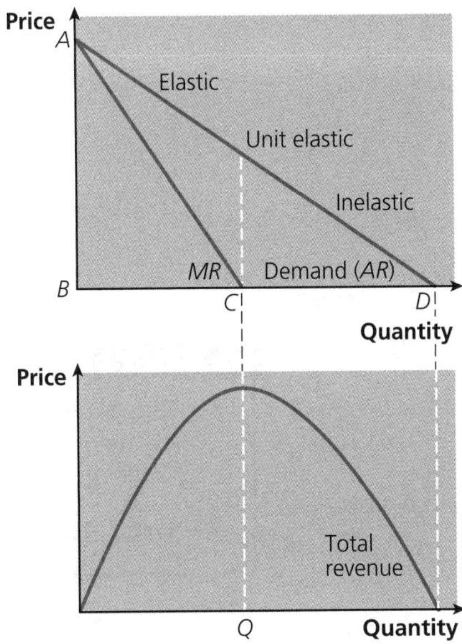

Figure 4 Elasticity and total revenue

Profit

Revised

It is generally assumed that the main objective of a firm is **profit maximisation**. **Profit** is defined as the difference between the total revenue received by a firm and the total costs involved in producing what is sold, i.e. it is equal to the total revenue minus the total costs. Profit maximisation is a situation where marginal cost is equal to marginal revenue.

It is important, however, to distinguish between **normal profit** and **abnormal profit**. Normal profit refers to the amount of profit that needs to be made by a firm to stay in a particular market. It is actually included in the average cost curve of a firm.

A firm may, however, wish to make a profit that is above normal profit. This level of profit that is over and above normal profit is known as abnormal or **supernormal profit.**

profit maximisation: the situation where marginal cost is equal to marginal revenue

profit: the difference between total revenue and total costs

normal profit: the level of profit that a firm requires to keep operating in the industry

abnormal profit: the level of profit (also known as supernormal profit) that is over and above normal profit

breakeven point: the level of output at which a firm is making neither a loss nor a profit

Expert tip

Candidates need to be able to clearly distinguish between *normal profit* and *abnormal/supernormal profit.*

The economist's and the accountant's definition of profit

The economist's definition of normal profit includes within it a rate of return that is needed for the firm to remain in that particular market or industry. An accountant, however, takes a different view, pointing out that this assumed rate of return cannot be formally and explicitly identified in the accounts of a firm.

An accountant is concerned with the actual figures that can be produced by a firm as a result of its various trading activities. An economist, on the other hand, is prepared to build into the assumptions that a firm will need to make a certain profit that is just enough to keep it in its present line of business. For an accountant, however, the fact that it is impossible to say precisely what the size of this normal profit will need to be is sufficient for such a figure not be included in any accounting data.

Now test yourself

7 Distinguish between normal profit and abnormal (or supernormal) profit.

Answer on p.157

Tested

Expert tip

Candidates need to be aware of the fact that an economist and an accountant will consider profit from different points of view.

Differing objectives of a firm

Other objectives of a firm

Revised

Although profit maximisation has traditionally been regarded as the main objective of a firm, it is necessary to consider that a firm may have other objectives. These are set out in Table 5.

Table 5 Other objectives of a firm

Model	Explanation
Satisficing profits	Where there is a distinction between ownership and control, managers may just want to deal in an appropriate manner with all of the stakeholders involved in a firm, with the result that the stakeholders are all satisfied with the situation. In such a situation, satisfactory profits, rather than maximum profits, may be the aim.
Revenue maximisation	This is likely to be the case where the salaries of managers are linked to revenue rather than to profits.
Sales maximisation	In this situation, managers aim to maximise the volume of sales rather than the revenue resulting from such sales.
Growth maximisation	This refers to a situation where managers aim to increase the size of the firm because this will make it less vulnerable to a takeover or merger and it is possible that salaries of managers may be linked to the size of a firm.

Now test yourself

8 Identify other possible objectives of a firm apart from profit maximisation.

Answer on p.157

Tested

satisficing profits: when the objective of a firm is to produce a level of profits that is satisfactory to stakeholders, such as shareholders and managers

revenue maximisation: when the objective of a firm is to maximise the total revenue, rather than the profits, of a firm

sales maximisation: when the objective of a firm is to maximise the volume of sales

Expert tip

In examination questions on the objectives of a firm, candidates need to remember not to write exclusively on profit maximisation, but also to consider other possible objectives of a firm.

Revision activity

Research a firm with which you are familiar. Outline its main objectives.

The concepts of firm and industry

Revised

It is important to distinguish between a **firm** and an **industry**. A firm is a distinct organisation that is owned separately from any other organisation. In a firm, an entrepreneur will bring together factors of production in order to produce particular products. An industry, on the other hand, involves a number of firms which produce broadly similar products.

firm: a particular and distinct organisation that is owned separately from any other organisation

industry: a collection of firms producing similar products

Expert tip

Candidates often confuse the terms 'firm' and 'industry', making it difficult sometimes for examiners to follow the logic of a candidate's answer. It is important that you clearly understand the difference between 'one firm' and 'a number of firms operating in an industry or market'.

Revision activity

Distinguish between a firm and an industry.

Different market structures

It is important to distinguish between the different types of market structure that can occur in an economy. There are four main market structures:

- perfect competition
- monopolistic competition
- oligopoly
- monopoly

Table 6 summarises the main distinguishing features of the four types of market structure.

Table 6 Different market structures

	Perfect competition	Monopolistic competition	Oligopoly	Monopoly
Number of firms	Many	Many	Dominated by a few	One
Freedom of entry	Not restricted	Not restricted	Some **barriers to entry**	High barriers to entry
Firm's influence over price	None	Some	Some	Price maker, subject to the demand curve
Nature of product	Homogeneous	Differentiated	Varied	No close substitutes
Examples	Cauliflowers Carrots	Fast-food outlets Travel agents	Cars Mobile phones	PC operating systems Local water supply

Monopolistic competition, oligopoly and monopoly are all part of what is generally referred to as **imperfect competition**.

barriers to exit and entry: various obstacles that make it very difficult, or impossible, for new firms to exit or enter an industry. For example, where a firm is benefiting from technical economies of scale, it may be difficult for a new firm to enter the industry because its average costs of production will be much higher. Another reason might because a firm already has legal control of production of a product through a patent. An example of a barrier to exit would be where a firm has already invested heavily in capital equipment and would be reluctant to just 'write off' this expenditure

imperfect competition: a market which lacks some, or all, of the features of perfect competition

Perfect competition

Revised

The market structure of **perfect competition** is based on a number of assumptions, which include the following:

- There are many buyers and sellers.
- The buyers and sellers are price takers, i.e. they just have to accept the price that prevails in the market and are unable to influence it in any way.
- There is perfect knowledge among producers and consumers, so the buyers and sellers know which products are for sale and at what price.
- The product is homogeneous, so there is no possibility of product differentiation.
- There are no barriers to entry or exit, so firms can enter or leave the industry in the long run, if they so wish.
- There is perfect factor mobility in the long run.
- There are no transport costs.
- All producers have access to the same technology.
- Each firm faces a perfectly elastic demand curve for its product (although the demand curve for the whole industry is downward sloping from left to right).
- Firms aim to maximise profits.
- Only normal profit can be earned in the long run.

In the short run, a firm could make abnormal/supernormal profits, normal profits or subnormal profits (i.e. losses). If it was unable to cover its short-run average variable cost, it would need to exit from the market.

perfect competition: a market or industry consisting of many virtually identical firms which all accept the market price in the industry

Figure 5 shows the equilibrium situation of a firm in perfect competition that is making abnormal/supernormal profits. The profit maximisation position, where *MC* equals *MR*, is at output *Q*, but at this point the price is shown by *P* and the average cost by *AC*. At this point, *AR* is greater than *AC* and this explains the existence of abnormal/supernormal profits in the short run, shown by the shaded area.

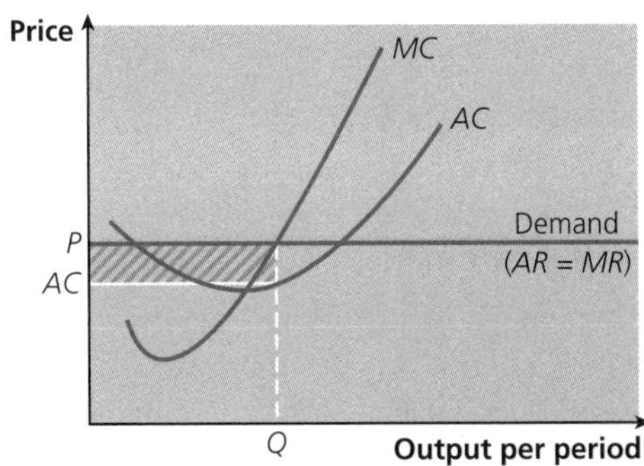

Figure 5 The firm in short-run supply equilibrium

In the long run, if a firm makes abnormal/supernormal profits, new firms will be attracted into the industry. If, however, a firm makes subnormal profits, i.e. where *AC* is greater than *AR*, such firms will decide to leave the industry. As a result of such changes, only normal profits will be made by the firms in the industry in the long run.

Figure 6 shows the equilibrium situation of firms in perfect competition in the long run. *AR* is equal to *AC* at a price of *P** and a quantity of *Q** and so only normal profits are made.

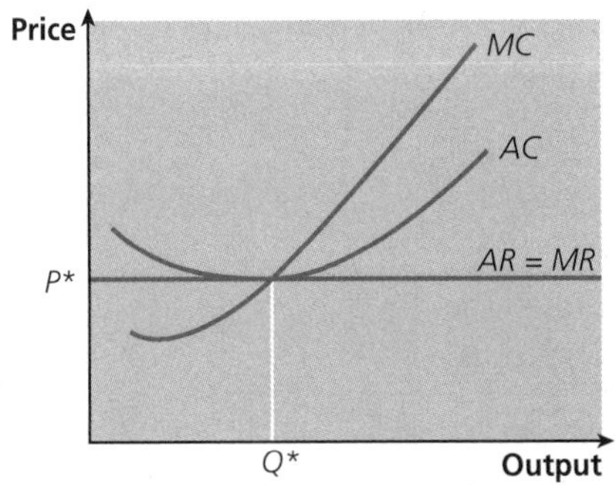

Figure 6 Long-run equilibrium under perfect competition

Perfect competition is very much a theoretical model of the behaviour of firms, based on a number of assumptions. It has therefore been criticised for being unrealistic, but it is still useful as a model of economic behaviour.

Now test yourself

9 Distinguish between the profits made in the short run and in the long run in perfect competition.

Answer on p.157

Tested

Expert tip

It would be easy for candidates to dismiss the theory of perfect competition for being unrealistic, but the theory is important in providing a benchmark to consider other theories of market structures.

Revision activity

How useful do you think the market structure of perfect competition is?

Monopolistic competition

Revised

The market structure of **monopolistic competition** is based on a number of assumptions, which include the following:

- There is a large number of firms.
- Products are differentiated, i.e. they are not homogeneous.
- Each firm faces a demand curve that is downward sloping from left to right.

- Demand for a product is relatively price elastic, but not perfectly elastic.
- Great use is made of advertising brand images to build up brand loyalty.
- There are no barriers to entry and exit, so firms can enter or leave the industry in the long run, if they so wish.
- Firms aim to maximise profits.
- Only normal profits can be earned in the long run.

In the short run, a firm could make abnormal/supernormal profits, normal profits or subnormal profits. As there are few barriers to entry or exit, this will enable firms to leave or enter the industry in response to these profits.

monopolistic competition: a market or industry where there is competition between a large number of firms which produce products which are similar but differentiated, usually through the use of brand images

Figure 7 shows the equilibrium situation of a firm in monopolistic competition that is making abnormal/supernormal profits. The profit maximisation position, where *MC* equals *MR*, is at output *Q* and price *P*. *AR* is above *AC* and so the firm is making abnormal profits, shown by the shaded area.

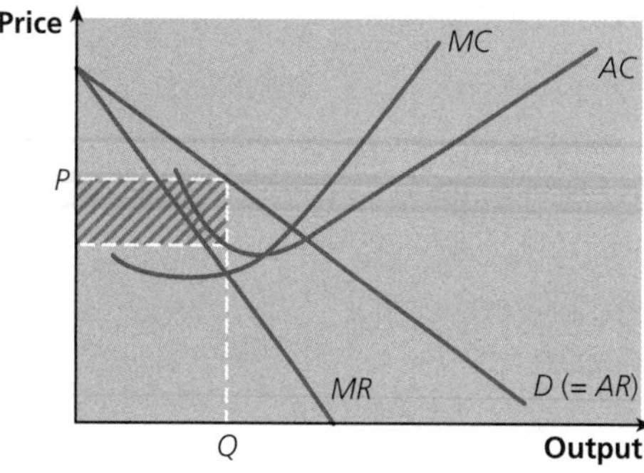

Figure 7 Short-run equilibrium under monopolistic competition

In the long run, if a firm makes abnormal/supernormal profits, new firms will be attracted into the industry. If, however, a firm makes subnormal profits, i.e. where *AC* is greater than *AR*, such firms will decide to leave the industry. As a result of such changes, only normal profits will be made by the firms in the industry in the long run.

Figure 8 shows the equilibrium situation of firms in monopolistic competition in the long run. *AR* (or *D*) is equal to *AC* at a price of *P* and a quantity of *Q** and so only normal profits are made.

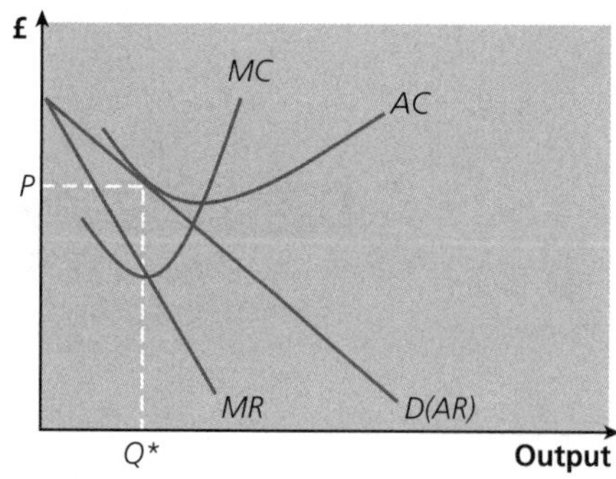

Figure 8 Long-run equilibrium under monopolistic competition

Monopolistic competition is generally regarded as a more realistic model of the behaviour of firms because it is often the case that there is a great deal of competition between firms that are selling products that are similar, but not identical.

Expert tip

In some questions which require candidates to compare monopolistic competition and monopoly, it is not always clear when a candidate is referring to monopolistic competition and when they are referring to monopoly. It is important that candidates clearly indicate which market structure they are referring to throughout their answer.

Revision activity

Distinguish between the market structures of perfect competition and monopolistic competition.

Oligopoly

Revised

The market structure of **oligopoly** is based on a number of assumptions, which include the following:

- There is a small number of firms. (If there are only two firms, it is called a duopoly.)
- There are differentiated products.
- Great use is made of advertising brand images to build up brand loyalty.
- Barriers to entry make it difficult for new entrants to enter the market.
- Firms can make abnormal/supernormal profits in the long run, as well as the short run.
- There could be a mixture of price makers and price takers.
- The firms are interdependent.
- There could be a degree of collusion between firms operating in a **cartel**.
- There is a kinked demand curve.
- There is a great deal of price stability/rigidity.

There are usually only a few large firms in an oligopolistic market structure, i.e. the **concentration ratio** of the largest firms is usually very high.

oligopoly: a market or industry in which there are a few large firms competing with each other

concentration ratio: the percentage of a market controlled by a given number of firms, e.g. the five largest firms in an industry might control 80% of the output of the industry

An important distinctive feature of oligopoly is the existence of a kinked demand curve. This results from the fact that firms in an oligopolistic market structure try to anticipate the reactions of rival firms to their actions.

It is assumed that if an oligopolistic firm increases its price, other firms in the market will not follow and so demand above the kink is elastic. It can also be assumed that if an oligopolistic firm reduces its price, other firms in the market will follow and so demand below the kink is inelastic.

Figure 9 shows the equilibrium situation of oligopolistic firms. The profit maximisation position, where *MC* equals *MR*, is at output *Q** and price *P**. Above the kink (i.e. to the left of *Q**), demand is elastic; below the kink (i.e. to the right of *Q**), demand is inelastic. It should be noted that that the marginal revenue line is discontinuous, shown by the dotted line between MC_1 and MC_0.

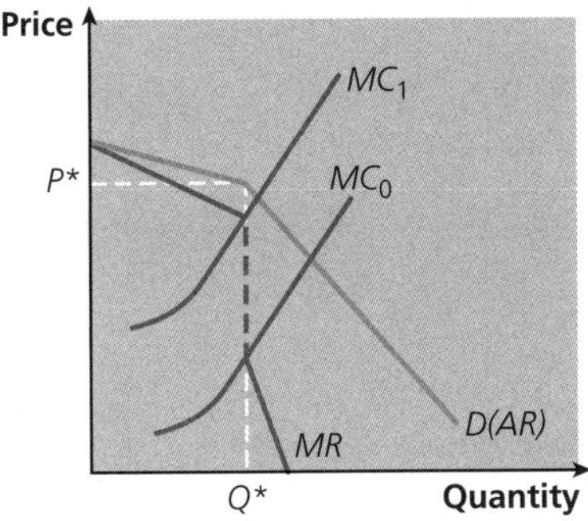

Figure 9 The kinked demand curve

Another important distinctive feature of oligopoly is that firms may sometimes act together, i.e. there will be collusion between two or more firms, such as through **price agreements**, giving rise to the existence of a **cartel**.

Oligopoly can sometimes give rise to **predatory pricing**. This is where a firm charges a price that is lower than those of competitors in a deliberate attempt to force other firms out of the industry.

Oligopoly is generally regarded as a reasonably realistic model of the behaviour of firms, but it is more complex than the other market models because there are many ways in which firms in such a market may interact with each other.

price agreements: where firms in an oligopolistic market agree to fix prices between themselves

cartel: a situation where a number of firms agree to collude, i.e. work together, such as by limiting output to keep price higher than would be the case if there was competition between the firms

predatory pricing: a deliberate attempt by a market leader to reduce prices in order to force other firms out of a market

Now test yourself

10 Explain what is meant by a 'kinked demand curve' in oligopoly.

Answer on p.157

Tested

Revision activity

Outline the main characteristics of oligopoly.

Monopoly

Revised

The market structure of **monopoly** is based on a number of assumptions, which include the following:

- There is one firm in an industry, i.e. there is just one single seller.
- Legally, a monopoly can be defined in terms of a percentage of market share, e.g. in the UK this is 25%.
- It is a price maker.
- There are no substitutes for the product.
- Barriers to entry make it virtually impossible for new firms to enter the market.
- Abnormal/supernormal profits can exist in both the short run and the long run.
- The demand for the firm's product is also the market or industry demand, so the demand curve is downward sloping from left to right.
- Marginal revenue is always less than average revenue.
- The firm aims to maximise profits.

monopoly: a market or industry where there is a single firm which controls the supply of the product

Figure 10 shows the equilibrium situation of a monopolistic firm. The profit maximisation position, where *MC* is equal to *MR*, is at price *P** and quantity *Q**. Abnormal/supernormal profits are being made, but because of the existence of barriers to entry, it is impossible for new firms to enter the market and so these profits can exist in the long run as well as the short run.

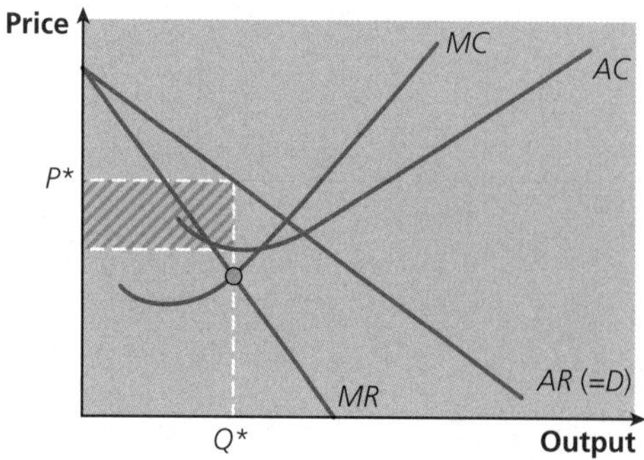

Figure 10 Profit maximisation and monopoly

A monopoly is generally regarded as a market structure that has disadvantages for the consumer, but this need not necessarily always be the case. For example, in the case of a **natural monopoly**, one firm will have sufficient economies of scale to satisfy market demand more efficiently than two or more firms.

natural monopoly: a situation where average cost will be lower with just one provider, avoiding the wasteful duplication of resources

Revision activity

Do you think that a monopoly is always bad? Explain your reasoning.

Expert tip

In examination questions on monopoly, especially those which require candidates to discuss or evaluate a monopoly market, it is important to include *both* the potential advantages *and* the possible disadvantages of monopoly before coming to a conclusion.

Contestable markets

The idea of **contestable markets** is based on a number of assumptions, including the following:

- There are no barriers to entry; entry into an industry is relatively easy.
- Firms already in the market continually face the threat of competition.
- This puts pressure on the firms to be efficient.
- Abnormal profits are made in the short run, but only normal profits in the long run.
- There are degrees of contestability; a perfectly contestable market will have no sunk costs (these are costs which have already been paid for when a firm enters a market and so are non-recoverable when a firm leaves an industry). For example, sunk costs are those costs which have already been paid for, so the costs of research and development will already have been paid for; if a firm leaves an industry, they will be non-recoverable.

The key feature of a contestable market is that because it is relatively easy for a new firm to enter a market, the existing firms in the market are continually influenced by the threat of the possible entry of such firms, making them behave as if these potential firms were actually already operating in the market.

contestable market: a situation where it may be relatively easy for new entrants to enter a market or industry; the effect of this is that existing firms in an industry face the threat of new firms coming into the industry and increasing the degree of competition

Expert tip

It is important that candidates clearly understand that in a contestable market, it is not so much the entry of new firms into a market that is important but the threat of such entry.

Now test yourself

11 What is meant by a 'contestable market'?

Answer on p.157

Tested

Conduct and performance of firms

It is possible to distinguish between firms in terms of pricing policy and non-price policy.

Pricing policy

Revised

Price discrimination

Price discrimination occurs where different prices can be charged to different customers where there are different price elasticities of demand and where the differences in price are not a reflection of differences in the costs of production.

This can happen in a situation of monopoly where the firm is able to keep different markets separate. This could be in terms of different geographical regions, different times of the day or different ages.

price discrimination: the process of charging different prices in different markets where there are differences in the price elasticities of demand

Expert tip

A common error in examination answers on this part of the syllabus is to assume that differences in price are because of differences in cost. The key point to emphasise in answers to questions about price discrimination is that the price differences do *not* reflect differences in cost.

Price leadership model

This can exist in an oligopoly market structure where there is collusion between firms in the market. There can be informal or tacit collusion between firms and this is usually seen when there is a situation of price leadership; in this situation, firms in the market will follow the lead of one firm. The aim of this behaviour is to maximise the profits of all these firms by behaving as if they were a monopolist, i.e. a single seller. As stated above, this agreement on price or output gives rise to a cartel arrangement.

Mutual interdependence

Another characteristic of firms in an oligopoly market structure is mutual interdependence. Firms in oligopoly take into account expectations about the behaviour of other firms in the market and it is this which gives rise to the existence of a kinked demand curve, a unique characteristic of oligopoly.

Now test yourself

12 What is meant by 'price discrimination'?

Answer on p.157

Tested

Non-price policy

Revised

The conduct of firms can also be compared in relation to whether they rely on pricing policies or non-price policies. In most markets, firms compete in terms of price, but in monopolistic competition and oligopoly there is a great deal of non-price competition, i.e. rather than using changes in price to compete, the firms use other ways to compete with each other.

Non-price competition involves any form of competitive activity, other than changes in price, and can include the following:

- advertising and product promotion
- branding and the creation/maintenance of brand and customer loyalty

- sales promotions, e.g. through such special offers as BOGOF ('buy one, get one free')
- distribution, e.g. controlling the distribution of products to particular retail outlets
- distinctive/exclusive packaging
- differences in quality or design

Now test yourself

13 Identify three examples of non-price competition.

Answer on p.157

Tested

The performance of firms

Revised

Table 7 summarises the main differences between firms in the four different market structures.

Table 7 The main differences between the market structures

	Profit	Efficiency	Barriers	Competition	Collusion
Perfect competition	Various in the short run; normal in the long run	Productive efficiency in the long run; allocative efficiency in both the short run and the long run	No barriers to entry or exit	Price competition	No collusion between firms
Monopolistic competition	Various in the short run; normal in the long run	Neither productive efficiency nor allocative efficiency is achieved	Very few barriers to entry or exit	Price competition and non-price competition	No collusion between firms
Oligopoly	Supernormal in the long run	Neither productive efficiency nor allocative efficiency is likely	Some barriers to entry	Price competition and non-price competition	Collusion between firms
Monopoly	Supernormal in the long run	Productive efficiency is most unlikely; allocative efficiency will not occur	High level of barriers to entry	Price competition	Only one firm

Growth and survival of firms

The survival of small firms

Revised

Despite the potential advantages of economies of scale, small firms still continue to exist in many economies.

The reasons for the continued survival of small firms include the following:

- The size of the market is small.
- The firm may be in a very specific niche market.
- The firm is providing customers with a service that requires personal attention.
- The firm may have only just started and so is relatively small at present.
- The owners of the firm prefer it to remain small.
- Small firms may receive specific financial support from government.
- Small firms may be more flexible in responding to changes in demand.
- Small firms may be more innovative and pioneering.
- The small firm may not be able to grow because of difficulties in raising the necessary finance.
- In some industries, there is an increase in the process of 'contracting out' and small firms may benefit from this.
- A small firm may be more efficient, e.g. labour relations and levels of motivation may be better than in a large firm.

The growth of firms

Revised

Internal and external growth

The internal growth of a firm comes about as a result of a firm increasing in size through producing and selling more products; the extent of this growth can be measured through volume of sales, sales revenue (turnover), the number of employees, market share and the size of profits.

The external growth of a firm comes about as a result of a merger, takeover or acquisition where two or more firms combine together, a process known as **integration**.

integration: the process whereby two or more firms come together through a takeover, merger or acquisition. A merger is where two or more firms combine together as a result of mutual agreement, whereas a takeover or acquisition usually involves some form of hostile bid by one firm for another

The reasons for the growth of firms

The reasons for the growth of firms include the following:

- to take advantage of possible economies of scale, leading to a decrease in the costs of production of a firm
- to be stronger and therefore safer from a hostile takeover or merger proposal (in the case of a firm becoming larger through internal growth)
- to take advantage of opportunities to gain from a larger market share, such as through greater profitability
- a possible desire of owners and/or managers to expand

Different types of external growth

Revised

Horizontal integration

One form of external growth is **horizontal integration**. This is where two or more firms at the same stage of the production process join together, such as two banks or two car manufacturing companies.

horizontal integration: where firms at the same stage of production merge

Vertical integration

Another form of external growth is **vertical integration**. This is where two or more firms at different stages of the production process join together. If this is going back to an earlier stage in the production process, such as a tyre (tire) producing country taking over rubber plantations, this is known as backward vertical integration. If this is going forward to a later stage in the production process, such as a car producer taking over a chain of petrol stations and garages to act as distributors of the vehicles, this is known as forward vertical integration.

vertical integration: where a firm joins with another firm at an earlier stage of the production process (backward vertical integration) or at a later stage of the production process (forward vertical integration)

Conglomerate integration

Both horizontal and vertical (whether backward or forward) integration involve mergers of firms operating in the same market. **Conglomerate integration**, however, is where two or more firms join together even though they are operating in entirely different markets that do not always have any relationship with each other. Although this may appear illogical, it has the benefit of spreading risks in different markets through the process of diversification. For example, the brewing company Guinness diversified into publishing, producing the *Guinness Book of Records* among other titles.

Now test yourself

14 Distinguish between backward and forward vertical integration.

Answer on p.157

Tested

conglomerate integration: where there is a merger between firms which are operating in completely different markets rather than in different stages of the same market

Expert tip

In examination questions on integration, candidates often write about horizontal and vertical integration only, making no reference at all to conglomerate integration. Candidates should consider all three types of integration in their answers. Conglomerate integration has the advantage of providing diversification and this spreading of risks in different markets can be of fundamental importance to a large number of firms.

Revision activity

Distinguish between the different types of integration that can exist in an economy.

Demand and supply for labour

The demand for labour

Revised

Labour is not demanded for its own sake, but for what it can contribute to the production process. This is known as **derived demand**.

The demand for labour is closely linked to the **marginal physical product** of labour. This refers to the additional output produced if a firm increases the labour input by one unit.

Firms are interested not only in the extra output that is produced by employing one more unit of labour, but also in the revenue obtained from selling the additional output that has been produced. The **marginal revenue product** of labour is obtained by multiplying the marginal physical product of labour by the marginal revenue received by a firm.

derived demand: where the demand by employers for labour is related to the demand for the product that the labour helps to produce, i.e. labour is not demanded for its own sake, but for its contribution to the production process

marginal physical product: the amount of extra output that is produced if a firm increases its input of labour by one unit

marginal revenue product: the extra revenue obtained by a firm as it increases its output by using an additional unit of labour

Figure 11 shows the profit maximising position where the marginal cost of labour (*MCL*) equals the marginal revenue product of labour (*MRPL*) at a wage of W^* and a quantity of Q^*.

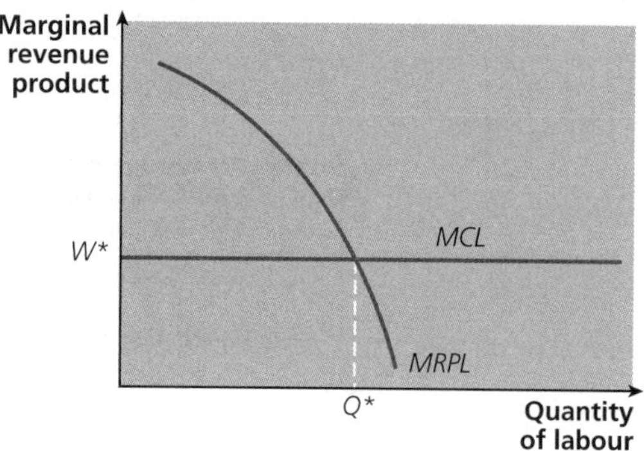

Figure 11 The labour input decision of a profit maximising firm under perfect competition

Now test yourself

15 Explain what is meant by the term 'derived demand'.

Answer on p.157

Tested

The supply of labour

Revised

In Figure 11, it is assumed that a firm is in a perfectly competitive market for labour and so cannot influence the price, i.e. the wage, of labour. The firm therefore regards labour supply as perfectly elastic, as shown by *MCL*.

For the industry as a whole, however, the supply curve of labour will be upward sloping from left to right because more people will make themselves available for work when the wage is increased.

For an individual worker, however, the increase in wages may persuade that worker to work fewer hours in order to enjoy more leisure time and this situation gives rise to a backward-bending supply curve for a particular individual.

This situation can be seen in Figure 12. Up to a wage of *W**, a worker decides to work more hours as the wage increases, but as the wage increases above *W**, the worker may decide to work fewer hours.

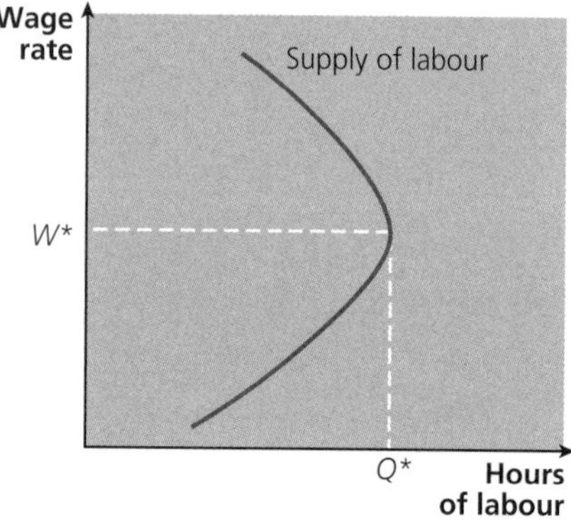

Figure 12 A backward-bending individual labour supply curve

The backward-bending supply curve of a particular worker reflects the importance of the **pecuniary advantages** of work to that employee, i.e. a reward or benefit that is paid in the form of money.

Of course, there are also **non-pecuniary** reasons why people work, i.e. reasons other than a financial reward.

pecuniary advantages: the advantages of employment that are in the form of financial rewards or benefits

non-pecuniary advantages: the advantages of employment, other than the money that is gained, such as the job satisfaction gained from a particular form of employment

Now test yourself

16 Distinguish between pecuniary and non-pecuniary advantages of employment.

Answer on p.157

Tested

Wage determination

Wage determination under free-market forces

Revised

Equilibrium in a labour market is just like equilibrium in any other market, i.e. it is where demand is equal to supply. This can be seen in Figure 13 where the downward-sloping demand curve for labour and the upward-sloping supply curve of labour intersect at a wage of W^* and a quantity of Q^*.

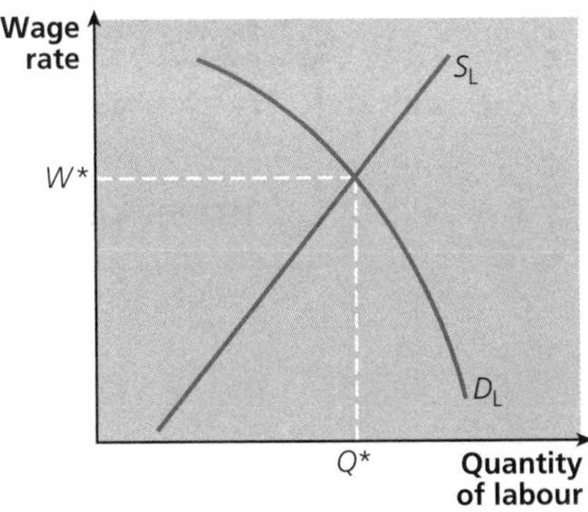

Figure 13 Labour market equilibrium

Transfer earnings and economic rent

Revised

Transfer earnings refer to those earnings that are the minimum that would be necessary to keep a factor of production in a particular use.

Economic rent is the additional payment that a worker receives above the transfer earnings. This can be seen in Figure 14, where an employee receives a wage of W^*. Some of this wage will be in the form of transfer earnings (shown by $OBAQ^*$) and some of it will be in the form of economic rent (shown by BAW^*).

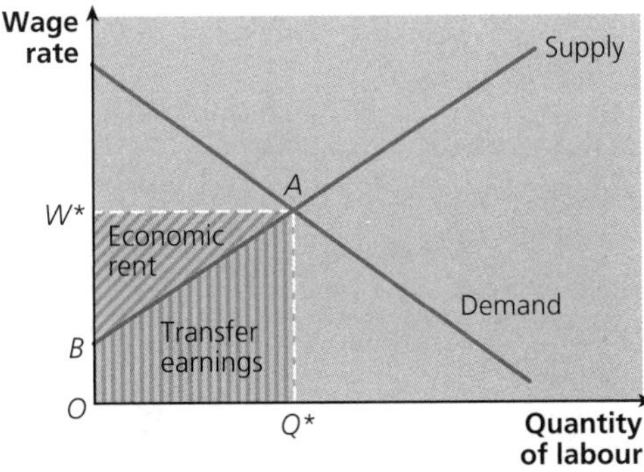

Figure 14 Transfer earnings and economic rent

transfer earnings: the minimum payment required to keep a factor of production in its present use

economic rent: the extra payment received by a factor of production that is above what would be needed to keep it in its present use

Expert tip

A common error in examinations is to confuse where *economic rent* and *transfer earnings* should be shown in the diagram, as they are often labelled the wrong way round. It is important that candidates include appropriate diagrams wherever possible in their examination answers, but the diagrams need to be accurately drawn and correctly labelled.

The amount of economic rent that a worker is able to obtain is limited by the fact that there is not usually a high level of **mobility of labour**; in fact, in many labour markets, there is a high degree of **immobility of labour**.

There can sometimes be differences in wages in an industry in different parts of a country. This is because although there might be an officially agreed wage rate in an industry that is supposed to apply across a whole country, specific demand and supply circumstances may mean that the actual earnings of some workers in some parts of the country are higher. This situation is known as **wage drift**.

mobility of labour: the degree to which labour finds it easy to move from one job to another (occupational mobility) and/or from one location to another (geographical mobility)

immobility of labour: the degree of occupational immobility and geographical immobility of labour which makes a labour market less flexible than it would otherwise be

wage drift: a situation where the average level of wages in an industry tends to rise faster than the supposed wage rates

Now test yourself

17 Distinguish between transfer earnings and economic rent.

Answer on p.157

Tested

Imperfect markets

Revised

A labour market may not necessarily operate under free-market conditions. For example, there may exist a single employer of labour, a government may intervene or the workers may be members of a trade union.

Monopsony

It has been assumed so far, in terms of wage determination, that the industry demand curve is made up of a number of firms in an industry. It could be the case, however, that there is just one firm in the market to employ a factor of production. Such a firm is known as a **monopsony**.

monopsony: a single buyer of a product or of a factor of production, such as labour

In a competitive market, there will be many firms in an industry and so each firm must accept the prevailing market wage. If a firm is a monopsonist, however, the situation will be different. This can be seen in Figure 15. If the market was a competitive one, the equilibrium position would be where demand is equal to supply; this would be wage W^* and quantity Q^*. A monopsonist, however, would be at an equilibrium position where marginal cost was equal to demand; this would lead to a lower wage of W_m and a lower quantity of Q_m.

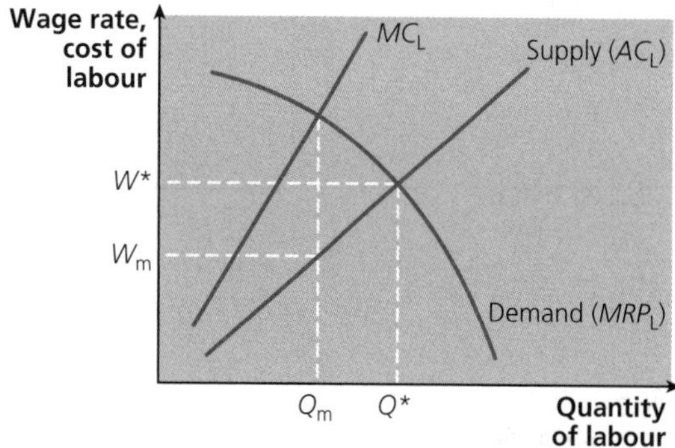

Figure 15 A monospony buyer of labour

Expert tip

A common error in examination answers on this part of the syllabus is to show the minimum wage below where supply and demand intersect, rather than above this point. Candidates should understand that there would be no point in having a minimum wage below what the wage in the economy would have been without any form of intervention.

Government intervention

In a free market, there would be no government intervention, but governments do intervene in economies, including in labour markets. For example, a government might decide to introduce a minimum wage to prevent employees being paid below a certain level.

The effect of this can be seen in Figure 16. Without government intervention, the equilibrium would be a wage of W^* and a quantity of Q^*, an equilibrium determined by the intersection of demand and supply. A government may decide, however, that the wage of W^* is too low and so intervenes in the market by introducing a national minimum wage. This will be set above W^* at a wage of W_{min}. The advantage of this is that those employed will gain a higher wage, but the disadvantage is that fewer workers will be employed (Q_{min} rather than Q^*).

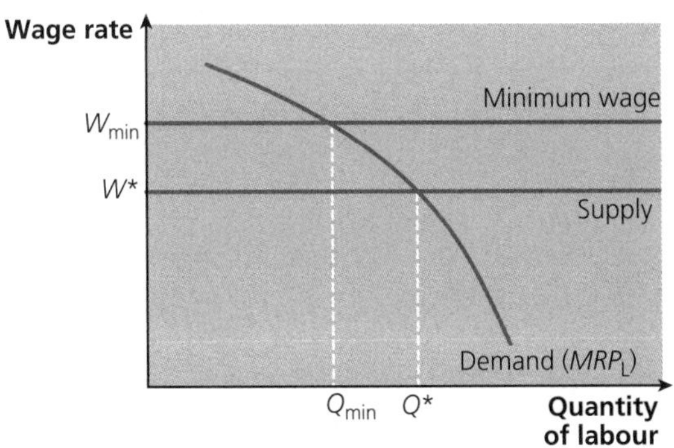

Figure 16 The effect of a minimum wage on a firm in a perfectly competitive labour market

Trade unions

It may be the case that workers belong to a **trade union** which is involved in **collective bargaining** with employers on behalf of the workers. A trade union may insist on the existence of a **closed shop** to increase its bargaining power with employers.

trade union: an organisation of workers which is involved in collective bargaining with employers to achieve certain objectives, such as improvements in pay and working conditions

collective bargaining: the process of negotiation between trade union representatives of the workers and their employers on such issues as remuneration (payment) and working conditions

closed shop: a requirement that all employees in a specific workplace belong to a particular trade union

The trade union can reduce the supply of labour, e.g. by pressurising governments and/or employers into making entry into particular employment more difficult, and this will have an effect on wages. This can be seen in Figure 17.

Without a trade union, the equilibrium position will be wage W^* and quantity Q^*. However, if a trade union makes it more difficult for people to enter employment in that particular industry, the wage will now be higher, at W_1, and the quantity of labour will now be lower, at Q_1.

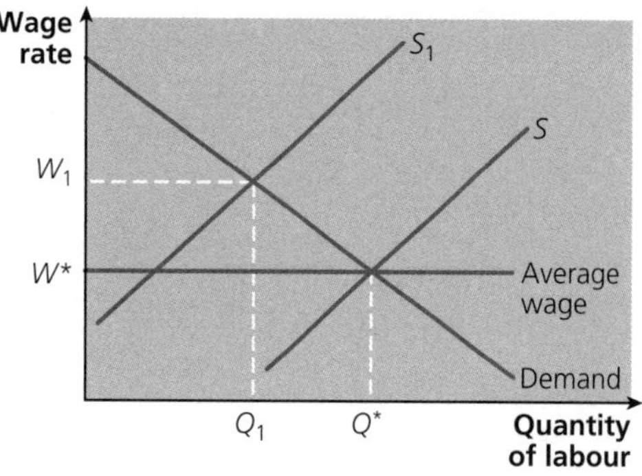

Figure 17 A trade union restricts the supply of labour

Revision activity

Find out to what extent government and trade unions influence wages in your country.

10 Government intervention in the price system

Sources of market failure

Many aspects of market failure are covered in the AS syllabus (see Topic 3); others, such as the implications of monopolistic elements in a market and of inequality of wealth and income, are dealt with later in this unit. Table 1 provides a summary of the main sources of market failure.

Table 1 Types of market failure

Type of market failure	Explanation
Merit goods	These are goods which are regarded as socially desirable and which would be under-produced and under-consumed in a free market.
Demerit goods	These are goods which are regarded as socially undesirable and which would be over-produced and over-consumed in a free market.
Public goods	These are goods which would not be provided at all in a free market because it would be impossible to charge a price for them.
Externalities	Externalities are costs and benefits which affect third parties. Negative externalities may result from the over-production of a good and positive externalities may result from the under-production of a good.
Information failure	There is a lack of full information and so the allocation of resources may not be as efficient as it otherwise would be.
Government failure	A government can intervene in a market to try to overcome a market failure, but there is always a chance that such intervention may create further distortions in the market.
Imperfect competition	This occurs when there is a departure from the situation of perfect competition. There can be different market imperfections and one of these is the existence of monopolistic elements in an economy where one firm can have monopoly power in a market.
Inequality in the distribution of income and wealth	A free market may lead to a very unequal distribution of income and wealth, giving some people more influence in a market than others.
Factor immobility	In a perfect market, the factors of production would be able to move easily from one market to another, but the existence of occupational and geographical immobility of factors of production means that this does not always happen.
Price instability	This occurs where prices can rapidly change in a relatively short period of time. In some markets, there can be a great deal of price instability, especially in agricultural markets.

Revision activity

Consider the different forms of market failure which exist in your country.

Market imperfections — existence of monopolistic elements

Revised

The topic of monopoly is discussed elsewhere in the A level syllabus (see Topic 9); in this topic it is important to see how monopoly is another possible example of market failure.

Monopoly power is regarded as a market imperfection because the equilibrium price is likely to be higher and the equilibrium quantity lower than would be the case in perfect competition. Unlike the situation in perfect competition, the abnormal profits are not competed away in the long run because there are significant barriers to entry, which make it very difficult, if not impossible, for new firms to enter the market. A particular form of inefficiency that can exist in monopoly is when a firm's average cost curve is not at its minimum level; monopoly power can mean that the lack of competition can reduce the level of efficiency, meaning that unit costs of production are not minimised. A particular example of such a market imperfection is the existence of deadweight losses.

technical monopoly: technically, a monopoly is said to exist where there is just one firm in an industry

X-inefficiency: a situation where average cost is not at its lowest point because monopoly power has given rise to inefficiency

Now test yourself

1 Explain what is meant by 'X-inefficiency'.

Answer on p.157

Tested

The meaning of deadweight losses

Revised

A **deadweight loss** occurs when there is a monopoly situation leading to a higher price and a lower quantity compared to the situation that would exist if the market was one of perfect competition. In this sense, a consumer is worse off and so there is said to be a welfare loss.

deadweight losses: the reduction in consumer surplus when a monopoly producer reduces output and raises price compared to what the situation would be in perfect competition; there is therefore a welfare loss to the consumer

This can be seen in Figure 1, which compares the situation of perfect competition with that of monopoly. In perfect competition, the equilibrium price will be P_{pc} and the equilibrium quantity will be Q_{pc}. The consumer surplus will be $AP_{pc}E$.

If, however, the market becomes one with just one firm, i.e. a monopoly, the equilibrium price will now be at P_m and the equilibrium quantity will now be at Q_m. The price will therefore be higher and the quantity lower than was the case in perfect competition. The consumer surplus is now much less, shown by the triangle AP_mB. This creates a loss to society shown by the triangle BCE; this is the deadweight loss.

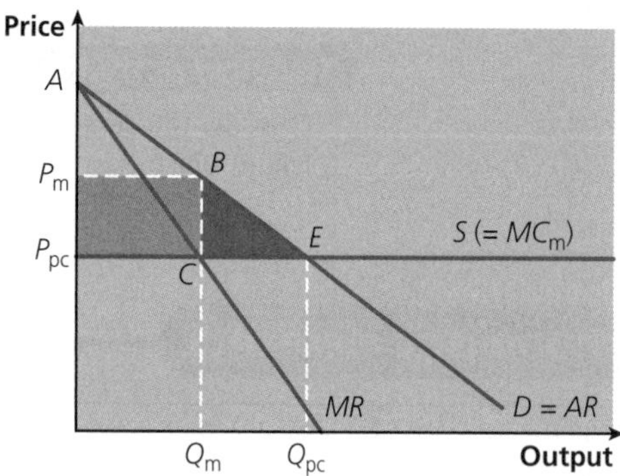

Figure 1 Comparing perfect competition and monopoly

Now test yourself

2 What is meant by a 'deadweight loss'?

Answer on p.157

Tested

Additional policies to correct market failure

Regulation

Revised

Topic 3 in the AS syllabus considers a number of ways that a government could intervene in a market, such as through taxes and subsidies; another way that a government could intervene is through **regulations**. For example, in some countries a government may establish regulations to control monopolies; if a firm has too much monopoly power in a market, it can be referred to a commission (a body which can look into a monopoly situation) which can investigate whether the monopoly is acting against the public interest. Regulations could also exist in relation to health and safety and consumer protection.

regulations: these cover a variety of legal and other rules which apply to firms in different circumstances

Policies towards income and wealth redistribution

Revised

Table 1 above indicates that another market failure is the fact that there is often a degree of inequality in the distribution of income and wealth in an economy. A government may, therefore, decide to intervene in an attempt to bring about a more equitable distribution of income and wealth.

Income tax, for example, could be used to redistribute income because an income tax is likely to be progressive, i.e. a higher income tax rate can be charged to those earning high incomes so that they pay not only more in tax but also a higher proportion of their income.

A **negative income tax** can also be used to redistribute income. This involves people on low incomes receiving money from a government instead of paying income tax to it.

negative income tax: the payment of money to those people on low incomes instead of taking part of their income from them through income tax

Expert tip

Candidates sometimes confuse an income tax and a negative income tax in their examination answers. An income tax involves taking money from people, whereas a negative income tax involves giving money to people.

Sometimes a government will provide **universal benefits** to people that do not take into account their need, but a government could also decide to prioritise the provision of benefits to those people who are less well off through **means tested benefits**. An example of a means tested benefit would be **tax credits**, which are paid to those people who have children or who have a job that pays a very low wage.

A potential problem of means tested benefits is that as people receive money in the form of benefits, they may no longer be entitled to as much support as was the case before. This gives rise to what has been termed the **poverty trap**.

A government may also decide to try to bring about a more equitable distribution of wealth, as well as income. Examples of taxes that can achieve this objective include inheritance tax and capital gains tax.

universal benefits: benefits that are provided to everyone who is entitled to them without taking into account the income of those people

means tested benefits: benefits that are provided to those people entitled to them after taking into account their income and, therefore, their need for the benefits

tax credits: a form of benefit that is paid to people on low incomes to boost their income and raise their standard of living

poverty trap: the situation which occurs when a person receives benefits, increasing income, but which then means the person is no longer entitled to receive as much as was the case before

Now test yourself

3 Explain what is meant by a 'progressive tax'.

4 What is meant by a 'poverty trap'?

Answers on p.157

Tested

Revision activity

Research how one country of your choice attempts to bring about a more equitable distribution of wealth and income.

Objectives of government microeconomic policy

Efficiency

Revised

One objective of government microeconomic policy is the achievement of efficiency. This would involve the achievement of both productive and allocative efficiency. The attainment of such efficiency would ensure that the scarce resources in an economy were allocated in the best possible way.

Equity

Revised

Another objective of government microeconomic policy is the achievement of equity. This can be seen in terms of government policies to bring about a fairer and more equitable distribution of income and wealth.

Effectiveness of government policies

Topic 3 in the AS syllabus and this topic have indicated a number of different ways in which a government can intervene to reduce the extent of market failure. The effectiveness of government policies, however, will depend on a number of factors, including the following:

- information — a government's policy will only be effective if it has all the necessary information, but this isn't always possible; for example, it is not easy to place a monetary value on a negative externality, such as pollution
- incentives — a government may decide to use a progressive income tax to bring about a more equitable distribution of income, but if the top rate of tax is very high, there may be a disincentive for the higher paid to work as much; some workers may even decide to leave the country and seek employment elsewhere

It is possible to consider the possibility of government failure where a government intervenes to correct market failure but, as a result of doing so, creates other distortions or imperfections in the market.

government failure: a situation where government intervention to correct market failure does not actually improve the level of economic efficiency; it is possible that such intervention may even reduce the efficiency of the allocation of scarce resources in the economy

Privatisation

As stated in Topic 3 in the AS syllabus, a government could decide to provide a particular service itself by providing it through a state-owned or nationalised industry.

However, a nationalised industry may not always be as efficient as one operating in the private sector, and so a government may decide to privatise an industry by transferring ownership from the public to the private sector.

The term **privatisation** can also apply to a number of other government initiatives, including **deregulation** and **contracting out**.

privatisation: the transfer of the ownership of an industry from the state or public sector to the private sector

deregulation: the reduction in the number of regulations, rules and laws that operate in an industry

contracting out: the transfer of responsibility for the provision of a service from the public to the private sector

Expert tip

Candidates need to understand that in an examination question on privatisation, it would be appropriate to include references to both deregulation and contracting out in their answers.

Deregulation refers to the process of reducing the regulations, laws and rules which can apply in an industry. When these are removed, it usually allows for a greater degree of competition to take place, which, so it is argued, should lead to a greater degree of efficiency in the industry.

Contracting out is another form of privatisation; this is where a service that was originally provided by an enterprise in the public or state sector is now provided by a firm in the private sector. This, again, should lead to a greater degree of efficiency.

Measures such as privatisation, deregulation and anything that leads to the promotion of competition can be regarded as **supply-side** measures, i.e. a government attempts to bring about change to improve efficiency in an economy by taking action on the supply, rather than on the demand, side.

supply-side economics: the approach to change in an economy that puts the focus on the supply side, rather than the demand side, e.g. privatisation, deregulation and contracting out

Now test yourself

5 Distinguish between privatisation and deregulation.

Answer on p.157

Tested

Revision activity

To what extent do the different forms of privatisation and deregulation exist in your country?

11 Theory and measurement in the macroeconomy

National income statistics

The different forms of the statistics

Revised

National income statistics actually involve a variety of different statistics. National income is often used as a generic term, but there are three different forms of the statistics — gross domestic product, gross national product and net national product.

national income: a general term for the total income of an economy over a particular period of time. More precisely, it refers to net national product (defined on page 115)

Gross domestic product

First, there is **gross domestic product (GDP)**. This refers to all that is produced within the geographical boundaries of a particular country. It does not matter whether the productive assets are owned locally or are foreign owned. There are three different ways of measuring the value of a country's GDP — the output method, the income method and the expenditure method. All the different methods, however, will produce the same figure because they all measure the flow of income in an economy over a particular period of time.

gross domestic product: the total value of all that has been produced over a given period of time within the geographical boundaries of a country

net domestic product: the gross domestic product of a country minus depreciation or capital consumption (this is the wear and tear of capital equipment over time, leading to a fall in its value)

Gross national product

Second, there is **gross national product (GNP)**. This is calculated by adding **net property income from abroad** to the figure for gross domestic product. The net property income from abroad takes into account the total interest payments, profits and dividends, both coming into, and leaving, a country. Generally, the figure for net property income from abroad tends to be positive for developed countries and negative for developing countries.

gross national product: the gross domestic product of a country plus net property income from abroad

net property income from abroad: the interest and profits on foreign investments. It refers to the total interest, profits and dividends received by the residents of one country on their foreign investments, minus the total interest, profits and dividends paid to foreign residents on their investments in this particular country

Net national product

Third, there is **net national product**. This is calculated by taking away the value of **capital depreciation** from the gross national product. This is done to take into account the money that will need to be spent on replacing machinery and equipment that has worn out during the course of the year.

net national product: the gross national product of a country minus depreciation or capital consumption

depreciation (of capital): the amount of capital that is needed to replace equipment that has depreciated, i.e. worn out, over a year

The use of national income statistics

Revised

National income statistics are used as measures of economic growth and living standards.

Gross domestic product is the value of everything that has been produced in a particular economy over a given period of time, usually a year. It is therefore the main statistic used in many countries as a measure of economic growth.

Gross national product gives a clear indication of the total spending power in a particular economy over a given period of time, usually a year. It is therefore the main statistic used in many countries as a measure of the standard of living.

Now test yourself

1 Distinguish between gross domestic product and gross national product.
2 Explain what is meant by 'depreciation'.

Answers on p.157

Tested

GDP deflator

It has already been pointed out that it is important to distinguish between nominal value and real value. If a country is experiencing inflation, the value of its GDP will rise, but this increase could be due solely to the rise in prices, i.e. there may not have been a real increase in value if the effect of inflation is eliminated from the figures. This is a limitation of any data that is expressed **at current prices**.

This is why economists usually produce national income statistics **at constant prices** so that changes in real output can be identified rather than changes in value that are purely due to the inflation that exists in a country.

The **GDP deflator** is a price index that is used to convert the figures into real GDP. It measures the prices of products produced in a country and not the prices of products consumed. It therefore includes the value not just of consumer products but also of the capital used in the production of the products. It includes the prices of exports, but not the prices of imports.

GDP deflator: a ratio of price indices that is used in national income statistics to take away the effect of price changes so that the figures can be seen as representing real changes in output

at current prices: data which is expressed in terms of the prices of a particular year, i.e. they have not been corrected to take account of inflation

at constant prices: data which has been adjusted to take into account the effects of inflation

Now test yourself

3 Explain the purpose of a GDP deflator.

Answer on p.157

Tested

Expert tip

It is important that you demonstrate a clear understanding of the difference between a real change in the value of a country's output, after taking into account the effect of inflation, and a change in the value of a country's output that is purely due to inflation in that economy.

Comparison of economic growth rates

The main method used to compare economic growth rates over time and between countries is changes in real GDP. There are, however, a number of potential problems in using real GDP data, as Table 1 indicates.

Table 1 Problems in using real GDP to compare living standards

Problem	Explanation
The hidden, informal or underground economy	These terms refer to economic activity that is not declared and so will not be included in the official GDP data, e.g. it may be illegal.
The level of literacy	The literacy rate can vary a great deal between countries and those countries with a relatively low rate of literacy may not produce very accurate data.
Non-marketed goods and services	The GDP data is likely to be reasonably accurate when the vast majority of economic output is recorded through market transactions, but in many economies there is a lot of economic activity that is not marketed, i.e. there is not a price attached.
The difficulties of measuring government spending	In some countries, it can be difficult to measure spending by the government because it is not always easy to value the output of something that is not sold in a market, e.g. defence.
Sustainability	A country may have a relatively high rate of economic growth, but this will not necessarily be regarded as good if the needs of future generations are not sufficiently taken into account, i.e. the growth is not sustainable because natural resources may be depleted and an unacceptable level of pollution created.
Unequal distribution of income and wealth	Real GDP can be divided by a country's population to give an indication of the average standard of living, but this average may be misleading if there is an unequal distribution of the GDP.
The products produced	A country's real GDP may increase, indicating economic growth and a rise in living standards, but this will not necessarily be the case, e.g. if a substantial proportion of the increase in GDP is the result of an increase in weapons.
The contrast between increases in consumer goods and increases in capital goods	A rise in living standards will come about as a result of an increase in consumer goods available, but in the short run there may be an increase in the production of capital goods which will eventually help to make this possible.
The quantity and quality of output	GDP statistics measure the quantity of a country's output, but they do not take into account the quality of that output.
The effect of exchange rate changes	When comparing standards of living between people in different countries, it is necessary to take into account the effect of changes in the exchange rates between countries which would otherwise distort any comparison; economists achieve this through the use of purchasing power parities.
Working hours and working conditions	The GDP data records the quantity of output produced in different countries, but they do not take into account the way in which that output is produced, e.g. a country's output may have increased substantially, but this may have been at a cost of a significant increase in working hours and a deterioration in working conditions.
Political freedom	Although not directly an economic example, it could be argued that political freedoms and civil/human rights also need to be taken into account when assessing the quality of life in different parts of the world.

Other indicators of living standards and economic development

As stated above, differences in real GDP are the most established way of comparing standards of living in different countries, but they are not the only method used to make such comparisons. Other approaches include the following composite measures:

- **Net Economic Welfare (NEW)**, also known as **Measurable Economic Welfare (MEW)** — this approach includes such elements as leisure hours, crime rates and levels of pollution.
- **Human Development Index** — this takes into account gross national income per head (at **purchasing power parities** in US$), life expectancy and years of schooling.
- **Human Poverty Index** — this approach measures longevity, adult literacy and deprivation; in 2010, it was replaced by the Multidimensional Poverty Index.
- **Multidimensional Poverty Index** — like the Human Poverty Index, which it has replaced, this focuses on the extent of deprivation in different countries.

Now test yourself

4 What is meant by the term 'sustainability'?

Answer on p.157

Tested

Net Economic Welfare (or Measurable Economic Welfare): a broader measure of economic welfare than real GDP per capita; it takes into account such aspects as the value of childcare and looking after the sick and elderly, any depletion of natural resources and changes in the natural environment

Human Development Index: a composite measure that combines life expectancy, average income in the form of gross national income per capita (PPP US$) and years of schooling

Human Poverty Index: this was developed by the United Nations to complement the Human Development Index; it puts more of a focus on the extent of deprivation in different countries

Multidimensional Poverty Index: replaced the Human Poverty Index in 2010; like its predecessor, it focuses on the extent of deprivation in different countries. It is made up of three dimensions and ten indicators

distribution of income: the degree to which income in a country is evenly distributed

Expert tip

Candidates should note that instead of the usual methods to measure income, i.e. GDP per capita, the Human Development Index was revised in 2010 and uses gross national income per capita.

Revision activity

Consider some of the main reasons why it is difficult to compare the standard of living and the quality of life in different countries.

The Multidimensional Poverty Index uses ten indicators in three categories, or dimensions as they are called, as Table 2 indicates.

Table 2 The Multidimensional Poverty Index

Dimension	Indicators
Health	• Child mortality • Nutrition
Education	• Years of schooling • Child school attendance
Living standards	• Electricity • Sanitation • Drinking water • Type of floor • Type of cooking fuel • Ownership of assets

Now test yourself

5 Name the ten indicators of the Multidimensional Poverty Index.

Answer on p.158

Tested

Expert tip

In examination questions on the comparison of living standards and economic development in different countries, it would be helpful if candidates brought in as many of the various indicators as possible into their answers.

Economists in the past have tended to focus on the concept of standard of living, especially when GDP per capita was the main measure. There has, however, been greater use of the concept of **quality of life** in recent years, reflecting the use of these composite measures. The concept of quality of life is a broader concept than standard of living and takes into account a wider range of criteria.

quality of life: a wider concept than the standard of living to compare living conditions in different countries; it could take into account such criteria as the number of doctors per thousand of population, the quality of drinking water and the average size of school classes

Expert tip

Candidates need to be clear about what is, and what is not, included in these various composite measures. For example, the quality of drinking water is *not* included in the Human Development Index, but *is* included in the Multidimensional Poverty Index.

The money supply

The **money supply** refers to the total amount of money in an economy at any one time. It is an important macroeconomic variable. It includes both broad money supply and narrow money supply.

money supply: the amount of money available to the general public and the banking system in an economy

Broad and narrow money supply

Revised

Different countries will have different definitions of the money supply, but a **broad money supply** will reflect the total purchasing power that is available in an economy at a particular time. It can often be termed M4 and would include the notes and coins plus all bank and building society deposits.

A **narrow money supply** will be mainly the cash that is available in an economy at a particular time. It can often be termed M0 and would include the notes and coins held by the general public, in cash machines and in balances that the financial institutions have with a country's central bank. This narrow money supply is also sometimes known as the **monetary base**.

broad money supply: a measure of the stock of money which reflects the total potential purchasing power in an economy

narrow money supply: a measure of the stock of money in an economy which is mainly cash

monetary base: the cash held by the general public and by the banking system, including the balances of the financial institutions with the central bank of the country. The monetary base acts as the basis for any expansion of bank lending in an economy

Government accounts

Revised

In each economy in the world, the government will produce its accounts in the form of a summary of its income and expenditure.

Government budget

In any economy, there will be one of three types of budget. First, there is a **balanced budget**.

In a balanced budget, the projected revenue, such as from taxation, is exactly equal to the government's planned expenditure. In this sense, where both sides of the budget are equal, it is neutral.

Second, there is a **budget surplus**.

In a budget surplus, the projected revenue is greater than the planned expenditure, i.e. less money is spent than is received. In such a situation, the government is taking more out of an economy than it is putting in and this is likely to be a deliberate policy to reduce the level of aggregate demand (known as deflation) in the economy, e.g. where there is a situation of high inflation.

Third, there is a **budget deficit**.

In a budget deficit, the projected revenue is less than the planned expenditure, i.e. more money is spent than is received. In such a situation, the government is putting more into an economy than it is taking out and this is likely to be a deliberate policy to increase the level of aggregate demand (known as reflation) in the economy, e.g. where there is a situation of high unemployment.

balanced budget: where projected revenue and planned government spending are equal

budget surplus: where projected revenue is greater than planned expenditure

budget deficit: where projected revenue is less than planned expenditure

Now test yourself

6 Explain what is meant by a 'budget deficit'.

Answer on p.158

Tested

Revision activity

Consider why it is important for a government to aim at achieving a balanced budget.

Deficit financing

If a government does have a budget deficit, it will need to think how it is going to finance that deficit. There are likely to be three possibilities.

- If the budget deficit is successful in stimulating the level of aggregate demand in the economy, this is likely to increase the revenue received from taxation and this will contribute towards financing the deficit.
- A country may have had a budget surplus in recent years, and the accumulated surpluses could be used to contribute towards financing the deficit.
- It is possible that both of these approaches will not bring in sufficient funds to finance the deficit and in this case the government will need to borrow money; this will lead to an increase in the **national debt**.

national debt: the total of all debt accumulated by a government

Expert tip

It is important that candidates are able to distinguish between a stock of money and a flow of money. A country's national debt is a stock of money that has been accumulated over many years. A budget deficit refers to a flow of money in one financial year. If a government is successful in reducing the size of a country's budget deficit in a particular year, the size of the country's national debt may still increase during the year.

Revision activity

Consider why the size of a country's national debt is important.

The circular flow of income

The **circular flow of income** refers to the flow of income around an economy. At any one time, there will be a number of **injections** into the economy and a number of **withdrawals** or **leakages** out of the economy.

circular flow of income: the flow of income around an economy, involving a mixture of injections and withdrawals or leakages

injection: spending which adds to the circular flow of income; this can come from investment, government expenditure and exports

leakage (or withdrawal): money which leaks out of the circular flow of income; this can be as a result of savings, taxation and money spent on imports

Expert tip

Candidates need to ensure that they understand, and can refer to, the different injections into, and the various leakages/withdrawals from, the circular flow of income.

Closed and open economies

Revised

A basic approach is to consider the circular flow of income in a closed economy.

In a **closed economy**, it is assumed that a country does not trade with any other countries in the world. If the circular flow of income is limited to the movement of incomes between households and firms, it is known as a 'two-sector economy'. If government is then added to the circular flow, it becomes a 'three-sector economy'.

A more realistic approach would be to consider the circular flow of income in an **open economy**.

> **closed economy:** an economy which does not trade with the rest of the world
>
> **open economy:** an economy which trades with the rest of the world

In an open economy, it is assumed that a country does trade with other countries in the world. The circular flow of income, therefore, involves four groups: households, firms, the government and the goods and services that are exported to, and imported from, other countries. This is why such an economy is known as a 'four-sector economy'.

The basis of aggregate demand in an economy is consumption expenditure by households and then the injections can be added to, and the withdrawals or leakages taken from, this expenditure, as can be seen in Table 3.

Now test yourself

7 Name the three injections into, and the three leakages or withdrawals out of, the circular flow of income.

Answer on p.158

Tested

Table 3 The circular flow of income in an open, or four-sector, economy

Injections	Withdrawals or leakages
Investment spending by private sector firms (*I*)	Savings (*S*)
Government spending (*G*)	Taxation (*T*)
Income from exports sold abroad (*X*)	Income spent on imports from abroad (*M*)

Revision activity

Contrast the circular flow of income in a two-sector (households and firms), a three-sector and a four-sector economy.

Keynesian and Monetarist schools

There are many different approaches to how the macroeconomy functions, but two economists have been very influential. They are **John Maynard Keynes** and **Milton Friedman**. The differences between the two approaches are many, but Table 4 offers a simplified comparison of these two distinct approaches to macroeconomics.

> **Keynesian:** an approach that is based on the views of the economist John Maynard Keynes (1883–1946)
>
> **Monetarist:** an approach that is based on the views of a number of economists, of which the most well known is Milton Friedman (1912–2006)

Table 4 Keynesian and Monetarist approaches

Keynesian	Monetarist
There is no guarantee that an economy, if left to market forces, would be able to achieve a full employment level of GDP; the reduction of unemployment is seen as the top priority in an economy.	The control of inflation is seen as the priority for a government; inflation is largely seen as the result of an excessive growth of the money supply in an economy.

(Continued)

(Continued)

Keynesian	Monetarist
It is therefore necessary for a government to intervene in an economy to influence the level of economic activity, e.g. by using a budget deficit to increase the level of aggregate demand in the economy.	It is therefore necessary for a government to intervene in an economy to control the rate of growth of the money supply. Attempts by a government to reduce unemployment through an increase in spending will only bring about a greater rate of inflation in the long run.
Markets do not easily clear and are slow to adjust, e.g. the labour market; this is why an economy can be in an equilibrium position below full employment, which is why a government needs to intervene to expand demand.	Markets do clear relatively easily and quickly and so it is appropriate to rely on market forces.
On the whole, fiscal policy is a more effective approach to demand management in an economy compared to monetary policy.	On the whole, monetary policy is a more effective approach to demand management in an economy compared to fiscal policy.
The rate of interest in an economy is determined by the liquidity preference theory (see page 129).	The rate of interest in an economy is determined by the loanable funds theory (see page 130).

Revision activity

Distinguish between Keynesian and Monetarist approaches to the management of an economy.

The aggregate expenditure function

Aggregate expenditure (*AE*), or demand, refers to the total demand for, and expenditure on, all that is produced in an economy. It can be represented in the following way:

$$AD = C + I + G + X - M$$

aggregate expenditure (or aggregate demand): the total demand for, and expenditure on, goods and services in an economy

Now test yourself

8 How is aggregate expenditure, or aggregate demand, usually represented?

Answer on p.158

Tested

Meaning, components of *AE* and their determinants

Revised

Consumption

Consumption refers to the expenditure by households in an economy over a period of time. The main influence on consumption is the level of disposable income in an economy and the consumption function shows the relationship between income and consumption.

The proportion of income that is spent on consumption can be measured in two ways. First, there is the **average propensity to consume**.

The average propensity to consume refers to the average proportion of income that is actually spent on buying goods and services in an economy. The proportion of income that is not spent is saved and so it is also possible to refer to the average propensity to save.

It is possible that consumption actually exceeds income and so would need to be financed by using past savings. This is known as **dissaving**.

Saving is generally regarded as a good thing, for an individual, providing the person with the opportunity to buy something in the future, but it is also possible to view it in a negative way in terms of a society because it is a leakage or withdrawal from

Revision activity

Consider whether saving is always a good thing for an individual and for an economy.

the circular flow of income in an economy and so could contribute to a fall in national income. This contradiction is known as the **paradox of thrift**.

consumption: the spending by consumers in an economy over a period of time

average propensity to consume: the proportion of income that is spent

dissaving: a situation that can occur when consumption exceeds income and so people have to rely on savings that have been accumulated in the past

saving: the amount of disposable income that is not spent on consumption

paradox of thrift: the contradiction between the potential advantages and the potential disadvantages of saving in an economy

Expert tip

Candidates need to demonstrate they understand what is meant by the *paradox of thrift*. Saving is generally regarded as a good thing to do in an economy, but it is important to recognise that there may be possible disadvantages to saving, given that it constitutes a leakage or withdrawal from the circular flow of income.

Second, there is the **marginal propensity to consume**. Whereas the average propensity to consume was concerned with a given income, the marginal propensity to consume is concerned with a change in income and, in particular, with the proportion of that extra income that is spent. The proportion of the extra income that is not spent is saved and so it is possible to refer to the marginal propensity to save.

Although the main influence on consumption is the level of disposable income in an economy, there are other possible determinants. These include:

- the distribution of income and wealth
- the rate of interest
- the availability of credit
- expectations about future economic prospects

marginal propensity to consume: the proportion of an increase in income that is spent

Investment

Investment refers to the expenditure by firms in an economy over a period of time, such as expenditure on factories, machinery and equipment. There are many influences on the investment decisions of firms, but the main determinants include:

- the rate of interest
- changes in technology
- the cost of capital goods
- changes in consumer demand
- expectations about future economic prospects
- government policies, such as in relation to taxes and subsidies

investment: the spending by firms in an economy over a period of time

Government spending

This can include government spending on the wages and salaries of people who work in the public sector and on investment projects, such as a new road. There are many influences on the spending decisions of a government, but the main determinants include:

- government policies on particular aspects of society
- tax revenue
- demographic changes

Net exports

The determinants of net exports can include the following:

- a country's GDP
- the GDP of other countries
- the relative prices of a country's exports
- the quality/reliability/reputation of a country's exports
- exchange rate movements

Income determination

Revised

The *AE*–income approach

The level of income in an economy is determined at the point where aggregate expenditure is equal to output. This can be shown in Figure 1 using the *AE*–income approach. Such a diagram can also be known as a 45-degree diagram. The economy is in equilibrium where *AE* crosses the 45-degree line, at Y_e. Money GDP is shown on the horizontal axis (indicated by *Y*) and aggregate expenditure on the vertical axis (indicated by *E*).

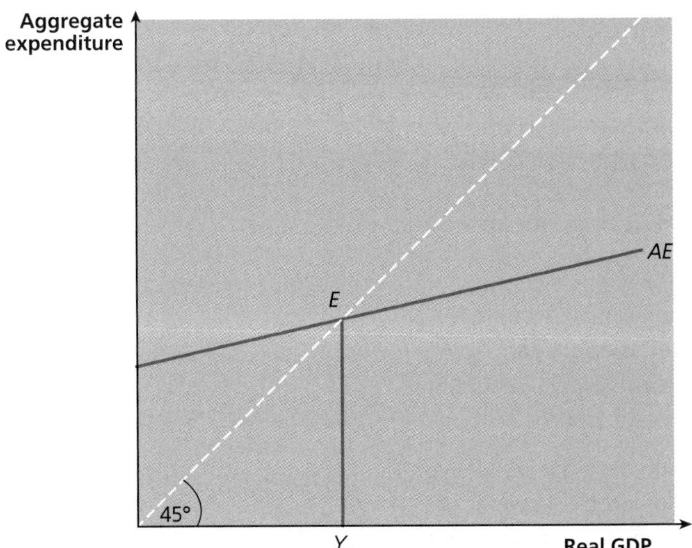

Figure 1 A Keynesian 45-degree diagram

The withdrawal/injection approach

Another way of showing equilibrium income in an economy is through the withdrawal/injection approach. For income to be in equilibrium in an economy, the injections into the circular flow of income need to be equal to the withdrawals from the circular flow of income. This can be seen in Figure 2 where the injections (*I*, *G* and *X*) are equal to the withdrawals (*S*, *T* and *M*) at the Y_e level of income.

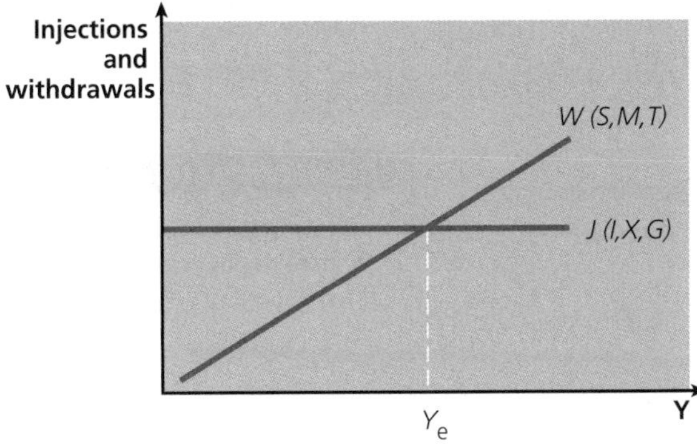

Figure 2 Equilibrium using the withdrawal/injection approach

Inflationary and deflationary gaps

Revised

Inflationary gap

It must be understood that an equilibrium level of income in an economy may not necessarily be at the full employment level of income. An **inflationary gap** shows a situation where equilibrium income is greater than the full employment equilibrium, i.e. aggregate demand in an economy is greater than aggregate supply.

This can be seen in Figure 3. Equilibrium income is at Y_e where the withdrawals are equal to the injections. The full employment level of income, however, is shown by Y_f. The vertical distance between *W* and *J* at this point shows the inflationary gap in the economy.

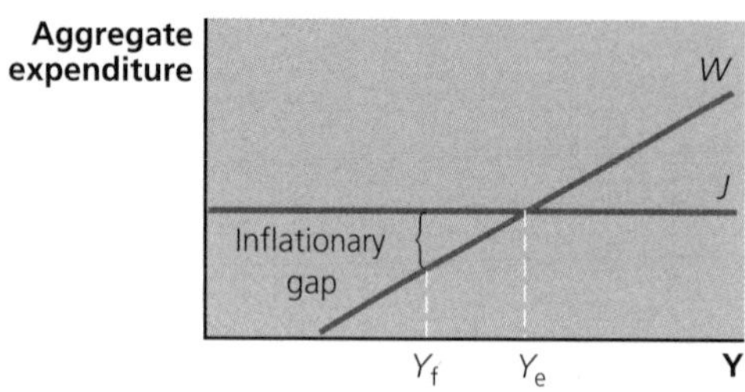

Figure 3 An inflationary gap

inflationary gap: a situation where the level of aggregate demand in an economy is greater than the aggregate supply at full employment, causing a rise in the general level of prices in the economy

Deflationary gap

Whereas an inflationary gap shows a situation where equilibrium income is greater than the full employment level of income, a **deflationary gap** shows a situation where equilibrium income is less than the full employment equilibrium, i.e. aggregate demand in an economy is less than aggregate supply.

This can be seen in Figure 4. Equilibrium income is at Y_e where the withdrawals are equal to the injections. The full employment level of income, however, is shown by Y_f. The vertical distance between *W* and *J* at this point shows the deflationary gap in the economy.

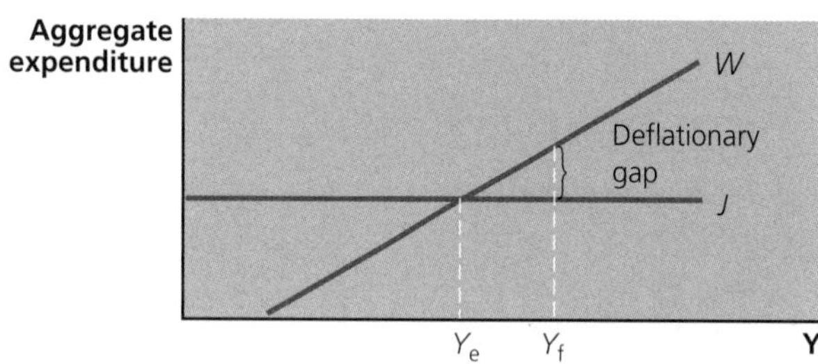

Figure 4 A deflationary gap

It should be noted that the terms 'inflationary gap' and 'deflationary gap' can also be referred to as an **output gap**.

deflationary gap: a situation where the level of aggregate demand in an economy is less than the aggregate supply at full employment, causing unemployment in the economy

output gap: the difference between the actual output and the potential output of an economy

Revision activity

Distinguish between an inflationary gap and a deflationary gap.

The multiplier

Revised

The **multiplier** is an important concept in the determination of the level of income in an economy. It measures the extent to which an increase in an injection into the circular flow of income brings about a magnified effect on the level of income. An increase in injections, however, is also likely to have an effect on the withdrawals out of the circular flow of income in an economy. Each successive increase in aggregate demand will therefore become progressively less.

multiplier: the amount by which an increase in an injection into the circular flow of income will bring about an increase of total income in an economy

Expert tip

Even if a particular examination question does not make explicit reference to the concept of the multiplier, this does not mean that it should not be included in answers. If a question is concerned with the determination of the level of income in an economy, candidates should assume that they should refer to the multiplier in their answers.

The size of an economy's multiplier will depend on how many sectors are involved, as Table 5 shows.

Table 5 The calculation of the size of the multiplier in an economy

Type of economy	Calculation
Two-sector economy (households and firms)	$\frac{1}{\text{marginal propensity to save}}$ or $\left[\frac{1}{MPS}\right]$
Three-sector economy (households, firms and government)	$\frac{1}{\text{marginal propensity to save + marginal rate of taxation}}$ or $\left[\frac{1}{MPS + MRT}\right]$
Four-sector economy (households, firms, government and foreign trade)	$\frac{1}{\text{marginal propensity to save + marginal rate of taxation + marginal propensity to import}}$ or $\left[\frac{1}{MPS + MRT + MPM}\right]$

Another way of expressing the multiplier is

$$\frac{1}{\text{marginal propensity to withdraw}}$$

The operation of the multiplier can be seen in Figure 5. The diagram shows the effect of an increase in injections into the circular flow of income in an economy; this can be seen by the vertical distance between J and J_1. The effect of this has been to increase national income from Y_1 to Y_2. The size of the multiplier (denoted by the symbol k) can be calculated by dividing the change in Y by the change in J.

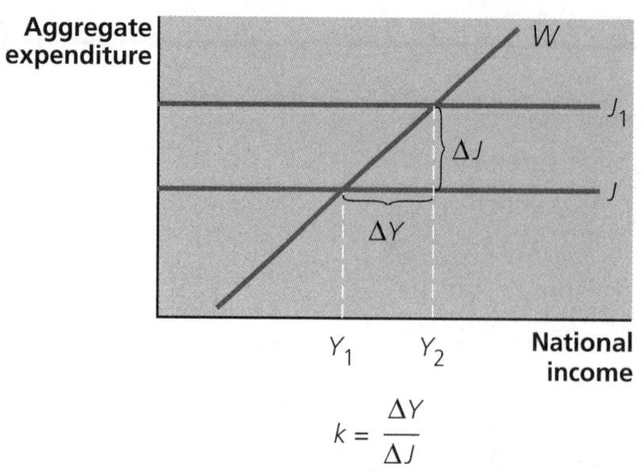

$$k = \frac{\Delta Y}{\Delta J}$$

Figure 5 The effect of an increase in injections into the circular flow of income

Now test yourself

9 Explain what is meant by the term 'multiplier'.

Answer on p.158

Tested

Autonomous and induced investment, and the accelerator

Revised

It is important to distinguish between two types of capital investment — autonomous and induced.

Autonomous investment

Autonomous investment refers to expenditure on capital investment that is not the result of any changes in the level of national income in an economy, i.e. it is independent of any such changes. An increase or decrease in autonomous investment can be shown in a diagram by the aggregate expenditure line shifting upwards or downwards.

autonomous investment: capital investment that is not related to changes in the level of national income in an economy

Induced investment

Whereas autonomous investment refers to expenditure on capital equipment that is unrelated to changes in income in an economy, **induced investment** refers to such expenditure that is directly related to changes in income. For example, a rise in national income will bring about an increase in induced investment. Induced investment is an important part of the accelerator theory of investment.

Now test yourself

10 Distinguish between autonomous and induced investment.

Answer on p.158

Tested

induced investment: capital investment that is related to changes in the level of national income in an economy

The accelerator

The concept of the **accelerator** is based on the link between changes in the level of national income in an economy and changes in induced investment. It states that investment is a function of a change in national income. It also assumes a fixed **capital:output ratio**.

It is important to understand that the accelerator is concerned with the relationship between investment and the rate of change of output, i.e. it is not the level of output that is important, but the rate of change of that output.

accelerator: a way of calculating the effect of a change in national income on investment in an economy

capital:output ratio: a way of measuring the amount of capital employed in the production of a given level of output

Expert tip

Candidates sometimes confuse the multiplier and the accelerator; it is important to be able to clearly distinguish between them. The multiplier shows the effect of a change in an injection, or in a withdrawal, on the level of national income in an economy; the accelerator, on the other hand, shows the effect of a change in the level of national income in an economy on the induced investment.

Revision activity

Distinguish between the multiplier and the accelerator.

Sources of money supply and the quantity theory of money

Sources of money supply

Revised

There are a number of different sources of money in an open economy.

Commercial banks/credit creation

Financial institutions are able to create 'new' money as a result of additional cash deposits. They know from experience that only a certain proportion of customers will want to take out money at any particular time; this means that a large proportion of money deposited can be loaned to people. The ratio of new money created to the initial money deposited is known as the **credit multiplier**.

credit creation: the process by which financial institutions make loans through what is known as fractional reserve banking, i.e. the requirement that such institutions only need to hold a certain percentage of their total liabilities, say 10%, in the form of cash reserves. The financial institutions are then able to expand their lending by a multiple of any new deposits received; this is known as the credit creation multiplier

credit multiplier: the relationship between new deposits created as a result of additional cash deposits

Revision activity

What is meant by 'credit creation'?

Expert tip

Despite financial institutions having a great deal of experience of knowing how much to lend, the decision of many financial institutions to lend out too much money was a major cause of the financial crisis in 2007–2008. This created a lack of confidence in financial institutions, some of which collapsed.

Central bank

A **central bank** may wish to control the ability of commercial banks to lend money, such as through open market operations. This is the process of buying or selling government securities, i.e. bonds and/or shares that are issued by the government. If a central bank wants to encourage bank lending, it will buy government securities.

This process of the central bank buying government securities, such as bills and bonds, is known as **quantitative easing**. These securities are bought by the central bank, leading to an increase in bank deposits, and this creates more liquidity in the system. In some countries, it is known as credit easing.

central bank: the main bank in a country that is responsible for oversight of the banking system

quantitative easing: the process by which a government buys securities to create more liquidity in the financial system

Now test yourself

11 Explain what is meant by quantitative easing.

Answer on p.158

Tested

Expert tip

Candidates should understand that quantitative easing has been used by a number of countries, including the USA and the UK, to stimulate economic activity in countries that have been suffering from recession since the credit crunch of 2007–08.

Deficit financing

Deficit financing is discussed above under 'Government accounts' on page 118. As pointed out, a government may need to borrow in order to finance a budget deficit and if money is borrowed from the commercial banks or the central bank, this will have the effect of increasing the money supply. This is because the liquid assets of the banks will be increased and this will increase their ability to lend.

Total currency flow

The **total currency flow** is a part of a country's balance of payments and shows the total inflow and outflow of money resulting from a country's international transactions with the rest of the world. If the flow is positive, it is likely to increase the foreign exchange reserves of a country. This net inflow of money into a country will have the effect of increasing its money supply.

total currency flow: an element of the balance of payments that refers to the total inflow or outflow of money which results from a country's international transactions with other countries

The quantity theory of money

Revised

The **quantity theory of money** shows the relationship between the money supply, the general price level and the level of output in an economy. It is usually expressed in terms of $MV = PT$ where M is the quantity of money, V is the velocity of circulation, P is the general price level and T is the number of transactions. V and T are assumed to be constant over a period of time because it is unlikely that there is going to be a great deal of difference in the velocity of circulation or in the number of transactions in an economy from one year to the next. In this case, M and P are directly linked. This means that if the money supply rises, people will have access to more funds, giving them greater purchasing power, and as a result of this, the general level of prices in the economy will rise, i.e. a situation of inflation will exist.

The theory has been widely discussed over the years, especially in relation to whether it is correct to assume that V and T are constant over a period of time. It has also been criticised for being less of a theory and more of an identity that is necessarily true, i.e. MV represents total spending in an economy and PT represents the total money received for the goods and services. It is the same situation, but looked at in different ways.

Now test yourself

12 How is the quantity theory of money usually stated?

Answer on p.158

Tested

quantity theory of money: a theory which links the quantity of money in circulation in an economy with the rate of inflation. It is stated as $MV = PT$ where M is the quantity of money, V is the velocity of circulation, P is the general price level and T is the number of transactions in an economy

Revision activity

How useful is the quantity theory of money as an explanation of inflation in an economy?

The demand for money

The demand for money in an economy, and the determination of interest rates, can be analysed through two alternative approaches, the liquidity preference theory and the loanable funds theory.

The liquidity preference theory

Revised

The Keynesian approach to the demand for money and the determination of interest rates is based on three motives.

First, there is a **transactions demand for money**. This is where money is used to pay for everyday purchases. This is an **active balance** and is interest inelastic, i.e. this demand for money does not respond to changes in interest rates.

liquidity preference theory: the Keynesian theory of interest rate determination, based on three motives for holding money — the transactions motive, the precautionary motive and the speculative motive

transactions demand for money: money that is required to pay for everyday purchases. It is an active balance and is interest inelastic

active balances: money which is flowing through the economy, underpinning the transactions and precautionary motives for holding money

Second, there is the **precautionary demand for money**. This is where money is used to pay for unexpected expenses. Like the transactions demand for money, it is an active balance and is interest inelastic.

precautionary demand for money: money that is required to pay for unexpected expenses. It is an active balance and is interest inelastic

Third, there is the **speculative demand for money**. This is where money is used to buy government bonds. Unlike the transactions and precautionary demand for money, it is regarded as an **idle balance** and one that is interest elastic. An important influence on the demand for a bond is the **yield**, which is the annual income obtained from the bond as a proportion of its current market price. The price of government bonds and the rate of interest will move in opposite directions because if the interest rate is high, this will reduce the desire to hold money. On the other hand, if the interest rate is low, there will be less of an incentive to switch out of money into other assets.

speculative demand for money: money that is required to buy government bonds. It is an idle balance and is interest elastic

idle balances: money which is withdrawn from the circular flow of money in an economy, underpinning the speculative motive for holding money

yield: the annual income obtained from a bond or a share as a proportion of its current market price

Another distinctive feature of this demand for money, unlike the other two motives, is that the demand curve is downward sloping. In fact, at low rates of interest, the liquidity preference (or demand) curve becomes horizontal, indicating that a change in the money supply will have no effect on the rate of interest. At this point, the demand for money is perfectly elastic. This is known as the **liquidity trap**.

A shift of the money supply to the right, e.g. from MS_0 to MS_1, would normally lead to a lowering of the rate of interest (see Figure 6). However, when there is a liquidity trap, an increase in the money supply does not affect the interest rate which beyond MS_0 remains at r_0.

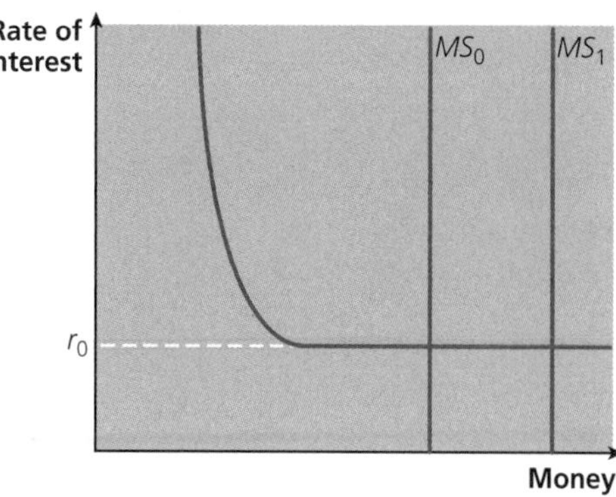

Figure 6 The liquidity trap

liquidity trap: a situation at low rates of interest when changes in the money supply will have no effect on the rate of interest and where the demand for money is perfectly elastic

The loanable funds theory

Revised

An alternative approach to the liquidity preference theory of explaining the demand for money and the determination of interest rates is the **loanable funds theory**. This states that the rate of interest is determined by the demand for, and the supply of, loanable funds in financial markets, i.e. the rate of interest is a price and, just like any other price in an economy, it is determined by the interaction of the demand for, and the supply of, loanable funds, i.e. the supply of funds from savings and the demand for funds for investment.

loanable funds theory: the idea that interest rates are determined by the demand for, and the supply of, loanable funds in financial markets

The demand for loanable funds comes from:

- firms wanting to invest
- households wanting to buy consumer products
- a government aiming to fund a budget deficit

The demand curve for loanable funds slopes down from left to right.

The supply of loanable funds comes from:

- savings

The supply curve for loanable funds slopes up from left to right. Figure 7 shows how the rate of interest is determined by the demand for, and the supply of, loanable funds. A rate of interest of *R* is established for a quantity *Q* of funds.

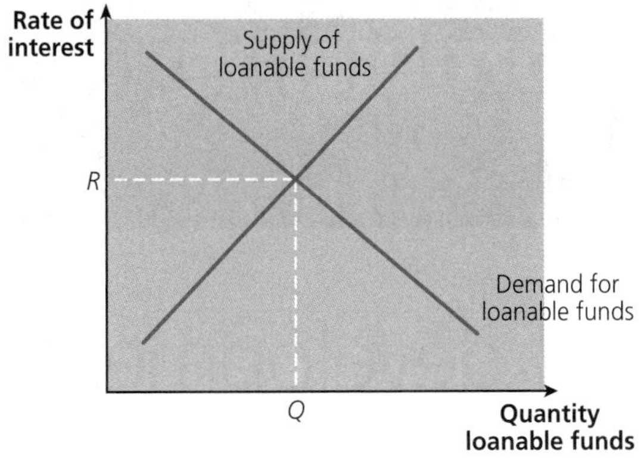

Figure 7 The loanable funds theory

The rate of interest will be determined at the point where demand and supply are equal.

Revision activity

Distinguish between the liquidity preference and the loanable funds theories.

12 Macroeconomic problems

Economic growth and development

Economic growth

Revised

Economic growth is defined as the increase in national output of a country over a period of time. It is usually measured in terms of a change in gross domestic product. It is important to distinguish between two types of economic growth in national output: actual growth and potential growth.

economic growth: an increase in the national output of an economy over a period of time, usually measured through changes in gross domestic product

Now test yourself

1 Define the term 'economic growth'.

Answer on p.158

Tested

Actual versus potential growth in national output

Economic growth in an economy can come about by using the existing factors of production more effectively, such as by reducing the number of people unemployed. This can be shown by a movement from *within* a country's production possibility curve or frontier to a position *on* the curve or frontier. This is known as **actual growth** in the national output of an economy.

In addition to a movement along a production possibility curve or frontier, it is also possible for the curve or frontier to shift outwards. This would be due to an increase in the quantity of the factors of production available in an economy and/or an increase in the quality of the factors of production available in an economy. This is known as **potential growth** in the national output of an economy.

actual growth in national output: a movement from within the production possibility frontier of an economy to a position on the frontier, resulting from the better utilisation of the existing factors of production

potential growth in national output: a shift outwards of the production possibility frontier, resulting from a greater quantity and/or quality of factors of production in an economy

This distinction between actual growth and potential growth of national output can be seen in Figure 1. The movement from *X*, within the production possibility curve, to *Y*, on PPC_1, shows actual growth. The movement from *Y* to *Z*, on PPC_2, shows potential growth.

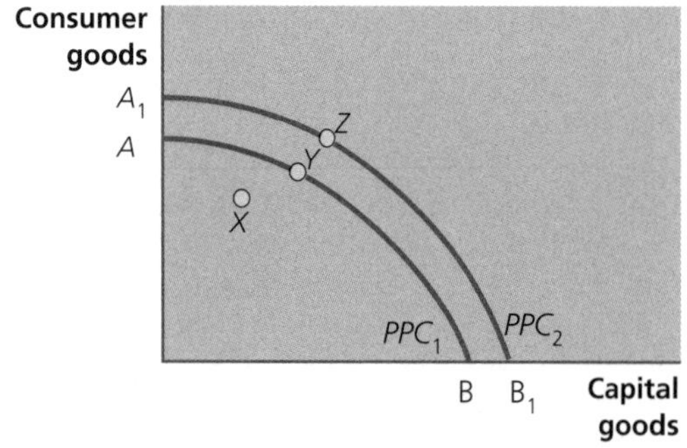

Figure 1 Production possibility curves

Now test yourself

2 Distinguish between actual growth and potential growth.

Answer on p.158

Tested

Expert tip

It is important to make sure that you understand this distinction between actual growth and potential growth, and the distinction between a movement from inside a production possibility curve to a position on a production possibility curve and an actual shift outwards of the whole curve.

Factors contributing to economic growth

Economic growth in an economy can be brought about by a number of factors, including the following:

- an increase in the number of workers
- an improvement in the quality of labour, e.g. through acquiring new skills leading to a higher level of productivity
- a greater commitment to research and development, both in terms of invention, i.e. the discovery of new products and new methods of production, and innovation, i.e. the bringing of these inventions to the marketplace
- an improvement in the state of technology
- investment in capital stock
- a move towards more capital-intensive production
- increased mobility and flexibility of factors of production
- a more efficient allocation of resources
- development of new markets to export to
- a reduction in taxes on company profits to allow firms to have more funds to finance investment
- an upturn in the **trade** (or **business) cycle**

trade (business) cycle: the fluctuations in the national output of a country, involving a succession of stages or phases, including boom, recession, slump and recovery

Now test yourself

3 Explain what is meant by a 'trade/business cycle'.

Answer on p.158

Tested

Expert tip

Don't forget that economic growth is not only concerned with the quantity of the factors of production used in the production process, but also with the quality of these economic resources.

Costs and benefits of growth

It is clear that economic growth can have benefits for a country, but it is also important to take into account that there can be costs of growth. These costs and benefits of economic growth can be seen in Table 1.

Expert tip

If an examination question asks for a discussion of the concept of economic growth, you should remember to include a consideration of both the benefits and the costs of growth for an economy.

Revision activity

Consider whether it is possible for a country to have too high a rate of economic growth.

Table 1 The benefits and costs of economic growth

Benefits	Costs
• Economic growth will lead to an increase in the standard of living of a country resulting from the greater number of goods and services produced in the economy. • An economy that is growing shows that the economy is doing well; this greater confidence in the economic prospects of the future can encourage investment. • Economic growth is likely to lead to a decrease in the level of unemployment in the country, although this will depend on the extent to which the extra output is produced through labour-intensive or capital-intensive methods of production. (Labour-intensive production refers to a process of production with a relatively high proportion of labour inputs, compared to other inputs, whereas capital-intensive production refers to a process of production with a relatively high proportion of capital inputs, compared to other inputs.) • An increase in output, much of which is exported to other countries, may lead to the reduction, or possibly the elimination, of a deficit in the balance of payments.	• There can sometimes be a shift away from consumer goods to capital goods in order to bring about economic growth; this will be good in the long run, but not necessarily in the short run. • Economic growth may lead to a depletion of natural resources and damage to the environment in terms of various forms of pollution; it is in this sense that a high rate of economic growth is sometimes said to be unsustainable. • The benefits of economic growth may not always be shared evenly among different people in the country. • There may be a reduction in the quality of life in the country, e.g. working hours may be longer, reducing the amount of leisure time.

The use and conservation of resources

The contrast between the potential benefits and costs of economic growth can also be seen in relation to the use or conservation of resources. The use of resources can contribute significantly to economic growth, but it needs to be remembered that many natural resources are finite in supply, i.e. they will eventually run out.

This is why it is strongly argued in many economies that there should be conservation of resources. It is stressed that this is a more **sustainable** approach, taking into account the needs not only of the present generation, but also of future generations.

sustainability: the capacity to endure; it is the potential for the long-term maintenance of wellbeing in an economic environment so that the interests of future, as well as present, generations are taken fully into account

Revision activity

Explain what is meant by 'sustainability'.

Expert tip

Sustainability is an important concept in economics, recognising the importance of the needs of future generations and not just those of the present generation. Candidates should include a consideration of sustainability in any answer to a question on the use and conservation of resources.

Economic development

Revised

Whereas economic growth is concerned with increases in the national output of a country, as measured by changes in gross domestic product, **economic development** is a broader concept that puts the emphasis on the quality of life of people in different countries.

economic development: a broader perspective that goes beyond increases in national output to take into account factors that influence the quality of life of people in particular countries

Expert tip

It is important to make sure that you demonstrate in the examination that you understand the difference between economic growth and economic development, stressing that development is a wider process.

Indicators of comparative development and underdevelopment

It is possible to use a number of indicators to compare development and underdevelopment in the world economy. These are shown in Table 2.

Table 2 Indicators of comparative development and underdevelopment in the world economy

Indicator	Explanation
Economic	Differences in the balance of the economic structure, i.e. the proportion of output produced in the primary, secondary and tertiary sectors of production
Monetary	Differences in the level of income, usually measured by GDP per capita; countries can be divided into high income, middle income and low income
Non-monetary	Differences in social factors, such as the percentage of GDP spent on education and health, the rate of adult literacy, the number of doctors per thousand population, the number of hospital beds per thousand of population and quality of water
Demographic	Differences in terms of population growth rates, birth rates, death rates, fertility rates, average age and life expectancy

Now test yourself

4 Distinguish between economic growth and economic development.

Answer on p.158

Tested

Expert tip

It is important that you demonstrate in the examination an understanding of the fact that features of different countries tend to be rather general and that there may be exceptions, e.g. there are some very rich people in economically developing countries and some very poor people in economically developed countries.

Characteristics of economically developing economies

Economically developing economies have a number of key characteristics. Table 3 summarises some of these.

Table 3 Characteristics of economically developing economies

Population growth	There will typically be a relatively high rate of population growth, resulting from the difference between the **birth rate** and the **death rate**, i.e. the **natural increase** in a country's population; this means that, in many economically developing countries, the size of the population is well above the **optimum population**.
Population structure	There is likely to be a relatively high proportion of young people, creating a high dependency ratio, i.e. a high proportion of people who are reliant on others in an economy, such as pensioners..
Income level and distribution	Income levels tend to be lower than in economically developed countries, and there is usually a great deal of inequality in the distribution of that income.
Economic structure	In many economically developing countries, there is a relatively large proportion of workers employed in the primary or extractive sector and a relatively low proportion of workers employed in the tertiary or services sector.
Employment composition	In many economically developing countries, there are social, cultural and religious reasons why a smaller proportion of women work compared with the situation in economically developed countries.
External trade	Many economically developing countries depend on the exportation of primary products and these often experience greater price variations than is the case with manufactured goods, creating a greater instability.
Urbanisation	The proportion of people who live in rural areas in economically developing countries tends to be relatively higher than is the case in economically developed countries, and where there has been rural–urban **migration**, this can put pressure on resources in the urban areas.
Dependency	Many economically developing countries have become dependent on economically developed countries, and the role of multinational corporations has been significant in this; although they bring employment to the economically developing countries, much of the profit made is repatriated to the home country
External debt	Many economically developing countries have a high level of external debt and debt repayment is a major burden; in some countries, the debt is over 100% of the gross national product.
Social	Many economically developing countries have greater social problems than is the case in economically developed countries, as can be seen through such indicators as life expectancy, literacy rate, the number of doctors per thousand of the population and access to good quality water.

birth rate: the average number of live births per thousand of population of a country in a given time period, usually a year

death rate: the number of people per thousand of population in a country who die in a given time period, usually a year

natural increase: a natural increase in the population of a country is determined by the crude birth rate minus the crude death rate of a population, i.e. it is the difference between the number of live births and the number of deaths in a country during a year

optimum population: the number of people in a country that will produce the highest per capita economic return, given the full utilisation of the resources available

migration: the movement of people from one area to another, either within a country or between countries

Now test yourself

5 Explain, with the use of examples, what is meant by 'demographic' indicators of economic development.

6 Explain what is meant by an 'optimum' population.

Answers on p.158

Tested

Revision activity

How useful is it to divide countries into economically developed and economically developing categories?

Unemployment

Full employment and the natural rate of unemployment

Revised

There is some debate as to what actually constitutes a situation of **full employment** in an economy, but is generally taken to be a situation where everyone who wants a job has a job, with the exception of those who are frictionally unemployed. In many economies, it is about 4% to 5% of the working population.

The **natural rate of unemployment** stresses the link between the level of unemployment and the rate of inflation in an economy. It is that level of unemployment which contributes towards a rate of inflation that is non-accelerating. It is essentially an equilibrium situation where aggregate demand for labour is equal to the aggregate supply of labour at the current wage rate; as a result of this situation of equilibrium, there is no upward pressure on the level of prices in the economy.

unemployment: a situation that occurs when a number of people in an economy are able and willing to work but are unable to gain employment

full employment: the level of employment as a result of everyone who is able and willing to work having a job, with the exception of those who are frictionally unemployed

natural rate of unemployment: the non-accelerating inflation rate of unemployment (NAIRU); it can also be described as equilibrium unemployment. This is the rate of unemployment in an economy which will prevent the rate of inflation increasing

Now test yourself

7 What is meant by 'the natural rate of unemployment'?

Answer on p.158

Tested

Revision activity

Does a situation of full employment mean that everyone in a country who wants a job has a job?

The causes and types of unemployment

Revised

Unemployment in an economy can be caused by a number of factors and this gives rise to a variety of different types of unemployment. These can be seen in Table 4.

Table 4 Causes and different types of unemployment

Type of unemployment	Explanation of cause
Structural	Workers lose their jobs as a result of the changing conditions of demand in an economy; this creates a change in the country's economic structure, and the declining industries will not need to employ as many people, causing a loss of jobs.
Regional	Sometimes these declining industries are concentrated in particular areas of a country and this can contribute to regional unemployment; this is especially the case where workers lack the skills and training to move from one job to another.
Cyclical (or demand deficiency)	Whereas structural unemployment tends to be concentrated in particular industries, cyclical unemployment tends to be more widespread in an economy; this is because it is associated with the trade cycle and periods of economic downturn. When the level of aggregate demand in an economy is low, this can lead to a recession, defined as two successive quarters of negative growth.
Frictional	At any one moment in an economy, some people will be between jobs, i.e. they have left one job and are waiting to start another; this type of unemployment reflects dynamic change in an economy, with some sectors expanding while others are declining. It is possible to distinguish between three different types of frictional unemployment: • search unemployment, where people are prepared to keep looking for the best possible job rather than take the first one offered • casual unemployment, where certain types of work are not regular and so at any one time some people will be out of work, e.g. an actor • seasonal unemployment, where people are out of work when it is 'out of season', such as in the tourism or agriculture industries
Technological	A situation where people lose their jobs because there has been a move away from labour-intensive towards capital-intensive production, i.e. machinery and equipment can be used instead of workers.
Real wage (or classical)	This is where people are out of work because real wages in an economy are too high, e.g. because of the power of trade unions.
Disguised	This is where there are people who do not have a job, but who are not registered for unemployment benefits; they are not included in the claimant count of the number of unemployed people in a country.
Voluntary	This describes those who are out of work but who have refused to take a job which is available, perhaps because they are waiting to be offered a better-paid job; the existence of unemployment benefits means that some people are rather selective in deciding which job to accept.

Now test yourself

8 Distinguish between structural and cyclical unemployment.

Answer on p.158

Tested

Revision activity

Distinguish between the different causes of unemployment.

The consequences of unemployment

Revised

Unemployment has a number of consequences, including the following:

- Economic resources are said to be scarce, and so any unemployment is a waste of scarce resources; an economy will be underperforming and the level of national output produced will be lower than would otherwise have been the case.
- A government will lose out on potential tax revenue, both in terms of direct taxes, such as income tax, and indirect taxes, such as goods and services tax.

- A government will also find its fiscal situation worsened, not only because of the likely reduction in revenue from taxation, but also because of the money that will need to be paid out in the form of benefits to those who are unemployed and the cost of training that a government might need to provide in order to make unemployed people more employable in the future.
- Higher levels of unemployment can be associated with a number of social problems, such as an increase in the crime rate of a country.

Expert tip

Make sure that you read a question on unemployment carefully, to ensure that you do not confuse the causes of unemployment with the consequences.

Revision activity

Why is unemployment regarded as such a serious economic problem?

Inter-connectedness of problems

It should be stressed that macroeconomic problems are not separate and distinct, but are often interrelated in different ways. Three examples will show how this inter-connectedness can come about.

The internal and the external value of money

Revised

It is important to distinguish between the internal and the external value of money, but it should also be recognised that the two values are interrelated. For example, if the internal value of a currency falls as a result of a high rate of inflation in a country, exports too will become more expensive. If demand is price elastic, the demand for these will fall, as will the demand for the currency to pay for them. In this situation, there will be a depreciation in the external value of the country's currency.

The balance of payments and the rate of inflation

Revised

A relatively high rate of inflation in a country will make exports more expensive, and therefore demand for them is likely to fall, but the demand for imports may remain unchanged, as many countries have a relatively high marginal propensity to consume imported products. In such a situation, the balance of payments is likely to deteriorate.

Inflation and unemployment

Revised

The relationship between the level of inflation and the rate of unemployment in an economy can be seen in the Phillips curve shown in Figure 2. Such a curve shows the trade-off between inflation and unemployment, i.e. as the rate of inflation increases, this will be accompanied by a fall in the rate of unemployment and as the rate of inflation decreases, this will be accompanied by a rise in the rate of unemployment. For example, if a government deliberately aims to bring down the rate of aggregate demand in an economy, such as through an increase in taxes or interest rates, this is likely to put some people out of work.

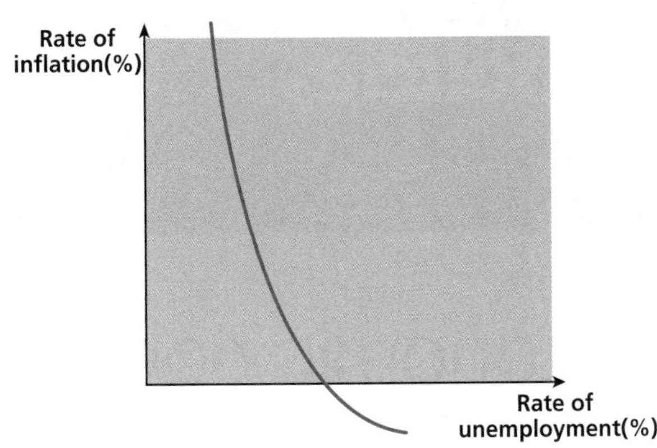

Figure 2 The Phillips curve

Now test yourself

9 Explain what is shown in a Phillips curve.

Answer on p.158

Tested

13 Macroeconomic policies

Objectives of macroeconomic policy

Governments generally have a wide range of objectives in relation to macroeconomic policy, but in most cases they tend to focus on a combination of the following six objectives:

- a relatively low and stable rate of inflation
- full employment
- a rate of economic growth that is regarded as sustainable
- equilibrium in the balance of payments over a period of time
- the avoidance of extreme fluctuations in the exchange rate
- the redistribution of income and wealth

At any one moment in time, the government of a particular country may have certain priorities in relation to the achievement of these objectives, but over a period of time all governments will aim to achieve a degree of success in each of these.

Now test yourself

1 State the six macroeconomic objectives that governments usually have.

Answer on p.158

Tested

Types of policy

There are broadly four different types of policy that a government could use to achieve these objectives, and these are:

- fiscal policy
- monetary policy
- exchange rate policy
- supply-side policy

Now test yourself

2 Identify the four different types of macroeconomic policy.

Answer on p.158

Tested

Fiscal policy

Revised

Fiscal policy is the deliberate use of revenue and expenditure decisions by a government to influence economic activity in a country, especially the level of aggregate demand. The idea is that by making changes to decisions about revenue and expenditure, an economy can be 'fine-tuned' to achieve particular aims. A government can deliberately plan for a balanced budget, a budget deficit or a budget surplus to achieve its objectives. For example, if an economy needed to be stimulated in order to reduce unemployment, taxation could be reduced and expenditure increased. On the other hand, if an economy needed to be deflated in order to reduce inflation, taxation could be increased and expenditure reduced.

fiscal policy: the use of public revenue and/or public expenditure to influence the level of aggregate demand in an economy

It is important to distinguish between discretionary fiscal policy and the use of automatic stabilisers.

Discretionary fiscal policy

Sometimes a government will deliberately change taxation and/or public expenditure to bring about a desired change in the level of economic activity in the economy. This is known as **discretionary fiscal policy**.

discretionary fiscal policy: the use of deliberate changes in taxation and/or public expenditure with the intention of changing the level of aggregate demand in an economy

Automatic stabilisers

Whereas discretionary fiscal policy involves deliberate action by a government, **automatic stabilisers** refer to a situation where changes in an economy take place without the need for deliberate action by a government. For example, in a recession, when the level of unemployment in an economy is likely to rise, the revenue received by a government from taxation is likely to fall, as fewer people are working, while at the same time government expenditure is likely to rise, such as in the form of unemployment benefits to those out of work.

automatic stabiliser: a situation where changes in the level of taxation and/or public expenditure automatically bring about changes in an economy without the need for deliberate action by a government

Canons of taxation

There are a number of principles or **canons of taxation**, as shown in Table 1.

Table 1 The canons of taxation

Principle	Explanation
Equity/fairness	The burden of taxation should take into account the ability of people to pay the tax.
Certainty/transparency	Information about taxation needs to be made available so that it is seen as transparent.
Convenience	The payment and collection of taxes need to be as convenient as possible.
Cost	The cost of administering and collecting taxes should be as low as possible.
Efficiency	Taxation should not lead to any disincentives, such as **work disincentives**.

canons of taxation: the main principles of taxation, i.e. any system of taxes should adhere to these principles in order to be effective

work disincentives: the possibility that taxation could lead to people being unwilling to work, e.g. there may be a disincentive to work if rates of income tax are too high

Laffer curve: this shows the relationship between the rate of tax and the revenue obtained from the tax

The poverty trap

One particular issue, arising from the combination of paying tax and receiving benefits, is that some people might actually become worse off as a result of working. This is because a worker may start paying tax above a certain level of income and, at the same time, no longer be able to claim benefits. This is known as the **poverty trap**.

poverty trap: the situation which occurs when a person receives benefits, increasing income, but which then means the person is no longer entitled to receive as much as was the case before

Expert tip

Candidates should be able to demonstrate an understanding of the idea that some people can actually be made worse off as a result of taking up employment because of the loss of benefits that they were previously entitled to. This situation is known as the poverty trap.

Progressive, regressive and proportional taxation

It is important to distinguish between **progressive**, **regressive** and **proportional taxation**.

Progressive taxation

Many economies make use of progressive taxation to achieve the macroeconomic objective of a fairer and more equitable distribution of income. An income tax, for example, will not only take more from a person as their income rises, but a higher proportion of that income.

Regressive taxation

Whereas a progressive direct tax, such as income tax, has different rates of tax depending on a person's income, a regressive indirect tax, such as a goods and services tax, has the same rate of tax. In such a situation, all people who buy a particular good or service will pay the same percentage, so this will have a greater impact on poor, compared to rich, people.

Proportional taxation

Another possible type of taxation is proportional taxation. This is where a tax takes an equal proportion of income from a person whatever that person's income is. In this situation, there is neither a progressive nor a regressive effect of the tax.

An example of a proportional tax is **flat-rate tax**, which has a constant marginal tax rate. A single tax rate is applied to all incomes with no deductions or exemptions.

progressive taxation: where taxation takes a higher proportion of a person's income as that income rises

regressive taxation: a situation where a tax takes a larger proportion of low incomes than it does of high incomes

proportional taxation: a tax which takes an equal proportion of income whatever a person's income level happens to be

flat-rate tax: a tax with a constant marginal rate

marginal tax rate: the proportion of an increase in income which is taken in tax

Revision activity

Consider the arguments for and against progressive taxation.

Issues in using fiscal policy

Although fiscal policy can be a very effective way to manage an economy, there are a number of issues involved in its use, including the following:

- A government needs to be able to estimate reasonably accurately the likely effects of any change in taxation and/or public expenditure, otherwise the desired objectives may not be achieved, e.g. if the size of the multiplier is underestimated or overestimated.
- There may be side-effects of any fiscal policy, e.g. unemployment may be reduced, but at the cost of a higher rate of inflation.
- There may be a significant time lag before a particular revenue or expenditure decision begins to take effect.
- Some decisions that may be justified by economic reasoning may not be taken by a government for political reasons, especially if an election is due in the not too distant future.

Now test yourself

3 Explain what is meant by the term 'fiscal policy'.

4 Distinguish between discretionary fiscal policy and automatic stabilisers.

5 Explain how taxation could become a disincentive to work.

6 Distinguish between a progressive tax, a regressive tax and a proportional tax.

Answers on p.158

Tested

Monetary policy

Revised

Monetary policy is concerned with the price and quantity of money in an economy. The **price of money** refers to the interest rate and the quantity of money refers to the money supply. For example, a government could reduce the interest rate in an economy to stimulate employment, but this could lead to an increase in the rate of inflation in that economy. If a government decided to increase the interest rate in an economy, this would attract 'hot money' into the country, raising the value of the exchange rate and making export prices more expensive and import prices less expensive, leading to the possibility of an adverse effect on the balance of payments.

monetary policy: the use of interest rates and/or the money supply to influence the level of aggregate demand in an economy

The other monetary approach is to influence the money supply in an economy. Many countries, since the credit crunch, have decided to increase the money supply in the economy through a process of **quantitative easing**. This is where a government buys bonds and bills, i.e. securities, giving the financial institutions more liquidity and so increasing the money supply in the economy. This process of a government buying bonds is known as **open market operations**.

quantitative easing: the process whereby the government of a country deliberately buys bonds and bills in order to increase the money supply in an economy

open market operations: the process of a government buying or selling bonds in order to influence the money supply in an economy

Issues in using monetary policy

Like fiscal policy, there are a number of issues that need to be taken into account in relation to monetary policy, and these include the following:

- There is a time lag between a change in an interest rate and the impact of that change on an economy; it is difficult to be precise about how long that time lag might be, but a number of economists have suggested that it could be as long as 18 months.
- Various people in an economy may react differently to a change in interest rates, i.e. not everyone will have the same interest elasticity of demand. For example, relatively rich people in an economy are likely to have a relatively inelastic interest elasticity of demand, whereas relatively poor people in an economy are likely to have a relatively elastic interest elasticity of demand. This makes it difficult to estimate the likely effects of a change in interest rates in an economy.
- Any increase in the money supply of an economy, such as through the process of quantitative easing, is likely to have an inflationary effect in that economy, resulting from the increase in the level of aggregate demand.

Now test yourself

7 Explain what is meant by the term 'monetary policy'.

8 Explain the term 'quantitative easing'.

Answers on p.159

Tested

Revision activity

Distinguish between fiscal policy and monetary policy.

Exchange rate policy

Revised

Exchange rate policy refers to the deliberate use of changes in a country's exchange rate to influence the level of activity in the economy. This is easier to achieve when there is a fixed exchange rate system, because a government can decide what an exchange rate will be, and then change it through a devaluation or a revaluation. It is more difficult to achieve when there is a floating exchange rate system, but even here a government can intervene in the foreign exchange market to ensure that the exchange rate does not rise or fall by too much; this situation is known as a **managed float**. Even if there is a genuine floating exchange rate system, a government can still influence the rate in some ways, such as through changes in the interest rate.

As with the other policies, there is likely to be some conflict between objectives when using exchange rate policy. For example, a reduction in the value of an exchange rate, making exports cheaper, is likely to lead to an increase in employment, but the increase in the price of imports is likely to have an adverse effect on the rate of inflation in the economy.

exchange rate policy: the deliberate use of changes in exchange rates to influence the level of aggregate demand in an economy

Issues in using exchange rate policy

As with the other policies, exchange rate policy involves a number of issues, including the following:

- A floating exchange rate can create uncertainty in an economy and this could have a negative effect on decisions to invest.
- A fixed exchange rate is likely to involve the use of foreign currency reserves to maintain a particular rate.
- It is not always clear what the 'best' exchange rate is for a currency.
- A country may be a member of a wider trading community, as a result of some form of economic integration, and in some cases a common exchange rate is used, so one economy would not be able to deviate from this agreed rate.

Now test yourself

9 Explain what is meant by 'exchange rate policy'.

Answer on p.159

Tested

Supply-side policy

Revised

Supply-side policy is a general term to refer to a number of different actions that a government could take in order to improve the efficiency of markets in the economy. It is different in approach from the other three types of macroeconomic policy because it approaches economic issues from the supply, rather than from the demand, side.

supply-side policy: policies which enable markets to work more efficiently

Examples of supply-side policies could include the following:

- increasing incentives to work by lowering income tax and unemployment benefits
- increasing expenditure on education to improve the quality, and therefore the productivity, of the labour force
- increasing expenditure on training to enable workers to move more easily from one type of work to another if they become unemployed; this is likely to improve the flexibility and occupational mobility of labour in an economy
- reforming trade unions so that labour is not in such a powerful bargaining position with employers; this could contribute to a reduction in the number of days lost through industrial action in an economy
- encouraging privatisation in an economy so that firms, needing to make a profit to survive, become more efficient
- encouraging deregulation, such as through a reduction in the barriers to entry into an industry, which will allow more private firms to enter a market
- providing more information about job vacancies in different parts of a country; this is likely to improve the geographical mobility of labour

Now test yourself

10 Explain, with the use of three examples, what is meant by 'supply-side policy'.

Answer on p.159

Tested

Issues in using supply-side policy

As indicated above, there are often issues in the use of any of the macroeconomic policies, and this is also the case with supply-side policy. Potential problems include the following:

- There is no guarantee that a firm in the private sector will be more efficient than one in the public sector; privatisation may involve the need to get rid of some workers, leading to an increase in the rate of unemployment in an economy.

- A privatised firm may be in a monopoly position in an economy, so all that has been achieved is a move from a state-owned to a privately owned monopoly.
- Lowering unemployment benefits might persuade more people to look for work, but this will have no effect if there are no jobs available for them.
- The effects of supply-side policies can take a long time to show, such as improvements to the education system.

Revision activity

Consider how supply-side policies differ from demand-side policies.

Evaluating policy options

As indicated above, there may well be problems arising from conflicts between the different policy objectives that a government might have. For example, a government might aim to reduce the rate of inflation in an economy by deflating the level of aggregate demand. This would also be useful if the country had a deficit in the balance of payments. There would, however, be an adverse impact in relation to unemployment and economic growth. Any dampening of aggregate demand in an economy is likely to reduce the level of employment and it is also likely to reduce the rate of economic growth. If an economy experiences two successive quarters of negative economic growth, the economy is said to be in a state of recession.

If, on the other hand, a government decided that it needed to reflate the economy, this would have a positive effect on the level of unemployment, which would be likely to fall, and on the rate of economic growth, which would be likely to rise, but if the increase in aggregate demand were greater than the increase in aggregate supply, this would be likely to be inflationary. Also, if there were a relatively high marginal propensity to import, this increase in demand would be likely to worsen the economy's balance of payments position.

A government, in attempting to achieve its macroeconomic objectives, has four types of policy that can be used but, as stated, each of these has its limitations. It is therefore the case that, in many situations, a government would be best advised to be willing to use all four types of policy in order to achieve its six macroeconomic objectives.

Policies towards economically developing economies

Policies towards economically developing economies are essentially of two types: trade and aid.

Trade

Revised

The theory of comparative advantage indicates that all countries can benefit from free trade as long as there are differences in opportunity cost ratios. International trade will therefore lead to an increase in world output and this will ultimately lead to an improvement in the quality of life and economic welfare in all countries, including economically developing economies.

A number of organisations have been established since 1944 to encourage free trade and to reduce the extent of trade protectionism in the world market. These include the International Monetary Fund, the World Bank (in particular the International Bank for Reconstruction and Development) and the World Trade Organisation. Policies should therefore aim to reduce the extent of protectionism, such as through the reduced use of tariffs, quotas and subsidies.

Economically developing economies, however, have experienced particular problems, which means that they have not gained from international trade as much as might have been expected. These problems include the following:

- Whereas economically developed economies have tended to specialise in the production of manufactured goods, economically developing economies have tended to specialise in the production of primary products; some economically developing economies rely on a single commodity for over half of their export earnings. The problem is that the prices of primary products have, on the whole, declined relative to the prices of manufactured goods, although many economically developing economies are now much less dependent on the exports of primary products than used to be the case.
- Primary production is likely to be more volatile in terms of supply conditions, with the effect that prices for primary products are usually less stable than for manufactured goods; a key issue is that the demand for, and the supply of, primary products is more price inelastic than is the case with secondary products.
- It is also the case that the demand for many primary products, such as different types of food, is more income inelastic than demand for manufactured goods.
- Much of the investment in economically developing economies has come from multinational corporations; much of their profit is repatriated back to their home countries.

A number of economically developing economies, given these problems, have actually introduced a number of different forms of trade protection to bring about import substitution in their economies, i.e. the aim is to replace imports with domestically produced goods. Some economically developing economies, however, recognising the enormous potential offered by free trade, have taken a different approach and have aimed for an export-led strategy in order to benefit from free trade.

Now test yourself

11 Explain whether the income elasticity of demand for primary products, such as food, is likely to be elastic or inelastic.

Answer on p.159

Tested

Aid

Revised

An alternative policy towards economically developing countries is the provision of **aid**. Aid from economically developed to economically developing economies can come in various forms, including grants and loans. Sometimes the aid is bilateral, i.e. involving just two countries, and sometimes it is multilateral, i.e. involving a number of countries and/or agencies.

aid: the process of economically developed countries providing financial support to economically developing economies

There have, however, been a number of problems in relation to such aid, including those listed below:

- Some aid has been used in investments which have become relatively unsuccessful. For example, some major construction projects, such as dams, have been criticised for not being in the long-term interests of particular countries. There is also some evidence that expenditure on aid has actually been spent on defence projects.
- Some of the aid has been 'tied' in some way, i.e. there are conditions attached to the aid and so the receiving country has not been totally free to decide how to spend the money.
- In some cases, there has been corruption in the receiving country, with the result that much of the money has been kept in the hands of a few, rather than spread across the whole economy.

- There have been some examples of the aid money being spent on defence, rather than on, say, education, healthcare or improving the water supply.
- Some aid has actually been counterproductive and has made the situation worse, e.g. supplies of large amounts of food to some countries have reduced the prices in the local economy, lowering incomes, and making it difficult for local farmers to survive.
- While in some cases the interest rate charged on the aid has been at a lower rate, i.e. concessional, in many cases it has been at market rates of interest.
- The loan repayments have, in many cases, been difficult for the economically developing countries to pay, although some debts have been rescheduled or cancelled; organisations, such as Jubilee 2000 and Make Poverty History, have been active in trying to persuade lenders to cancel, or at least reschedule, the debts.

Now test yourself

12 Explain what is meant by 'tied aid'.

Answer on p.159

Tested

Revision activity

Consider the arguments for and against aid.

A level questions and answers

This section contains A level exam-style questions. The key to the multiple-choice answers is given on p. 142. The data-response and essay questions are followed by expert comments (shown by the icon ⓔ) that indicate where credit is due and where there are areas for improvement.

Multiple-choice questions

Question 1

Which of the following explains potential economic growth?

A **A movement from within a production possibility curve to a position on the curve**
B **A movement upwards along a production possibility curve**
C **A movement downwards along a production possibility curve**
D **A movement from a position on a production possibility curve to a position outside the curve** [1]

Question 2

Which of the following could explain a shift of a supply curve to the right?

A **An increase in the price of a product**
B **An increase in the cost of production**
C **An increase in technology**
D **An increase in an indirect tax on a product** [1]

Question 3

Sustainability refers to the need to take into account primarily the needs of:

A **past generations**
B **the unskilled**
C **future generations**
D **the unemployed** [1]

Question 4

Which of the following would indicate the existence of a contestable market?

A **The threat of new firms entering the market**
B **The existence of very effective barriers to entry**
C **The establishment of very high prices**
D **The existence of very high sunk costs** [1]

Question 5

A competitive market becomes a monopoly. Which of the following is likely to happen as a result of this?

A **Price is likely to be reduced.**
B **The consumer surplus will be reduced.**
C **The producer surplus will be reduced.**
D **Output is likely to be increased.** [1]

Question 6

Which of the following is an example of fiscal policy?

A **An increase in the interest rate**
B **A decrease in the money supply**
C **A restriction on trade unions**
D **An increase in taxation** [1]

Question 7

Which of the following is an injection into the circular flow of income?

A **Taxation**
B **Investment**
C **Savings**
D **Expenditure on imports** [1]

Question 8

A worker receives an increased wage of 4% in an economy which is experiencing a rate of inflation of 2%. What is the real increase in the wage?

A **−6%**
B **−2%**
C **2%**
D **6%** [1]

Question 9

Which of the following policies is most likely to reduce a balance of payments deficit without, at the same time, causing inflation?

A An increase in direct taxes
B An increase in indirect taxes
C An increase in import tariffs
D An increase in the exchange rate [1]

Question 10

Which of the following is most likely to lead to an increase in the natural rate of unemployment in an economy?

A A decrease in government expenditure
B A decrease in unemployment benefits
C An increase in the membership of trade unions
D An increase in interest rates [1]

Key to the answers

1 D
2 C
3 C
4 A
5 B
6 D
7 B
8 C
9 A
10 D

Data-response question

Question 11

FISCAL POLICY IN PAKISTAN

Elements of fiscal policy in Pakistan are designed to help the poor, such as the use of subsidies to keep down the cost of electricity and gas. The aim is to reduce the number of people living below the poverty line. However, some economists have pointed out that the use of such subsidies may lead to a decrease in productivity. They have also questioned whether Pakistan can afford to provide such subsidies, given that the fiscal deficit is increasing and public expenditure is rapidly rising. One suggestion is that Pakistan should work harder to widen the tax base by bringing more people into the tax net. A major worry in Pakistan is that the economy may be facing the threat of recession and so one proposal has been to lower the interest rates in order to stimulate the economy.

(a) Describe what is meant by a subsidy. [4]
(b) Explain how a subsidy could lead to a reduction in productivity. [4]
(c) Explain what is meant by a fiscal deficit? [4]
(d) Discuss whether a reduction in interest rates should always be encouraged. [8]

Candidate answer

(a) A subsidy is an amount of money paid to a producer by a government. The effect of this is that the price to the consumer will be lower than would otherwise have been the case. The effect is to keep down the prices of essential goods, as in the Case Study where subsidies have been used to keep down the cost and, therefore, the price of electricity and gas with the aim of reducing the number of people living below the poverty line. The effect of the provision of a subsidy can be shown by a shift of the supply curve to the right, causing equilibrium price to fall and equilibrium quantity to rise.

The candidate clearly describes what is meant by a subsidy and goes on to outline its likely effects on both a producer and a consumer, using appropriate information from the Case Study to support the answer, especially in reducing the number of people living below the poverty line. There is a reference to what would happen in a diagram to show the effect of a provision of a subsidy, but no diagram has actually been drawn. It would be useful to include this diagram in the answer. Mark: 3/4.

(b) A subsidy is a form of support to a producer and therefore, to some extent, gives the producer some protection from the reality of market forces. There is always a danger that a producer might decide to hide behind this protective subsidy, leading to a decrease in levels of efficiency. Productivity is the output per factor (e.g. labour or machinery) per period of time. If the subsidy brings about a fall in efficiency, the level of productivity will also be expected to decrease.

The candidate is able to explain how a subsidy could lead to a reduction in efficiency and, therefore, to a lower level of productivity. The term 'productivity' is clearly explained, distinguishing it from production. Mark: 3/4.

(c) Fiscal policy is concerned with the money received by a government, i.e. revenue, and money spent by a government, i.e. public expenditure. Sometimes these two figures will be equal, giving rise to a balanced budget. In this case of a fiscal deficit, it means that the expenditure is greater than the revenue, i.e. the government is spending more than it has got. In order to overcome this deficit, the government will need to reduce expenditure and/or increase revenue.

The candidate begins the explanation of the term 'fiscal deficit' by putting it into the context of fiscal policy and then goes on to explain that it refers to a situation of expenditure exceeding revenue. However, to gain full marks, the answer could be developed by adding at the end that if it proved difficult to reduce expenditure and/or increase revenue, the government would need to resort to borrowing to cover the difference between revenue and expenditure. Mark: 3/4.

(d) The Case Study states that Pakistan is facing the threat of recession and so one possible way to stimulate the economy is to lower the interest rate. If interest rates are lowered, this will reduce the cost of borrowing. This will apply to both producers and consumers and this should lead to an increase in aggregate demand in the economy. One problem, however, is that a reduction in interest rates can sometimes take a while to have an effect, so there is not usually an immediate change in the level of demand in an economy. Also, the interest elasticity of demand may be quite low because the interest rate is only one of a number of factors that producers and consumers take into account in deciding whether to spend or not. For example, expectations about the future of the economy can have a major effect. Another factor to take into account is if the fall in interest rates leads to an increase in demand, how easy will it be to increase supply? This will, to some extent, depend on the extent of spare capacity in the economy. If supply responds very slowly to the increase in demand, this could lead to a situation of inflation with too much money chasing too few goods. If Pakistan's rate of inflation is higher than that of its main competitors, it will make its exports less competitive and this could lead to problems in the current account of the balance of payments and there would also be likely to be a rise in the unemployment rate in the country.

In conclusion, a decision to reduce interest rates to stimulate the economy should be encouraged if it is thought that the interest elasticity of demand is quite elastic and if there is a degree of spare capacity in the economy. However, if this is not the case, such a move could be inflationary, leading to a worsening of the current account position of the balance of payments and a possible increase in unemployment, so it should not always be encouraged.

The candidate offers a useful discussion of whether a reduction in interest rates should always be encouraged. The argument in favour of a cut in interest rates to stimulate demand is clearly put forward and then the candidate balances this with the view that it might not always be an ideal situation, partly because its effect may not be immediate and partly because there may be inflationary consequences. The answer finishes with a conclusion, always important in a 'discuss' question, that states that a fall in interest rates should not always be encouraged as it would be necessary to take into account the possible negative effects in terms of inflation, the current account of the balance of payments and the rate of unemployment. Mark: 8/8.

Overall, the answers to the four parts of the question are of a reasonable standard. The total mark is 17/20, equivalent to a Grade A.

Essay questions

Question 12

Explain the meaning of the term 'equilibrium level of national income'. Discuss the factors that could cause this equilibrium to change in a developing economy. [25]

Candidate answer

The term 'equilibrium level of national income' refers to a situation where the injections into the circular flow of income are equal to the leakages or withdrawals from the circular flow of income. It is possible to make a distinction between a two-sector, a three-sector and a four-sector model of an economy. If there were just two sectors, this would be a closed economy without a government sector, and would consist of one injection, investment, and one withdrawal, savings. If there were three sectors, this would be a closed economy with a government sector, so there would be two injections, investment and government expenditure, and two withdrawals or leakages, savings and taxation. If there were three sectors, this would be an open economy. The injections would be investment, government expenditure and the income from exports; the leakages or withdrawals would be savings, taxation and the money paid for imports. When all of these injections and leakages are equal, there is an equilibrium level of national income.

The candidate demonstrates a sound knowledge and understanding of the circular flow of income, discussing the various injections into, and leakages or withdrawals out of, the circular flow. There is a clear distinction between the two-sector, three-sector and four-sector economies. It would be helpful to include a diagram to show the 'equilibrium level of national income' in an economy. Examiners are keen for candidates to include appropriate diagrams to support the points being made in an answer, as long as these diagrams are relevant, clear and accurately drawn.

When there is a change, this will upset the equilibrium. This change would need to be seen in relation to the existence of a multiplier effect. This emphasises that an injection may well bring about a change in national income that is greater than the initial injection. The size of the multiplier in an economy can be determined by the formula

$$\frac{1}{MPS + MPT + MPM}$$

where *MPS* is the marginal propensity to save, *MPT* is the marginal propensity to tax and *MPM* is the marginal propensity to import.

In this paragraph, the candidate focuses on the importance of the multiplier. It is clear that the candidate understands that the eventual change in national income could be greater than the size of the initial injection into the circular flow, such as an increase in government expenditure. The candidate appreciates how the multiplier is calculated, although the answer could demonstrate a greater recognition of how the multiplier process operates through a series of stages with the size of the multiplier gradually becoming smaller as money is taken out of the economy through savings, taxation or expenditure on imports.

In a developing economy, there could be an injection in the form of investment by private sector firms. In many developing countries, a lot of investment is undertaken by multinational companies and this could contribute to an increase in the level of national income. It could be that the injection has come about through spending by the government. In a developing country, the government might have received aid, through either a bilateral or a multilateral arrangement, and this could have contributed to an increase in the level of national income. Finally, the injection could have come about as a result of the spending by people in other countries to buy this country's exports.

e *The candidate now moves on to focus attention on the economically developing country, although there is no introductory sentence to indicate more clearly what is meant by an economically developing country. There is a recognition, however, of the potential importance of multinational companies in economically developing countries. The potential importance of government expenditure is recognised and there is a useful reference to the possible importance of aid, of either a bilateral or a multilateral nature. A further potential recognition of an injection is in relation to expenditure on a country's exports. Although there is a reference to aid, much of this paragraph could apply to almost any country; it really needs to be more sharply focused on economically developing countries.*

It needs to be remembered that although the level of national income in a country can change as a result of the multiplier effect, the actual size of the multiplier is determined by the marginal rate to withdraw, so it is important to understand the marginal propensities to save, tax and import in a developing country.

e *This is an important point to make, but it might be better to include it at the end of the second paragraph, before moving on to a consideration of the special features of economically developing countries.*

In conclusion, when the injections into the circular flow of income are equal to the leakages from it, there will be a situation of national income equilibrium. This situation, however, can easily change in a developing economy, in relation to the extent of both the injections and the leakages.

e *The candidate offers a conclusion, but it is rather brief and really should be developed more fully. The link between the circular flow of income and national income equilibrium is briefly considered, but the reference to what could happen in an economically developing country is somewhat superficial.*

e *The candidate has made an attempt to answer the question, and the sections on the circular flow of income and the multiplier are good. The major limitation, however, is that the references to developing economies are rather limited and need to be developed more fully. The answer would gain a Grade B with a mark of 15/25.*

Question 13

Discuss whether a wage is determined just like any other price in an economy. [25]

Candidate answer

The wage of labour is to some extent determined, just like any other price in a market, by the forces of demand and supply. Demand for labour will be a derived demand, i.e. it will not be demanded for its own sake, but for what it can contribute to the production of finished goods. The supply of labour is determined not just by the quantity that is available, but also by the quality, i.e. the skills, training, qualifications, education and experience of the workers. The wage that prevails in a market will reflect the forces of demand and supply. For example, if the supply of skilled labour is in relatively short supply, this will increase the wage; if the supply of unskilled labour is in relatively large supply, this will lower the wage.

e *The candidate begins by recognising that a wage is, to some extent, determined just like any other price in an economy, i.e. by the interaction of the influences of demand and supply. It is stressed, however, that the demand for labour is unlike the demand for consumer goods or services in that it is not determined for its own sake, but in relation to what it can produce. It would be helpful if the candidate said more on this. The treatment of the supply of labour is also rather limited. This section should be developed more fully, such as in relation to the elasticity of supply of labour.*

The demand curve for labour is actually related to the marginal revenue product of labour, i.e. the extra sales revenue that is generated by the use of one more input of a factor of production. This will be equal to the marginal physical product multiplied by the price of the product, i.e. $MRP = MPP \times P$, where P is price.

e *There is some consideration of the importance of marginal physical product and marginal revenue product, but this paragraph is rather limited in scope and discussion of marginal revenue product, in particular, needs to be developed much more fully. It would be helpful to include a diagram to support the points being made about this. This would show how the demand curve, i.e. the* MRP *curve, for labour is eventually downward sloping from left to right.*

However, all this assumes that the wages of workers are determined in competitive markets, but this is not always the case. It could be that imperfections exist in the labour market. For example, a situation of monopsony could exist, where there is just one buyer of the labour and this single buyer is able to have considerable power and influence, i.e. it is a wage maker rather than a wage taker. Also, instead of wage levels being determined in a free market, the government could decide to intervene to establish a national minimum wage above what a free-market wage would be, determined just by the forces of demand and supply. A further imperfection could be that the workers are organised in trades unions and so instead of wages being established with individual workers, the trade unions intervene in the process of collective bargaining. This 'strength in numbers' would be likely to bring the wages up from what they otherwise would be expected to be.

e *The candidate clearly shows an understanding of the distinction that needs to be made between perfect and imperfect markets. There is a reference to the possible existence of a monopsonist, but the discussion here is rather limited. For example, there is a reference to a monopsonist having 'considerable power and influence' and to the situation of being 'a wage maker rather than a wage taker', but this doesn't really take the discussion very far. There is a lot more that could be written on the influence of a monopsonist on wages, and a diagram would be extremely helpful in showing how a monopsonist situation would be different from the situation prevailing in a perfect market. Again, there is a reference to another imperfection in the form of government intervention, such as through the establishment of a national minimum wage, but the discussion of such intervention is again somewhat limited. The inclusion of a diagram would show how the imposition of a national minimum wage would create a 'labour price' above what it would otherwise have been. At the end of the paragraph, there is some discussion of the potential importance of trade unions in the determination of wages, but this too needs to be expanded. For example, there is a reference to 'collective bargaining', but this term is not discussed more fully.*

In conclusion, the wage of a worker could be determined, just like any other price in an economy, by the forces of demand and supply, but this assumes a free market. Often this is not the case, and there are many possible situations where there are significant market imperfections, including monopsony, government intervention and the role of trade unions in the process of collective bargaining; in such cases, wages are not determined like other prices in an economy.

e *The candidate ends with a conclusion, vitally important in a 'discuss' question, but it is a rather limited conclusion. The distinction between a free or perfect market and an imperfect market is made clear, and the candidate does focus on the question in stating that whether a wage is determined just like any other price in an economy depends on whether the process of wage determination is taking place in a perfect or imperfect market. The conclusion could have been improved, however, by discussing to what extent the market imperfections are significant.*

e *On the whole, this is a reasonable attempt to answer the question. The answer is well structured and the candidate clearly understands the difference between a perfect and an imperfect market in relation to wage determination. However, there are a number of areas where the answer needs to be developed more fully, especially in relation to the existence of monopsony, government intervention and the potential role of trade unions. This answer would gain a Grade C with a mark of 13/25.*

Question 14

Discuss how useful GDP is in comparing living standards in different countries. [25]

GDP refers to the gross domestic product of a country, i.e. the value of what has been produced within its geographical boundaries over a period of time, usually one year. This statistic is of some use in comparing living standards in different countries, but it does not take into account the size of a country's population. In order to make effective comparisons between the living standards of different countries, it is necessary to divide the GDP by the size of population; this will produce a per head or per capita figure.

e *The candidate starts with a useful definition of what GDP is and then goes on to begin discussing the limitations of this method of comparison by stressing the importance of taking into account the size of a country's population. It would be helpful to contrast two countries with very different population sizes to support this point, such as Singapore with a population of 4.7 million and China with a population of 1.4 billion.*

Another issue is whether GDP or GNP would be a better statistic to use. GDP only includes the value of production that takes place within the geographical boundaries of a country, whereas GNP (gross national product) includes net property income from abroad, i.e. it includes the value of production that takes place in other countries using resources that are owned domestically. With some countries, this would be a more useful approach.

e *The candidate demonstrates some understanding of different ways of approaching the measurement of national income, contrasting GDP with GNP and stressing that the former excludes net property income from abroad whereas the latter includes it.*

It also needs to be stated that GDP only refers to the value of what has been produced over a period of time. It is, therefore, a quantitative measure. It includes all forms of production and yet some of this production might not positively affect standards of living. For example, it could include expenditure on military equipment. It could also include production that leads to the creation of negative externalities, such as pollution, which would not contribute to an increase in living standards.

e *The candidate usefully contrasts quantitative and qualitative approaches to the consideration of standards of living, stressing that GDP simply provides a figure for the value of production in a country; it does not make any comment on the quality of life brought about by whatever has been produced.*

Another limitation of the GDP statistics is that they only include economic activity which has taken place officially. In many countries, however, a significant amount of economic activity goes unrecorded in what can be termed the hidden, informal or underground economy. Such economic activity is not included within markets and so it goes unrecorded. Work carried out at home by a person, called DIY (Do It Yourself), would not be recorded, but if a person paid somebody to do such work, it would be recorded.

It is important to have stressed that GDP only includes economic activity that goes through a market. In many economies, there may be a large amount of economic activity that goes unrecorded.

A further limitation of GDP statistics is that a per capita or per head figure only provides an average for that country. It does not take into account the distribution of the GDP and in some countries there may be a very unequal distribution of income.

This is also an important point for the candidate to have stressed. A GDP per capita or per head figure simply provides an average by dividing a country's GDP by its population. The degree to which this is distributed equally in different countries can vary enormously.

Another factor to take into account is the distinction between real GDP and nominal GDP. Nominal GDP simply refers to the value of GDP over a period of time, but it does not take into account the effect of changes in the rate of inflation. For example, if the GDP of a country has increased by 5% over a period of time, but it has experienced a rate of inflation of 3% over this period, the increase in real GDP would only have been 2%.

This is an important point to stress. The candidate has demonstrated a clear knowledge and understanding of the distinction between real and nominal data and has used an appropriate mathematical example to indicate the difference between the two.

As a result of these limitations of using GDP statistics, other measures have been adopted to give a better indication of the differences in living standards between various countries. One of these is the Human Development Index. This was created by the United Nations to try to give a broader view of the quality of life than just GDP. It includes GDP as well as life expectancy and years of schooling. The highest HDI value that a country can be given is 1.00.

It is good that the candidate has gone beyond GDP to consider alternative measures of welfare, such as the HDI. However, the construction of the HDI was changed in 2010 and it now includes gross national income per capita rather than gross domestic product per capita. The HDI figures are also measured in terms of purchasing power parity. This concept is not referred to in the candidate's answer; it would be useful to bring this in as it is a way of taking into account the price levels in different countries.

Other measures of the quality of life could also be used, other than HDI, such as the Human Poverty Index (HPI). The HPI has now largely been replaced by the Multidimensional Poverty Index.

It would be good to develop this reference to the Multidimensional Poverty Index more fully by referring to the ten criteria that are used: child mortality, nutrition, years of schooling, children enrolled in school, cooking fuel, access to a toilet, water, electricity, the type of floor in the home and assets. This would show just how much wider this measure of welfare is when compared to GDP or HDI.

In conclusion, GDP statistics are clearly of some use in comparing living standards in different countries, especially when the figures used are real GDP per capita figures, but there are a number of limitations in their use. This is why alternative measures of welfare have been introduced to give a wider view of living standards and quality of life, especially the Human Development Index and the Multidimensional Poverty Index.

It is always important to end a 'discuss' question with a reasoned and logical conclusion. The candidate does this by focusing on the fact that GDP statistics are of some value, especially when expressed in terms of real per capita data, but then stresses the fact that there are a number of limitations which is why other measures have been adopted to provide a wider perspective.

This is a very good attempt to answer the question. The candidate's answer demonstrates a sound knowledge and understanding of the issue of comparing living standards in different countries. There are areas where the answer could be improved, as indicated in the comments, but there is a clear focus on the question and the answer is well structured. It would gain a Grade A with a mark of 18/25.

Now test yourself answers

Topic 1

1. The 'economic problem' refers to a situation where there are not enough resources in an economy to satisfy all the needs and wants of the people and, given this situation of scarcity, a choice will need to be made in terms of the allocation and use of those scarce resources.
2. Opportunity cost means that when you choose the best option, you forego the next best alternative.
3. A market economy allocates resources through demand and supply; a planned economy allocates resources through the government; and a mixed economy allocates them through a mixture of demand and supply and the government.
4. A transitional economy is one which is in the process of moving away from being a planned economy towards one which allows a greater role for market forces.
5. A production possibility curve identifies the combination of two products that can be produced in an economy when the available resources are fully used.
6. The primary sector of production refers to production that has taken place in an extractive industry, such as agriculture. The secondary sector of production refers to production that has taken place in manufacturing and construction, such as car production. The tertiary sector of production refers to the provision of services, such as education (e.g. a teacher).
7. The term 'capital', when used as a factor of production, refers to the human-made aids to production that are used in the production process, such as tools, equipment and machinery.
8. The four functions of money are to act as a medium of exchange, a unit of account or measure of value, a store of value or wealth and a standard of deferred payment.

Topic 2

1. There is an inverse relationship between the quantity demanded of a product and the price of a product, assuming that the condition of ceteris paribus exists. This is why a demand curve is usually downward sloping from left to right.
2. A movement along a demand curve, known as an extension of demand or a contraction of demand, is caused by a change in the price of a product, assuming that all other influences on demand are kept constant (ceteris paribus). A shift of a demand curve, known as an increase or a decrease in demand, is caused by any of the other influences on demand, apart from price, such as changes in incomes or in the tastes and preferences of consumers.
3. A normal good is one for which the demand will rise as a result of an increase in income. An inferior good is one for which the demand will fall as a result of an increase in income.
4. This situation exists when the percentage change in the quantity demanded of a product is greater than the percentage change in the price of a product. In terms of the figure for price elasticity of demand, it is greater than one.
5. The concept of price elasticity of demand indicates the relationship between a change in the price of a product and the quantity demanded of that product, whereas the concept of income elasticity of demand shows the relationship between a change in income and the quantity demanded of a product.
6. The formula for cross elasticity of demand is the percentage change in the quantity demanded of good A divided by the percentage change in the price of good B.
7. There is a direct relationship between the quantity supplied of a product and the price of a product, assuming that the condition of ceteris paribus exists. This is why a supply curve is usually upward sloping from left to right.
8. A subsidy is a payment, often by a government, to reduce the cost of production to a firm in order to encourage it to produce more at a lower price to consumers. It causes the supply curve for a product to shift to the right, so that the new equilibrium will be at a lower price and at a higher output.
9. If everything else remains constant, and only the price of a product changes, there will be a movement *along* a supply curve. If any of the other influences on supply changes, such as the cost of raw materials, there will be a *shift* of the whole supply curve.
10. The formula for price elasticity of supply is the percentage change in the quantity supplied of a product divided by the percentage change in the price of a product.
11. A market equilibrium exists when the quantity demanded in a market is exactly equal to the quantity supplied. There is neither an excess demand nor an excess supply.
12. An equilibrium position in a market occurs where the market is said to be 'in a state of rest'. Demand and supply are equal and there are no pressures for this to change, so an equilibrium price and an equilibrium quantity are established.
13. Consumer surplus is a situation in a market where many consumers would be willing to pay a higher price for a product, but they do not need to because the market price is the same for all consumers. This extra satisfaction gained by these consumers is shown in a diagram by the triangle between the horizontal price line and the downward-sloping demand curve.
14. The importance of price in a market was recognised by the Scottish economist Adam Smith who stressed that it plays a crucial role in providing a signal for any changes in demand and/or supply. In this way, price acts as an 'invisible hand' in decisions about the allocation of scarce resources.

Topic 3

1. An externality is a cost or a benefit which has a spillover effect on a third party and which is not paid for by a

consumer or a producer. Externalities can therefore relate to either production or consumption and can be either positive or negative.

2 A social cost is the combined cost of private costs and external costs.

3 Cost–benefit analysis refers to the analysis of a project that takes into account all the possible costs and benefits involved, i.e. private costs, external costs, private benefits and external benefits. As a result of this, a decision can then be taken as to whether the project is worthwhile.

4 A private good is one that is bought by an individual for their own benefit, whereas a public good is one that is provided by a government for the whole community so that all can benefit.

5 A merit good is one that, if left to a free market, would be likely to be under-produced and under-consumed; a government may therefore intervene in a market to provide, or to encourage the consumption of, such a good. Examples could include education and healthcare. A demerit good is one that, if left to a free market, would be likely to be over-produced and over-consumed; a government may therefore intervene in a market to discourage the consumption of such a good. Examples could include alcohol and tobacco.

6 Prices are usually determined by the forces of demand and supply, but sometimes a government may intervene by establishing a maximum price. This will prevent the prices of certain goods rising above a particular level, making them more affordable for people in a society on relatively low incomes.

Topic 4

1 Absolute advantage is where a country can produce a good using fewer resources or inputs than any other country. Comparative advantage is where another country has an absolute disadvantage in producing something, but there may still be a case for it producing certain products which it is least efficient at producing, as long as there are differences in the opportunity cost ratios of production in two countries.

2 Bilateral trade refers to trade between two countries, whereas multilateral trade refers to trade between a number of countries and/or agencies.

3 The World Trade Organisation has the purpose of promoting free trade through the reduction of protectionist barriers. Its negotiations take place through a series of 'rounds', the most recent of which is the Doha Round which began in 2001.

4 A sunrise industry is one which is just beginning to develop, i.e. it is in its infancy. A sunset industry is a declining one that is gradually producing less. It is argued that trade protection for both of these types of industry can be justified, at least for a limited period of time.

5 A tariff is a tax that is placed on imports to reduce the demand for imported goods, assuming that the price elasticity of demand for such goods is elastic. A quota is a restriction on the imports into a country; a quota can take the form of a physical limit on units imported, a limit in terms of the value of imports or a limit in relation to the market share that they represent.

6 Both encourage the development of free trade among their members, but whereas a free trade area retains a separate set of trade barriers against other countries, a customs union imposes a common external tariff on imports from countries that are outside the union.

7 The calculation of the terms of trade for a country involves the following formula:

$$\frac{\text{index number showing the average price of exports}}{\text{index number showing the average price of imports}}$$

8 A visible refers to the import or export of a tangible, physical product, such as a car or a television. An invisible refers to money coming into, or leaving, a country as a result of a service, such as banking, insurance or tourism.

Topic 5

1 The labour force is the number of people in an economy who are available for work. It is therefore made up of both the employed and the unemployed.

2 Labour productivity refers to the efficiency of labour in terms of the output per worker per period of time.

3 One way to measure the number of people in a country who are unemployed is through the claimant count, i.e. the number of people who are officially registered as unemployed in order to be able to claim benefits. The other method is through the labour force survey, i.e. those who will appear on the claimant count and also others who are available for work but who have not officially registered as unemployed. Clearly the figure produced through the labour force survey will be higher than that arrived at through the claimant count.

4 Weighting refers to the fact that not all the items included in a basket of expenditure on household goods will be of the same importance. For example, expenditure on food, housing and transport is going to be more important than expenditure on newspapers or magazines. Each of the different items in the basket will be given a 'weighting' to indicate the relative importance of these items in the spending patterns of people.

5 Nominal data refers to data that has not been adjusted to take into account the effects of inflation. Real data, however, refers to information that has been adjusted to take account the effects of inflation. For example, if a person's wage has increased by 5%, and there is an inflation rate of 3%, then the person has had a real increase in wages of 2% (5% – 3%).

6 The four elements that make up aggregate demand are consumption, investment, government spending and net exports.

Topic 6

1 Inflation refers to a situation where there is a persistent or sustained increase in the general or average level of prices in an economy over a given period of time.

2 Hyperinflation is a situation where the rate of inflation in an economy is very high, e.g. it is over 100%. It is a serious problem because it can undermine confidence in an economy, especially its currency, and can lead to the currency having to be replaced by another, as happened in Zimbabwe.

3 Menu costs refer to the costs involved in the constant need to keep changing prices that are being advertised for products in a situation of inflation. Shoe leather costs refer to the costs involved in the constant need to keep searching for the best possible returns so as to keep ahead of inflation.

4 Demand-pull inflation is where the level of demand in an economy is greater than supply, pulling the general level of prices up. Cost-push inflation is where the increase in the general level of prices is caused by an increase in the costs of production; as a result of these increases in costs, producers increase the prices charged for their products.

5 Fiscal drag refers to a situation where an increasing number of people are 'dragged' into the tax net if the tax allowances are not increased in line with the rate of inflation that is prevailing in an economy.

6 The International Monetary Fund (IMF) was set up to promote world trade. The IMF can help countries which have a persistent deficit in their balance of payments by providing loans to help a country over a difficult period, giving time for appropriate policies to be adopted to overcome the long-term reasons for such deficits.

7 A balance of payments deficit can lead to an increase in unemployment and a reduction of business confidence. If action is taken to try to reduce the deficit, this could lead to a reduction in choice for consumers and possibly an increase in the rate of inflation.

8 Purchasing power parity refers to the idea that the value of a currency needs to be seen in relation to what it would be able to buy, i.e. its purchasing power, in another country.

9 A depreciation of a currency refers to a situation where the value of the currency on the foreign exchange market is allowed to fall in a floating exchange rate system. A devaluation of a currency refers to a situation where the value of the currency on the foreign exchange market is deliberately lowered by a government in a fixed exchange rate system.

10 The term 'hot money' refers to money that is moved from the financial institutions of one country to those of another country to take advantage of the differences in interest rates in the two countries, i.e. the money will move away from countries with relatively low interest rates to countries with relatively high interest rates.

11 The J-curve effect is the idea that, after a depreciation or a devaluation of a currency, the balance of payments position will initially get worse before it begins to get better.

12 The Marshall-Lerner condition refers to the situation where, for a depreciation or devaluation of an exchange rate to be effective in terms of bringing about an improvement in a country's balance of payments position, the sum of the price elasticity of demand for imports and the price elasticity of demand for exports must be more than one.

Topic 7

1 Expenditure switching refers to a situation in an economy where policies are adopted to change the pattern of demand by increasing the demand for exports and reducing the demand for imports. Possible policies that could be adopted to try to achieve this aim are tariffs, quotas, subsidies, embargoes, exchange controls and administrative restrictions.

2 Expenditure dampening refers to a situation in an economy where policies are adopted to try to bring about a reduction in aggregate demand. Possible policies that could be adopted to try to achieve this aim are fiscal, such as reducing expenditure and/or increasing taxation, and monetary, such as an increase in the interest rate and/or a reduction in the money supply.

3 A balance of payments disequilibrium refers to a situation where there is a persistent, long-term imbalance in the balance of payments of an economy. This could be in terms of either a deficit or a surplus.

Topic 8

1 In terms of an individual firm, productive efficiency is where a firm is producing at the lowest point on its average cost curve, reflecting a situation of both technical and cost efficiency. In terms of the whole economy, it is where production is operating on the economy's production possibility curve, frontier or boundary.

Allocative efficiency, on the other hand, is where the allocation of resources matches the preferences of consumers; this can be seen where price is equal to marginal cost.

2 The idea of optimum indicates that this is the 'best' possible allocation of resources in an economy, given the particular circumstances of that economy. Optimum resource allocation is where both productive and allocative efficiency exist.

3 A Pareto optimal situation is where it is not possible to make one person better off without making another person worse off. This type of optimality is named after the Italian economist, Vilfredo Pareto.

Topic 9

1 This is the idea that the consumption of successive units of a product will lead to a decreasing level of utility or satisfaction from each unit consumed.

2 The equi-marginal principle is the idea that a consumer will maximise total satisfaction by equating the utility or satisfaction per unit of money spent on the marginal unit of each product consumed. It can be shown by

$$\frac{MUa}{Pa} = \frac{MUb}{Pb} = \frac{MUc}{Pc}$$

3 A budget line shows all the possible combinations of two products that a consumer would be able to buy, given a situation of a fixed income and prices.

4 Average product is the output per unit of a variable factor in the production process, e.g. the output per worker per period of time. Average product is also known as the productivity of a factor of production.

5 An economy of scale is where an increase of output in the long run brings about a decrease in the average cost of production. If it is an internal economy, it is concerned with

cost savings in a particular firm, such as a financial economy of scale that relates to just one firm. A diseconomy of scale is where an increase of output in the long run eventually brings about an increase in the average cost of production. If it is an external diseconomy, such as congestion in a particular area, it is concerned with the effects of the congestion on all firms in the area.

6 Average cost refers to the total cost of producing a number of items divided by the number of items produced. Economists, however, are often interested not in the average cost of producing a number of items, but in the cost of producing just one extra unit; this is known as the marginal cost.

7 Normal profit is the level of profit that is just sufficient to keep a firm in an industry, whereas abnormal (or supernormal) profit is the extra profit that is above the normal profit.

8 Economists are generally of the belief that profit maximisation is the main objective of a firm, but there are other possible objectives. These could include satisficing profits, revenue maximisation, sales maximisation or growth maximisation.

9 In the short run, a firm in perfect competition could make normal profits, abnormal/supernormal profits or subnormal profits. In the long run, however, a firm in perfect competition could only make normal profits.

10 A distinctive feature of oligopoly is that firms usually take into account the likely reactions of other firms in the industry to any actions they take. If a firm raises price, it is assumed that other firms will not follow this lead, and so demand is elastic. If a firm lowers price, it is assumed that other firms will follow this lead, and so demand is inelastic. This mixture of elastic demand above a certain price and inelastic demand below a certain price causes the demand curve to be kinked at this price.

11 A contestable market is one where it is relatively easy for a firm to enter and so firms in the market continually face the threat of new firms entering the market, so bringing about greater competition.

12 Price discrimination is where different prices can be charged in a market where there are different price elasticities of demand and where the difference in price is not due to a difference in cost.

13 There are a number of possible examples of non-price competition and these could include sales promotions, packaging or branding.

14 Backward vertical integration is where one firm integrates with another at an earlier stage of the production process to ensure the supply of raw materials. Forward vertical integration is where one firm integrates with another at a later stage of the production process to ensure the supply of products through appropriate retail outlets.

15 Derived demand refers to the fact that labour is not demanded for its own sake, but for what it can produce.

16 Pecuniary advantages of employment refer to monetary gains, whereas non-pecuniary advantages of employment refer to non-monetary gains, such as the job satisfaction gained.

17 Transfer earnings are the minimum payment required to keep a factor of production in its present use, whereas economic rent refers to the extra payment received by a factor of production that is above what would be required to keep it in its present use.

Topic 10

1 X-inefficiency refers to a situation where the average cost of production is not at its lowest point because there is inefficiency in the industry. It is a situation that is particularly associated with monopoly.

2 A deadweight loss refers to a reduction in the extent of a consumer surplus in a monopoly because the price is higher than it would be, and the quantity lower than it would be, in a perfectly competitive market. As a result of this situation, there is a welfare loss to the consumer.

3 A progressive tax, such as income tax, is one where an increasing percentage of a person's income is taken in tax as their income rises. It is not simply that more taxation is taken from a high income than a low one — a higher *percentage* of tax is taken from a high income than a low one.

4 A poverty trap is where a person who receives an increase in income can actually become worse off as a result of this income rise because, above a certain level of income, a person is no longer entitled to certain benefits from the state.

5 Privatisation refers to the process whereby a firm or industry is sold to the private sector, i.e. there is a transfer of ownership from the public sector to the private sector. Deregulation refers to a situation where there is a reduction in the number of regulations, laws and rules that operate in an industry, bringing about a greater degree of flexibility and, hopefully, efficiency.

Topic 11

1 Gross domestic product is the value of all that has been produced within the geographical boundaries of a country over a period of time. Gross national product is gross domestic product plus net property income from abroad, which is the net value of the interest, profits and dividends paid and received. This takes into account the fact that some of a country's economic activities will take place abroad.

2 Depreciation refers to the value that has been lost over a period of time, usually a year, and which will be needed to replace the capital equipment and machinery that has worn out during the year.

3 A GDP deflator is used to adjust the value of GDP to take into account the effects of inflation. If a country is experiencing inflation, the value of its GDP will go up by the rate of inflation, but this will not mean that there has been a 'real' increase in the value of the output. A deflator is used to adjust GDP so that it represents a 'real' value.

4 Sustainability refers to a situation where the interests of future generations, and not just the interests of the current population, are taken into account when decisions are taken on the allocation of scarce resources. For example, if scarce resources are used extensively by the present population, there will be a more rapid depletion of resources compared to a situation where a more considered approach was taken to the use of scarce resources, balancing the use of the resources with the conservation of them.

5 The ten MPI indicators are: child mortality, nutrition, years of schooling, child school attendance, electricity, sanitation, drinking water, type of floor, type of cooking fuel and the ownership of assets.

6 A budget deficit is where public expenditure is greater than public revenue. A budget shows the balance between public revenue and public expenditure. Sometimes a government may deliberately decide to operate a budget deficit to simulate the economy.

7 The three injections into the circular flow of income are investment spending, government expenditure and income received from exports. The three leakages or withdrawals out of the circular flow of income are savings, taxation and the money spent on imports.

8 Aggregate expenditure, or aggregate demand, is usually represented by $AD = C + I + G + X - M$.

9 The multiplier is the term used to denote the degree to which an injection into the circular flow of money brings about a greater increase in the total national income of an economy. It is calculated by

$$\frac{1}{\text{marginal propensity to withdraw}}$$

10 Autonomous investment takes place irrespective of any changes in the national income of an economy, whereas induced investment takes place as a result of changes in an economy's national income.

11 The term 'quantitative easing' refers to a situation where a country's central bank increases the amount of money available, or liquidity, by buying securities. The money used to buy them then becomes available in the economy, making it easier for people in the economy to borrow money.

12 The quantity theory of money is usually stated as $MV = PT$ where M is the money supply or stock of money, V is the velocity of circulation of money, P is the general price level in an economy and T is the number of transactions financed by the money over a period of time.

Topic 12

1 Economic growth is the increase in the national output of an economy over a period of time. It is usually measured through changes in gross domestic product over a year.

2 Actual growth refers to the movement from *within* the production possibility curve of an economy to a position *on* the production possibility curve. Potential growth refers to a shift outwards of an economy's production possibility curve as a result of an increase in the quantity and/or quality of a country's factors of production.

3 A trade/business cycle refers to a situation where the national output of an economy fluctuates through a number of stages or phases, such as boom, slump, recession and recovery.

4 Economic growth refers to the increase in a country's national income over a period of time, as measured by changes in gross domestic product. Economic development is a broader concept. It includes changes in gross domestic product, but it also includes other factors that affect the quality of life of people in a country.

5 Demography is concerned with the study of population; examples of such an approach include such indicators as the birth rate, the death rate, the fertility rate, the average age and life expectancy.

6 An optimum population is one which is the most appropriate population for a particular country, given its available resources.

7 The natural rate of unemployment, or equilibrium unemployment as it can also be called, is the non-accelerating inflation rate of unemployment, i.e. it is that rate of unemployment in an economy which is necessary to prevent the rate of inflation from increasing.

8 Structural unemployment refers to those people who have lost their jobs because of changes in the structure of a country's economy, i.e. because of the decline in traditional or sunset industries. Cyclical unemployment refers to those people who have lost their jobs because of changes in the trade/business cycle, i.e. because of the onset of a recession.

9 A Phillips curve is used to show the relationship between changes in the rate of inflation and changes in the rate of unemployment in an economy.

Topic 13

1 The six macroeconomic objectives that governments usually have are low inflation, full employment, sustainable economic growth, balance of payments equilibrium, exchange rate stability and as equitable a distribution of income and wealth as possible.

2 The four different types of macroeconomic policy are fiscal policy, monetary policy, exchange rate policy and supply-side policy.

3 Fiscal policy refers to the use of public revenue and/or public expenditure to influence the level of aggregate demand in an economy.

4 Discretionary fiscal policy refers to a situation where specific policy decisions are taken by a government in terms of revenue and/or expenditure to deliberately influence the level of demand in an economy. Automatic stabilisers refer to a situation where changes in public revenue and public expenditure in an economy come about automatically without the need for a government to deliberately take action.

5 If a direct tax, such as income tax, became too high, a person might become less inclined to work because they would feel that the marginal rate of tax, i.e. the amount of tax paid on the last unit of currency earned, was excessive.

6 A progressive tax is one which takes an increasingly greater proportion of the income of a rich person. A regressive tax is one which takes an larger portion of low incomes than high incomes. A proportional tax is one which takes an equal proportion of everyone's income.

7 Monetary policy refers to the use of interest rates and/or the quantity of money to influence the level of aggregate demand in an economy.

8 Quantitative easing refers to the deliberate policy of a government to increase the money supply through the purchase of bonds and bills to create more liquidity in the system.

9 Exchange rate policy refers to a situation where a country's exchange rate is deliberately changed to influence the level of aggregate demand in the economy.

10 Whereas many macroeconomic policies focus on influencing the level of demand in an economy, supply-side policy focuses on trying to improve the degree of efficiency and flexibility in markets. Examples could include lowering income tax, lowering unemployment benefits, improvements in the provision of education and training, reform of trade unions to reduce their power and influence, the encouragement of privatisation and deregulation and the improvement of information about job vacancies.

11 An increase in income is unlikely to lead to a significant increase in the demand for food, because there is only so much that people can eat, and so the income elasticity of demand for food is likely to be inelastic rather than elastic. Of course, the income elasticity of demand for particular types of food may well be elastic, e.g. people with higher incomes are more likely to purchase more exclusive types and brands of food.

12 Tied aid refers to aid that is provided by countries or agencies with certain conditions attached and so the country receiving the aid has not been entirely free in terms of how the aid is to be allocated.

Key terms

abnormal profit: the level of profit (also known as supernormal profit) that is over and above normal profit

absolute advantage: a situation where a country can produce a particular good using fewer resources than another country

accelerating inflation: a situation where the rate of inflation is rising, say from 5% to 25%, and is beginning to become a serious problem in an economy

accelerator: a way of calculating the effect of a change in national income on investment in an economy

active balances: money which is flowing through the economy, underpinning the transactions and precautionary motives for holding money

actual growth in national output: a movement from within the production possibility frontier of an economy to a position on the frontier, resulting from the better utilisation of the existing factors of production

ad valorem tax: an indirect tax with a percentage rate, e.g. a tax rate of 20% per product sold

Adam Smith: one of the founding fathers of Economics (1723–90) and author of The Wealth of Nations, published in 1776

aggregate demand: the total amount that is spent on an economy's goods and services over a given period of time; it is made up of four elements — consumption, investment, government spending and net exports

aggregate expenditure (or aggregate demand): the total demand for, and expenditure on, goods and services in an economy

aggregate supply: the total output that the various firms in an economy are able and willing to supply at different price levels in a given period of time; it includes both consumer and capital products

aid: the process of developed countries providing financial support to developing economies

allocative efficiency: a situation that describes the extent to which the allocation of resources in an economy matches consumer preferences

allocative mechanism: an allocative mechanism is a method of taking decisions about the different uses that can be made of factors of production. A mechanism is needed for economic goods that are scarce. Free goods in sufficient supply to satisfy demand, such as air or sunshine, do not need an allocative mechanism.

anticipated inflation: the expected future rate of inflation in an economy

appreciation: the rise in value of a currency that is floating

at constant prices: data which has been adjusted to take into account the effects of inflation

at current prices: data which is expressed in terms of the prices of a particular year, i.e. they have not been corrected to take account of inflation

automatic stabiliser: a situation where changes in the level of taxation and/or public expenditure automatically bring about changes in an economy without the need for deliberate action by a government

autonomous investment: capital investment that is not related to changes in the level of national income in an economy

average cost: the total cost divided by the number of units produced; also known as average total cost (ATC)

average fixed cost: the total fixed cost of production divided by the number of units produced

average product: the output per unit of the variable factor, e.g. output per worker per period of time. This is also referred to as productivity

average propensity to consume: the proportion of income that is spent

average revenue: the total revenue obtained from sales divided by the number of units sold

average variable cost: the total variable cost of production divided by the number of units produce

balance of payments: a record of all transactions linked with exports and imports, together with international capital movements. It consists of the current account, the capital account and the financial account

balanced budget: where projected revenue and planned government spending are equal

barriers to exit and entry: various obstacles that make it very difficult, or impossible, for new firms to exit or enter an industry. For example, where a firm is benefiting from technical economies of scale, it may be difficult for a new firm to enter the industry because its average costs of production will be much higher. Another reason might because a firm already has legal control of production of a product through a patent. An example of a barrier to exit would be where a firm has already invested heavily in capital equipment and would be reluctant to just 'write off' this expenditure

barter: the direct exchange of one good or service for another

base year: a year chosen so that comparisons can be made over a period of time; the base year for an index is given a value of 100

bilateral trade: where trade takes place between two countries

birth rate: the average number of live births per thousand of population of a country in a given time period, usually a year

breakeven point: the level of output at which a firm is making neither a loss nor a profit

broad money supply: a measure of the stock of money which reflects the total potential purchasing power in an economy

budget deficit: where projected revenue is less than planned expenditure

budget line: a line that shows all the possible combinations of two products that a consumer would be able to purchase with fixed prices and a given income. It is also sometimes known as a consumption possibility line

budget surplus: where projected revenue is greater than planned expenditure

buffer stock: a stock of a commodity which is held back from the market in times of high production and released onto the market in times of low production

canons of taxation: the main principles of taxation, i.e. any system of taxes should adhere to these principles in order to be effective

capital account of the balance of payments: this is made up of transactions where there is a transfer of financial assets between one country and another. For example, such a financial asset could include the purchase of a physical asset such as land

capital: the factor of production that includes all the human-made aids to production, such as tools, equipment and machinery

capital:output ratio: a way of measuring the amount of capital employed in the production of a given level of output

cartel: a situation where a number of firms agree to collude, i.e. work together, such as by limiting output to keep price higher than would be the case if there was competition between the firms

central bank: the main bank in a country that is responsible for oversight of the banking system

ceteris paribus: a Latin term that literally means 'other things being equal'

change in demand: this is where there is a change in the conditions of demand, i.e. something other than a change in the price of a product; this is shown by a shift of a demand curve

change in quantity demanded: this is where demand for a product changes as a result of a change in the price of the product; change in quantity demanded is shown by a movement along a demand curve

cheques: cheques are a method of payment, i.e. they are a means of transferring money from one account to another. They are not, however, a form of money

circular flow of income: the flow of income around an economy, involving a mixture of injections and withdrawals or leakages

claimant count: the number of people who officially register as unemployed

closed economy: an economy which does not trade with the rest of the world

closed shop: a requirement that all employees in a specific workplace belong to a particular trade union

collective bargaining: the process of negotiation between trade union representatives of the workers and their employers on such issues as remuneration (payment) and working conditions

common external tariff: where all of the countries in an economic organisation impose the same tariff with other countries outside of the organisation

comparative advantage: a situation where a country might be more efficient at producing everything compared to another country, but where there would still be an advantage if it produced something that it was least bad at producing

complementary goods: goods which are consumed together, e.g. DVDs and DVD players. These goods have a negative cross elasticity of demand, i.e. a rise in the price of one of them will lead to a decrease in the demand for the other

composite demand: this refers to the demand for a product which can be used for more than one purpose. Stone, for example, could be used for building purposes and could also be used in the construction of roads; a particular piece of land could be demanded to build both shops and houses

concentration ratio: the percentage of a market controlled by a given number of firms, e.g. the five largest firms in an industry might control 80% of the output of the industry

conglomerate integration: where there is a merger between firms which are operating in completely different markets rather than in different stages of the same market

constant returns to scale: whereas economies of scale give rise to decreasing costs, it may be that there is a level of output where costs remain the same. This is known as constant returns to scale

consumer prices index: a way of measuring changes in the prices of a number of consumer goods and services in an economy over a period of time

consumer surplus: a situation that comes about because some consumers will value a particular product more highly than other consumers and yet they will pay exactly the same price for it as the other consumers. Consumer surplus refers to the value of this extra satisfaction; it is shown on a demand and supply diagram by the triangle between the price line and the demand curve

consumption: the spending by consumers in an economy over a period of time

contestable market: a situation where it may be relatively easy for new entrants to enter a market or industry; the effect of this is that existing firms in an industry face the threat of new firms coming into the industry and increasing the degree of competition

contracting out: the transfer of responsibility for the provision of a service from the public to the private sector

cost efficiency: a situation where a firm uses the most appropriate combination of inputs of factors of production, given the relative costs of those factors

cost of living: the cost of a selection of goods and services that are consumed by an average household in an economy at a given period of time

cost-push inflation: a rise in the general level of prices in an economy, caused primarily by a significant rise in the costs of production

cost–benefit analysis: an analysis of a project which includes a valuation of the total costs and total benefits involved, i.e. including private and external costs and private and external benefits

costs of production: these are the various costs involved in the production process and can be generally divided into fixed costs, which do not vary with changes in output, and variable costs, which do vary with changes in output

credit creation: the process by which financial institutions make loans through what is known as fractional reserve banking, i.e. the requirement that such institutions only need to hold a certain percentage of their total liabilities, say 10%, in the form of cash reserves. The financial institutions are then able to expand their lending by a multiple of any new deposits received; this is known as the credit creation multiplier

credit multiplier: the relationship between new deposits created as a result of additional cash deposits

credit: refers to a situation where a person can take possession of a product immediately, but not be required to pay for it until a later time

creeping inflation: a situation where the rate of inflation is reasonably low, say about 2%

cross elasticity of demand (or cross price elasticity of demand): this measures the degree to which a change in the price of one product leads to a change in the quantity demanded of another product

current account of balance of payments: this is made up of four elements — the trade in goods, the trade in services, income and current transfers

current transfers: this refers to the net payments by governments and private individuals, such as grants for overseas aid or cash remittances sent home to their own countries by migrant workers

customs union: a group of countries which promote free trade between themselves, and which impose a common external tariff on imports from countries outside the area

D

deadweight losses: the reduction in consumer surplus when a monopoly producer reduces output and raises price compared to what the situation would be in perfect competition; there is therefore a welfare loss to the consumer

death rate: the number of people per thousand of population in a country who die in a given time period, usually a year

decreasing returns to scale: where the same proportional increase in productive factors gives rise to decreasing additions to total output; this gives rise to diseconomies of scale

deficit: a negative balance when expenditure exceeds income

deflation: a general decrease in the average level of prices in an economy over a period of time. Deflation can also mean a reduction in the level of aggregate demand in an economy, in contrast to reflation which means an increase in the level of aggregate demand in an economy

deflationary gap: a situation where the level of aggregate demand in an economy is less than the aggregate supply at full employment, causing unemployment in the economy

demand curve: a curve that shows how much of a good or service will be demanded by consumers at a given price in a given period of time

demand schedule: this gives the quantities sold of a product at different prices and enables a demand curve to be drawn from the information in the schedule

demand-pull inflation: a rise in the general level of prices in an economy, caused primarily by too much demand for products

demand: the quantity of a product that consumers are willing to buy at a given price in a given period of time

demerit goods: products which are rivalrous and excludable which, if left to a free market, would be likely to be over-produced and over-consumed. The social costs of production/consumption outweigh the private costs

dependency ratio: the ratio of those people in a country who are unable to work divided by those who are able to work

depreciation: the fall in value of a currency that is floating

depreciation (of capital): the amount of capital that is needed to replace equipment that has depreciated, i.e. worn out, over a year

deregulation: the reduction in the number of regulations, rules and laws that operate in an industry

derived demand: this is where the demand for a component depends upon the final demand for a product that uses that component. For example, the demand for rubber is derived from the demand for car tyres. Derived demand can also be used in relation to the demand for workers, e.g. the demand for bus drivers derives from the demand for bus transport from people

devaluation: the fall in value of a currency that is fixed

direct taxation: whereas an indirect tax is imposed on expenditure, a direct tax is imposed on the incomes of individuals and firms. Examples of direct taxation include income tax (on the incomes of individuals), corporation tax (on the profits of companies) and inheritance tax (on the wealth of individuals)

discretionary fiscal policy: the use of deliberate changes in taxation and/or public expenditure with the intention of changing the level of aggregate demand in an economy

diseconomies of scale: a situation where the average cost of production rises with an increase in the level of output

disequilibrium: a situation where there is an imbalance between demand and supply in a market, i.e. there will be a situation of excess demand or excess supply

dissaving: a situation that can occur when consumption exceeds income and so people have to rely on savings that have been accumulated in the past

distribution of income: the degree to which income in a country is evenly distributed

diversification: a situation where a firm decides to operate in a number of markets to spread risk

division of labour: the way in which production is divided into a sequence of specific tasks which enables workers to specialise in a particular type of job

double coincidence of wants: a situation in a system of barter where a seller needs to find a buyer who wants what is being sold and where the seller also wants something that the buyer has got and is willing to trade in exchange

dumping: the practice of selling a product at a price that is less than the cost of production

economic development: a broader perspective that goes beyond increases in national output to take into account factors that influence the quality of life of people in particular countries

economic growth: an increase in the national output of an economy over a period of time, usually measured through changes in gross domestic product

economic law: an economic theory put forward by economists, such as the laws of demand and supply

economic problem: a situation where there are not enough resources to satisfy all human needs and wants

economic rent: the extra payment received by a factor of production that is above what would be needed to keep it in its present use

economic union: a group of countries which agree to integrate their economies as much as possible through various rules, laws, policies and regulations

economies of large dimensions: the reduction in average cost as a result of using larger factors of production, such as larger containers in the transportation process

effective demand: consumers must not only want to buy a particular product but be able to afford to pay for it. Effective demand refers to demand that is backed by the ability and the willingness to pay for a product

efficient resource allocation: the optimal use of scarce inputs to produce the largest possible output

elastic: if the response of demand (or supply) is proportionately greater than the change in the independent variable, then the calculation is greater than one and is thus described as elastic

embargoes: bans on imports from particular countries. They can either apply to particular products or to all products from particular countries. They are usually imposed for political, diplomatic or military, rather than economic, reasons

enterprise: the factor of production that refers to the taking of a risk in organising the other three factors of production

entrepreneur: the individual who takes a risk in combining the other factors of production

equi-marginal principle: this states that a consumer will maximise total satisfaction by equating the utility or satisfaction per unit of money spent on the marginal unit of each product consumed

equilibrium: a situation where the quantity demanded in the marketplace is exactly equal to the quantity supplied. There is neither excess demand nor excess supply in the market. It is sometimes referred to as a state of rest or balance

equilibrium price: the price at which a market clears. The process of market clearing arises because the price is free to change and settle at the equilibrium level

equilibrium quantity: a situation where a market clears, with consumers getting all they want at the equilibrium price and producers not being left with unsold products, i.e. there is no excess demand or excess supply in the market

exchange rate policy: the deliberate use of changes in exchange rates to influence the level of aggregate demand in an economy

excise duties: an indirect tax on expenditure

excludable: a situation that occurs with private goods in that when a product is consumed by one person, all others are excluded from it

expenditure dampening (or expenditure reducing): a policy which attempts to bring about a reduction in the level of aggregate demand in an economy

expenditure switching: a policy which attempts to bring about a change in the pattern of demand in an economy by reducing the demand for imports and increasing the demand for exports

exports: goods and/or services that are produced domestically in one country and sold to other countries

external balance: the balance between receipts and payments in relation to international transactions between one country and other countries in the world

external benefits: the advantages gained by third parties, not just the consumer or the producer

external costs: the costs imposed on third parties

external diseconomies of scale: these are when costs of production rise because of developments outside a particular firm

external economies of scale: these are when costs of production fall because of developments outside a particular firm

externalities: costs or benefits of either consumption or production which have spillover or third party effects that are not paid for by the consumer or by the producer

financial account of the balance of payments: this is made up of the capital inflows and capital outflows resulting from investment in different countries

financial economies of scale: the reduction in average cost as a result of a firm being larger, such as the ability of a larger firm to negotiate more favourable borrowing terms on a loan

firm: a particular and distinct organisation that is owned separately from any other organisation

fiscal drag: the idea that more people will be dragged into the 'tax net' in a situation of inflation if the tax allowances are not increased in line with the rate of inflation

fiscal policy: the use of public revenue and/or public expenditure to influence the level of aggregate demand in an economy

fixed capital formation: buildings, plant, machinery and vehicles for commercial use that are used in the production process

fixed costs: the costs of production that remain constant at all levels of output, including zero production; examples include rent and interest payments

fixed exchange rate: an exchange rate that is determined at a particular level by a government

fixed factors of production: resource inputs that exist in the short run when the quantity of the factors used cannot be changed, e.g. capital equipment

flat-rate tax: a tax with a constant marginal rate

floating exchange rate: an exchange rate that is determined, like any other price, by the market forces of demand and supply

foreign exchange: the foreign currency that is used in other countries as a medium of exchange

Forex (or Foreign Exchange) Market: the coming together of buyers and sellers of currencies to establish a price

free rider: the idea that it would be impossible to charge people for the use of something because it would be virtually impossible to charge each person for the use of a product; this is why street lighting, for example, is provided as a public good rather than as a private good

free trade: trade which is not restricted or limited by different types of import controls

free trade area: a group of countries which promote free trade between themselves, but which retain a separate set of trade barriers against other countries

full employment: the level of employment as a result of everyone who is able and willing to work having a job, with the exception of those who are frictionally unemployed

GDP deflator: a ratio of price indices that is used in national income statistics to take away the effect of price changes so that the figures can be seen as representing real changes in output

general price level: the average level of prices of all consumer goods and services in an economy at a given period of time

globalisation: the process whereby there is an increasing world market in goods and services, making an increase in multilateral trade more likely. It has been made possible by a number of factors, including progress in trade liberalisation

government expenditure: the total of all spending by a government

government failure: a situation where government intervention to correct market failure does not actually improve the level of economic efficiency; it is possible that such intervention may even reduce the efficiency of the allocation of scarce resources in the economy

gross domestic product: the total value of all that has been produced over a given period of time within the geographical boundaries of a country

gross national product: the gross domestic product of a country plus net property income from abroad

horizontal integration: where firms at the same stage of production merge

hot money: flows of money that move from one country to another to take advantage of different rates of interest in various countries

household expenditure: a survey is taken on a regular basis (usually every month) to record changes in the prices of a selection of goods and services that constitutes a representative basket

Human Development Index: a composite measure that combines life expectancy, average income in the form of gross national income per capita (PPP US$) and years of schooling

Human Poverty Index: this was developed by the United Nations to complement the Human Development Index; it puts more of a focus on the extent of deprivation in different countries

hyperinflation: a situation where the rate of inflation is becoming very high, say over 100%, and is damaging confidence in the country's economy

idle balances: money which is withdrawn from the circular flow of money in an economy, underpinning the speculative motive for holding money

immobility of labour: the degree of occupational immobility and geographical immobility of labour which makes a labour market less flexible than it would otherwise be

impact of tax: this refers to the person, company or transaction on which a tax is levied, i.e. someone is responsible for handing the money to the tax authorities. The impact of a tax, therefore, is essentially concerned with the legal situation. As indicated above, the eventual incidence of a tax could be different if the burden of the tax is passed to someone else

imperfect competition: a market which lacks some, or all, of the features of perfect competition

imported inflation: a rise in the general level of prices in an economy, caused primarily by a significant increase in the price of imports

imports: goods and/or services that are produced in foreign countries and consumed by people in the domestic economy

incidence of tax: this refers to the burden of taxation. For example, with an indirect tax on expenditure, the burden of the tax is likely to be shared between the producer and the consumer. However, if the price elasticity of demand is perfectly inelastic, and there is a vertical demand curve, the incidence of the tax will be entirely on the consumer. On the other hand, if the price elasticity of demand is perfectly elastic, and there is a horizontal demand curve, the incidence of the tax will be entirely on the producer

income effect: the effect on consumption of a change in real income which occurs as a result of a price change

income elasticity of demand: this measures the degree to which a change in incomes leads to a change in the quantity demanded of a product

income tax: a direct tax on the incomes of individuals. There is usually a personal allowance, which is tax free, and then different tax rates for different levels of income over the tax-free allowance. Income tax, therefore, is usually progressive as the tax rates change as incomes rise, i.e. it takes a higher proportion of a higher income and a lower proportion of a lower income

increasing returns to scale: where output can be increased using proportionately fewer inputs; this gives rise to economies of scale

indirect tax: a tax that is imposed on expenditure; it is indirect in that the tax is only paid when the product on which the tax is levied is purchased

induced investment: capital investment that is related to changes in the level of national income in an economy

industry: a collection of firms producing similar products

inelastic: if the response of demand (or supply) is proportionately less than the change in the independent variable, then the calculation is less than one and is thus described as inelastic

infant industry argument: the idea that a newly established industry should be given time to establish itself; it will, therefore, need to be protected, at least temporarily

inferior good: a good for which the demand falls with an increase in income

inflation: a general increase in the average level of prices in an economy over a period of time

inflationary gap: a situation where the level of aggregate demand in an economy is greater than the aggregate supply at full employment, causing a rise in the general level of prices in the economy

information failure: a situation where people lack the full information that would allow them to make the best decisions about consumption

injection: spending which adds to the circular flow of income; this can come from investment, government expenditure and exports

integration: the process whereby two or more firms come together through a takeover, merger or acquisition A merger is where two or more firms combine together as a result of mutual agreement, whereas a takeover or acquisition usually involves some form of hostile bid by one firm for another

interest: the reward for parting with liquidity. This means that if a person deposits cash in a savings account, which they can no longer use for a period of time, their reward is an additional sum of money that they will get back with the amount of money originally deposited

interest rate policy: the use of changes in interest rates in an economy to bring about particular objectives, such as a change in the exchange rate

internal diseconomies of scale: these are the disadvantages of a firm growing in size in the form of an increase in the average cost of production

internal economies of scale: these are the advantages of a firm growing in size in the form of a reduction in the average cost of production

International Monetary Fund: set up in 1944 to promote international trade through such measures as providing financial support in the form of a loan which will help a country to overcome, or at least reduce, a deficit in the balance of payments; it now has 188 member countries

investment: (1) spending on capital equipment, such as a machine or a piece of equipment that can be used in the production process; (2) the spending by firms in an economy over a period of time

invisible balance: this refers to the trade in invisible services, such as banking, between countries

J-curve effect: the period of time, after a depreciation, when the current account of the balance of payments gets worse before it gets better

joint demand: this is a situation where two items are consumed together, i.e. they are complements. An example would be shoes and shoe laces

joint supply: a situation where the process of producing one product leads to the production of another product, such as meat and leather. It can sometimes happen in the chemical industry where one chemical can be produced as a byproduct of the production of another

Keynesian: an approach that is based on the views of the economist John Maynard Keynes (1883–1946)

labour: the factor of production that includes all the human effort that goes into the process of production, both mental and physical

labour force: the number of people that are available for work in a country

labour force survey: this will include not only those who are officially registered as unemployed but also those who are available for work but who have not officially registered themselves as unemployed

labour productivity: productivity measures the level of efficiency in the use of resources. Labour productivity, therefore, measures the efficiency of labour in terms of the output per person per period of time

Laffer curve: this shows the relationship between the rate of tax and the revenue obtained from the tax

land: the factor of production that includes all the gifts of nature, or natural resources, that can be used in the process of production, such as minerals, forests and the sea

law of demand: a law (or theory) which states that there is an inverse relationship between the quantity demanded of a product and the price of the product, ceteris paribus

law of diminishing marginal utility: the principle (or law) that the marginal utility of consuming successive units of the same product will fall

law of diminishing returns: as additional units of a variable factor, such as labour, are added to a fixed factor, such as capital, the additional output (or marginal product) of the variable factor will eventually diminish.

law of supply: a law (or theory) which states that there is a direct relationship between the quantity supplied of a product and the price of the product, ceteris paribus

leakage (or withdrawal): money which leaks out of the circular flow of income; this can be as a result of savings, taxation and money spent on imports

liquidity: the extent to which a financial asset can be turned into cash. For example, if some shares in a company are sold, the paper asset becomes money

liquidity preference theory: the Keynesian theory of interest rate determination, based on three motives for holding money — the transactions motive, the precautionary motive and the speculative motive

liquidity trap: a situation at low rates of interest when changes in the money supply will have no effect on the rate of interest and where the demand for money is perfectly elastic

loanable funds theory: the idea that interest rates are determined by the demand for, and the supply of, loanable funds in financial markets

macroeconomics: the study of economics at the national and international levels

managed (dirty) float: an exchange rate that is determined, to some extent, by the forces of demand and supply, but where the rate is managed by a government, i.e. it will only be allowed to float between certain parameters

margin: the point at which the last unit of a product is produced or consumed

marginal cost: the additional cost of producing an extra unit of a product

marginal physical product: the amount of extra output that is produced if a firm increases its input of labour by one unit

marginal product: the additional output that is produced from employing another unit of a variable factor, e.g. the extra output from employing an additional worker

marginal propensity to consume: the proportion of an increase in income that is spent

marginal revenue: the extra revenue obtained from the sale of an additional unit of a product

marginal revenue product: the extra revenue obtained by a firm as it increases its output by using an additional unit of labour

marginal tax rate: the proportion of an increase in income which is taken in tax

marginal utility: the additional utility or satisfaction obtained from the consumption of an extra unit of a product

market: a way in which buyers and sellers come together to exchange products

market economy (or market system): an economy where decisions about the allocation of resources are taken through the price mechanism

market failure: a market imperfection which gives rise to an allocation of scarce resources which is not as efficient as it might have otherwise been

market imperfections: these occur in an imperfect market, such as a need for government intervention in a market

Marshall-Lerner condition: the requirement that for a depreciation to be successful, the sum of the price elasticity of demand for exports and the price elasticity of demand for imports must be greater than one

maximum price controls: controls which establish a maximum price for a product; price is not allowed to rise above this specific level

means tested benefits: benefits that are provided to those people entitled to them after taking into account their income and, therefore, their need for the benefits

medium of exchange: the use of money as an acceptable means of payment between buyers and sellers of a product

menu costs: the costs of continually having to change the prices of goods and services as a result of an inflationary situation

merit goods: products which are rivalrous and excludable but, if left to a free market, would be likely to be under-produced and under-consumed

microeconomics: the study of the behaviour of relatively small economic units, such as particular individuals, households or firms

migration: the movement of people from one area to another, either within a country or between countries

minimum efficient scale: the lowest level of output where average cost is at the minimum

mixed economy: an economy where the allocation of resources is decided both by market forces and by the state

mobility of labour: the degree to which labour finds it easy to move from one job to another (occupational mobility) and/or from one location to another (geographical mobility)

Monetarist: an approach that is based on the views of a number of economists, of which the most well known is Milton Friedman (1912–2006)

monetary base: the cash held by the general public and by the banking system, including the balances of the financial institutions with the central bank of the country. The monetary base acts as the basis for any expansion of bank lending in an economy

monetary inflation: a rise in the general level of prices in an economy, caused primarily by too much money in an economy

monetary policy: the use of interest rates and/or the money supply to influence the level of aggregate demand in an economy

monetary union: a group of countries who decide to bring their economies closer together through the adoption of a single currency

money: anything which is generally acceptable in a society as a means of payment

money supply: the amount of money available to the general public and the banking system in an economy

monopolistic competition: a market or industry where there is competition between a large number of firms which produce products which are similar but differentiated, usually through the use of brand images

monopoly: a market or industry where there is a single firm which controls the supply of the product

monopsony: a single buyer of a product or of a factor of production, such as labour

Multidimensional Poverty Index: replaced the Human Poverty Index in 2010; like its predecessor, it focuses on the extent of deprivation in different countries. It is made up of three dimensions and ten indicators

multilateral trade: a more realistic situation where trade takes place between a number of countries

multiplier: the amount by which an increase in an injection into the circular flow of income will bring about an increase of total income in an economy

narrow money supply: a measure of the stock of money in an economy which is mainly cash

national debt: the total of all debt accumulated by a government

national income: a general term for the total income of an economy over a particular period of time. More precisely, it refers to net national product

natural increase: a natural increase in the population of a country is determined by the crude birth rate minus the crude death rate of a population, i.e. it is the difference between the number of live births and the number of deaths in a country during a year

natural monopoly: a situation where average cost will be lower with just one provider, avoiding the wasteful duplication of resources

natural rate of unemployment: the non-accelerating inflation rate of unemployment (NAIRU); it can also be described as equilibrium unemployment. This is the rate of unemployment in an economy which will prevent the rate of inflation increasing

needs: things that are essential for human survival, e.g. food or shelter

negative consumption externality: an externality that affects the consumption side of a market in a negative or disadvantageous way

negative externality: the external cost that may occur as a result of an action, bringing some disadvantage to a third party

negative income tax: the payment of money to those people on low incomes instead of taking part of their income from them through income tax

negative production externality: an externality that affects the production side of a market in a negative or disadvantageous way

net domestic product: the gross domestic product of a country minus depreciation or capital consumption (this is the wear and tear of capital equipment over time, leading to a fall in its value)

Net Economic Welfare (or Measurable Economic Welfare): a broader measure of economic welfare than real GDP per capita; it takes into account such aspects as the value of childcare and looking after the sick and elderly, any depletion of natural resources and changes in the natural environment

net errors and omissions: those transactions in the balance of payments that go unrecorded

net investment income: this refers to the net income that relates to investments, such as dividends on shares or interest payments

net national product: the gross national product of a country minus depreciation or capital consumption

net property income from abroad: the interest and profits on foreign investments. It refers to the total interest, profits and dividends received by the residents of one country on their foreign investments, minus the total interest, profits and dividends paid to foreign residents on their investments in this particular country

nominal value: the value of a sum of money without taking into account the effect of inflation

non-excludability (or non-excludable): where the consumption of a product by one person does not exclude others from consuming the same product

non-pecuniary advantages: the advantages of employment, other than the money that is gained, such as the job satisfaction gained from a particular form of employment

non-rejectability: a situation where individuals cannot actually abstain from the consumption of a public good, even if they wanted to, e.g. an individual cannot reject being defended by the armed forces of a country

non-rivalness (or non-rivalry): where the consumption of one product does not prevent its consumption by someone else

normal good: a good for which the demand rises with an increase in income

normal profit: the level of profit that a firm requires to keep operating in the industry

normative statement: a statement which is subjective and expresses a value judgement

O

oligopoly: a market or industry in which there are a few large firms competing with each other

open economy: an economy which trades with the rest of the world

open market operations: the process of a government buying or selling bonds in order to influence the money supply in an economy

opportunity cost: the benefit foregone from not choosing the next best alternative

optimum population: the number of people in a country that will produce the highest per capita economic return, given the full utilisation of the resources available

optimum resource allocation: the best allocation of resources possible in given circumstances

output gap: the difference between the actual output and the potential output of an economy

paradox of thrift: the contradiction between the potential advantages and the potential disadvantages of saving in an economy

paradox of value: the fact that certain products that are essential to survival, such as water, are cheaper than less important products to survival, such as diamonds

Pareto optimality: a particular use of the term 'optimality' associated with the Italian economist Vilfredo Pareto, who stated that this situation existed when it was not possible to reallocate resources to make someone better off without making someone else worse off

participation rate: the proportion of the population which is either in employment or officially registered as unemployed

pecuniary advantages: the advantages of employment that are in the form of financial rewards or benefits

perfect competition: a market or industry consisting of many virtually identical firms which all accept the market price in the industry

perfectly elastic: this refers to a situation where all that is produced is sold/bought at a given price; it is shown as a horizontal straight line

perfectly inelastic: this is where a change in price has no effect on the quantity demanded (or supplied); the calculation will be zero and it is shown as a vertical straight line

perishability: the length of time in which a product is likely to decay or go bad; the shorter the time, the more perishable the product. For example, cheese will usually have a sell-by date and a date by which it should be consumed

planned (or command) economy: an economy where decisions about the allocation of resources are taken by the state

positive consumption externality: an externality that affects the consumption side of a market in a positive or beneficial way

positive externality: the external benefit that may occur as a result of an action, bringing some benefit to a third party

positive production externality: an externality that affects the production side of a market in a positive or beneficial way

positive statement: a statement which is factual and objective

potential growth in national output: a shift outwards of the production possibility frontier, resulting from a greater quantity and/or quality of factors of production in an economy

poverty trap: the situation which occurs when a person receives benefits, increasing income, but which then means the person is no longer entitled to receive as much as was the case before

precautionary demand for money: money that is required to pay for unexpected expenses. It is an active balance and is interest inelastic

predatory pricing: a deliberate attempt by a market leader to reduce prices in order to force other firms out of a market

price agreements: where firms in an oligopolistic market agree to fix prices between themselves

price discrimination: the process of charging different prices in different markets where there are differences in the price elasticities of demand

price elasticity of demand: this measures the degree to which a change in the price of a product leads to a change in the quantity demanded of a product

price elasticity of supply: measures the degree to which a change in the price of a product leads to a change in the quantity supplied of a product

price mechanism: the operation of changes in prices in a market to act as signals to producers to allocate resources according to changes in consumer demand

price stabilisation: a situation where a government intervenes to purchase stocks of a product when supply is high and to sell stocks of a product when supply is low

primary sector: production that takes place in agriculture, fishing, forestry, mining, quarrying and oil extraction

private goods: goods that are bought and consumed by individuals for their own benefit

privatisation: the transfer of the ownership of an industry from the state or public sector to the private sector

producer surplus: the difference between the price that consumers are willing to pay for a particular product and the price that producers require in order to supply the product. Firms will stop increasing supply if the price is just equal to the marginal cost of production, but for all the output that firms have supplied up to that point they have received a price above the cost of production. This is the producer surplus; it is shown on a demand and supply diagram by the triangle between the price line and the supply curve

production function: refers to the ratio of inputs to output over a given time period. It shows the resources that will be needed to produce a maximum level of output, assuming that the inputs are used efficiently

production possibility curve (or frontier): a graphic representation showing the maximum combination of goods or services which can be produced from given resources

productive efficiency: a situation where a firm operates at the minimum of the average cost curve. It is made up of two elements: technical efficiency and cost efficiency. It can also be seen in terms of a whole economy when that economy is operating on its production possibility curve or frontier

profit: the difference between total revenue and total costs

profit maximisation: (1) the idea that the main aim of a firm is profit maximisation; (2) the situation where marginal cost is equal to marginal revenue

progressive taxation: where taxation takes a higher proportion of a person's income as that income rises

proportional taxation: a tax which takes an equal proportion of income whatever a person's income level happens to be

public goods: goods and services that are provided by the public sector, otherwise they would not be provided

purchasing power parity: the value of a currency in terms of what it would be able to buy in other countries

quality of life: a wider concept than the standard of living to compare living conditions in different countries; it could take into account such criteria as the number of doctors per thousand of population, the quality of drinking water and the average size of school classes

quantitative easing: the process by which a government buys securities to create more liquidity in the financial system

quantity theory of money: a theory which links the quantity of money in circulation in an economy with the rate of inflation. It is stated as $MV = PT$ where M is the quantity of money, V is the velocity of circulation, P is the general price level and T is the number of transactions in an economy

quota: a limit on the imported products that are allowed to enter a country; a quota can be in the form of a limited quantity, a limited value or a limited market share

real value: the value of a sum of money after taking into account the effect of inflation, i.e. the effects of inflation have been removed

rectangular hyperbola: this is how unitary elasticity of demand is represented in a diagram; a movement up or down a demand curve will leave total revenue unchanged

regressive taxation: a situation where a tax takes a larger proportion of low incomes than it does of high incomes

regulations: these cover a variety of legal and other rules which apply to firms in different circumstances

resources: the inputs available to an economy for use in the production of goods and services

retail prices index: an index, just like the consumer prices index, which measures changes in the prices of a number of goods and services in an economy over a period of time, but it includes a number of items that are not included in the CPI, such as the costs of housing

returns to scale: the relationship between the level of output produced by a firm and the quantity of inputs required to produce that output

revaluation: the rise in value of a currency that is fixed

revenue maximisation: when the objective of a firm is to maximise the total revenue, rather than the profits, of a firm

risk-bearing economies of scale: a situation where there is diversification so that a firm is not reliant on what happens in just one market. By diversifying into different markets, the overall pattern of demand is more predictable and so a firm can save costs, such as by reducing the amount of stocks held in reserve

rivalry: rivalry in consumption means that when a product is consumed by one person, it cannot be consumed by another

sales maximisation: when the objective of a firm is to maximise the volume of sales

sampling: the use of a representative sample of goods and services consumed in an economy to give an indication of changes in the cost of living

satisficing profits: when the objective of a firm is to produce a level of profits that is satisfactory to stakeholders, such as shareholders and managers

saving: the amount of disposable income that is not spent on consumption

secondary sector: production that takes place in manufacturing, construction and energy

shoe leather costs: in a situation of very high inflation, people need to ensure that their money is gaining interest and so will be less inclined to have large cash deposits. These costs are, in fact, search costs that are caused by the high rate of inflation in an economy

social benefits: the sum of private benefits and external benefits

social costs: the sum of private costs and external costs

specialisation: the process whereby individuals, firms and economies concentrate on producing those products in which they have an advantage. Individuals working for a particular firm are an example, in the form of division of labour. Whole economies can also benefit from specialisation through the principle of comparative advantage

specific tax: an indirect tax that is a fixed amount per unit of output

speculative demand for money: money that is required to buy government bonds. It is an idle balance and is interest elastic

spillover effect: the effect of certain decisions which have an impact on third parties, i.e. those who are neither the producers nor the consumers of a particular product

stagflation: a situation where an economy is experiencing high inflation and high unemployment at the same time

standard of deferred payment: the use of money to purchase a product now and repay the debt in the future

stocks: goods which have been produced, but which are unsold and stored for sale in the future. For example, a firm which sells car tyres will usually have considerable stocks of tyres to fit a wide range of different cars

store of value or wealth: the use of money to store wealth

subsidy: an amount of money that is paid by a government to a producer. This is done so that the price charged to the customer will be lower than would otherwise have been the case without the subsidy

substitute goods: goods which are possible alternatives, e.g. gas or electricity as a source of energy in a home. These goods have a positive cross elasticity of demand, i.e. a rise in the price of one of them will lead to an increase in the demand for the other good

substitution effect: this shows the effect of a rise or fall in the price of a product on the utility or satisfaction obtained from each unit of money spent on that product. As a result of the price changes, expenditure can be rearranged to maximise the utility or satisfaction gained

sunrise industries: industries that are new, or relatively new, and which are growing fast. It is also expected that they will become very important in the future

sunset industries: industries that have passed their peak and are now in decline, with no realistic hope of recovery

supply: the quantity of a product that producers are willing to sell at a given price in a given period of time

supply curve: a curve that shows how much of a good or service will be supplied by producers at a given price in a given period of time

supply-side economics: the approach to change in an economy that puts the focus on the supply side, rather than the demand side, e.g. privatisation, deregulation and contracting out

supply-side policy: policies which enable markets to work more efficiently

surplus: a positive balance when income exceeds expenditure

sustainability: the capacity to endure; it is the potential for the long-term maintenance of wellbeing in an economic environment so that the interests of future, as well as present, generations are taken fully into account

tariff: a tax or duty that is imposed on an imported product to make it more expensive in the hope that this will reduce demand for the product

tax credits: a form of benefit that is paid to people on low incomes to boost their income and raise their standard of living

technical economies: the reduction in average cost as a result of the application of advanced technology in a firm which brings about a greater degree of efficiency

technical efficiency: a situation where a firm produces the maximum output possible from given inputs

technical monopoly: technically, a monopoly is said to exist where there is just one firm in an industry

terms of trade: the price of exports in relation to the price of imports

tertiary sector: production that takes place through the provision of services

third party: individuals or groups that are not the main parties in a transaction, but are still affected by it

total currency flow: an element of the balance of payments that refers to the total inflow or outflow of money which results from a country's international transactions with other countries

total product: the total output produced by the factors of production

total revenue: the total income that firms receive from sales; it is calculated by the price of a product multiplied by the number of products sold

total utility: the total amount of satisfaction obtained from the purchase of a number of units of a product

trade (business) cycle: the fluctuations in the national output of a country, involving a succession of stages or phases, including boom, recession, slump and recovery

trade creation: the creation of new trade as a result of the reduction or elimination of trade barriers

trade diversion: where a certain amount of trade is lost as a result of the imposition of trade barriers

trade union: an organisation of workers which is involved in collective bargaining with employers to achieve certain objectives, such as improvements in pay and working conditions

trade-weighted exchange rate: a way of measuring changes in an exchange rate in terms of a weighted average of changes in other currencies

trading possibility curve: a means of showing the advantages of two countries trading with each other as long as the opportunity costs of production are different

transactions demand for money: money that is required to pay for everyday purchases. It is an active balance and is interest inelastic

transfer earnings: the minimum payment required to keep a factor of production in its present use

transitional economy: an economy which was previously a command or planned economy and which is now allowing a greater degree of scope for market forces to operate

unanticipated inflation: the actual rate of inflation in an economy minus the anticipated or expected rate of inflation

unemployment: a situation where people who are able and willing to work are unable to find work

unemployment rate: the number of unemployed people divided by the labour force

unit of account (or measure of value): the use of money to establish the value of a product

unitary elasticity: this is where the proportionate change in demand (or supply) is exactly equal to the change in the independent variable; the calculation will be equal to one

universal benefits: benefits that are provided to everyone who is entitled to them without taking into account the income of those people

value judgement: an opinion which reflects a particular point of view

variable costs: the costs of production that vary with changes in output, i.e. the cost is zero if nothing is produced; examples include the cost of raw materials and component parts

variable factors of production: factors or resource inputs that can be varied in the short run, when at least one factor of production is fixed, e.g. raw materials

velocity of circulation: the average number of times one particular unit of money is used over a given period of time

vertical integration: where a firm joins with another firm at an earlier stage of the production process (backward vertical integration) or at a later stage of theproduction process (forward vertical integration)

visible balance: this refers to the trade in visible goods, such as cars, between countries

voluntary export restraints: a decision, taken by an exporting country, to voluntarily restrict its exports in the hope that a country that it exports to will decide against imposing import controls

wage drift: a situation where the average level of wages in an industry tends to rise faster than the supposed wage rates

wants: things that are not essential, e.g. a new car or television

weights: the items in a representative sample of goods and services bought by people in an economy will not all be of the same importance; weights are given to each of the items to reflect the relative importance of the different components in the basket, and so a price index involves a weighted average

welfare gain: an additional benefit resulting from more being produced in a market

welfare loss: a situation which arises when MSC exceeds MSB, leading to a socially inefficient allocation of resources

work disincentives: the possibility that taxation could lead to people being unwilling to work, e.g. there may be a disincentive to work if rates of income tax are too high

working capital: the part of the capital of a business that is available to pay for wages and materials and not tied up in fixed capital, such as land, buildings or equipment

working population: the people in a country who are working or who are actively seeking work

World Trade Organisation: an organisation set up in 1995 to promote free trade in the world through the reduction of trade barriers

X-inefficiency: a situation where average cost is not at its lowest point because monopoly power has given rise to inefficiency

yield: the annual income obtained from a bond or a share as a proportion of its current market price